9ÈME CONCEPT PAINTS FOR PLANET REEF –

At the outset, my background was organizing sporting events, in particular, profes-
sional surf competitions. That activity provided me with contacts in a wide variety
of fields. As a result, I had the good fortune to meet the 9ème Concept, a collective
of French artists. Our association began when, as an events promoter, I commis-
sioned them to do live pieces for Reef. The Collective subsequently created artistic
labyrinths, including a 20 meter long fresco, and animated soirées. The artists were
invited to express themselves freely at competition sites.

After ten years of events, I left for California to join Reef. On the eve of my depar-
ture, I promised never to forget the Collective. I wanted to continue to work with
them because over the years, we had developed a friendship well beyond our pro-
fessional relationship, and I admire their talent. A few months after my arrival,
 I developed a project, Planet Reef, creating a series of events, blending together
sports, art, and music. The 9ème Concept began by painting directly onto Reef
shoes. Then they worked on the walls of Reef's tradeshow booths and participated
in a traveling advertising campaign. The Reef team had complete confidence in the
artists, who expressed themselves with total liberty. This book is the culmination
of two years of collaboration between Reef and the 9ème Concept. What began as
a marketing idea resulted in the creation of veritable works of art and a collection
of shoes, which we are delighted to present here.

JC Clenet

What makes for the beauty of board sports is the concentration of powerful images, choreographic movements, physical performance, indescribable sensations and strikingly bright colors. A wave... seen from the interior! The lifestyle of "riders" is closely related to that of artists: in perpetual movement, always open to new things, relentless efforts, systematically pushing the possibilities of their work and play to their absolute limits. The very nature of board sports is filled with contradictions: several worlds, both rebellious and organized, coexist. There are those who are hunting for rewards, those who are seeking gold, those who are out for the sensa-tional, and those who are happy with the simple pleasure of sliding on their boards, when adrenalin obscures worries and gravity is mastered and time stretches out.

The time has come where this prolific scene has reached maturity and has as many active participants as it has fans. A generation of artists, inspired by this world, has achieved recognition.

Ce qui fait la beauté des sports de glisse, c'est ce concentré d'images fortes, de mouvements chorégraphiques, de performances physiques, de sensations indes-criptibles, de couleurs aux éclats éblouissants ! Une vague... vue de l'intérieur ! Le mode de vie des « riders » est un parent proche de celui des artistes : toujours en mouvement, à l'affût de la nouveauté, travaillant sans cesse, s'amusant à mettre systématiquement à l'épreuve le potentiel de leurs outils-jouets... La nature même des « boardsports » est faite de contradictions : plusieurs mondes, à la fois rebelles et organisés, coexistent sur une même planche. Il y a les chasseurs de médailles, les chercheurs d'or qui poursuivent des sensations toujours plus fortes, et les autres, ceux qui se satisfont du plaisir simple de glisser, quand l'adrénaline domine les soucis, que la pesanteur est maîtrisée et que le temps s'étire.

Voici venu l'âge de la maturité pour cette scène prolifique qui compte autant de pra-tiquants que de sympathisants. Une génération d'artistes s'inspirant de ce monde est désormais reconnue.

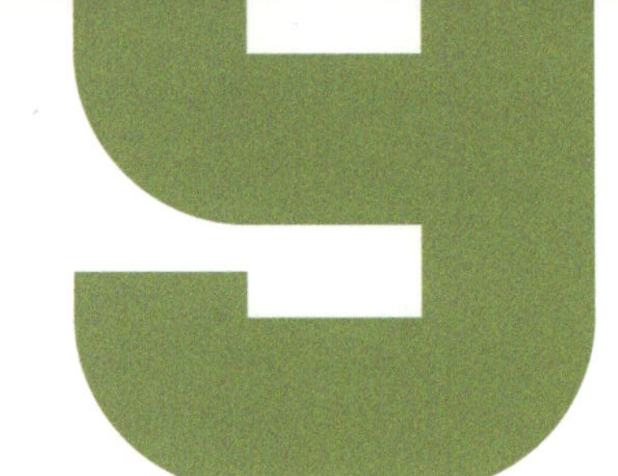

What is the 9ème Concept ?

Twelve brains, 24 hands, too many ideas! Collaboration among artists is not always easy. It is undoubtedly in an explosion of images and above all in the accomplishment of collective pieces that the 12 members of the 9ème find their equilibrium. They use a multiplicity of supports and reveal a sensitivity which facilitates the relationship between the creator and the spectator. The collective scatters colored messages everywhere it goes: the street, galleries, nightclubs, surf boards, tee-shirts. If you run into them, you will be subjugated...from head to toe.

Le 9ème concept, qu'est ce que c'est ?

12 cerveaux, 24 mains, trop d'idées ! La collaboration artistique n'est pas toujours chose aisée. C'est sans doute dans une explosion d'images et surtout dans la réalisation d'œuvres collectives que les 12 du 9ème trouvent leur équilibre. Ils aiment une multiplicité de supports et dévoilent une sensibilité qui simplifie les rapports entre le créateur et le spectateur. Le collectif sème ses messages colorés partout sur son passage : rue, galerie, boîte de nuit, planche à voile, tee-shirts... Si vous les croisez vous serez conquis... de la tête aux pieds.

Alexis Deforges

Steph grew up in an environment in the Paris area propitious for artistic and graphic development. Even if he is perfectly at ease with the computer, he continues to wield the paintbrush. His most obvious theme, and what interests him the most, is the human face. His drawings stage his personal preoccupations : life, human energy. "The face is at the heart of my thoughts along with life, and the energy which surrounds us." His primary inspiration : masks and primitive African art. Carricondo is one of the three founders of the 9ème Concept : "A huge part of my life. Family-Encounters-Energy, a child's dream become reality."

Steph a grandi dans un environnement propice à l'éveil artistique et graphique aux abords de Paris. Même s'il est parfaitement à l'aise avec l'informatique, il continue à jouer du pinceau. Son thème le plus évident, ce qui l'intéresse le plus, c'est le visage humain. Ses dessins mettent en scène ses préoccupations personnelles : la vie, l'énergie humaine. « Le visage est au coeur de ma réflexion, la vie, les énergies qui nous entourent…» Sa source d'inspiration première : les masques et l'art primitif africain. Carricondo est l'un des trois fondateurs du 9ème Concept : « Une grosse partie de ma vie. Famille-Rencontres-Energie. Un rêve d'enfant devenu réalité ».

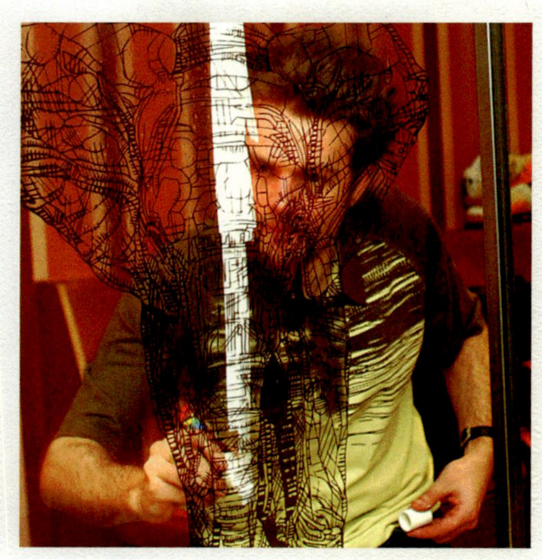

STEPH CARRICONDO

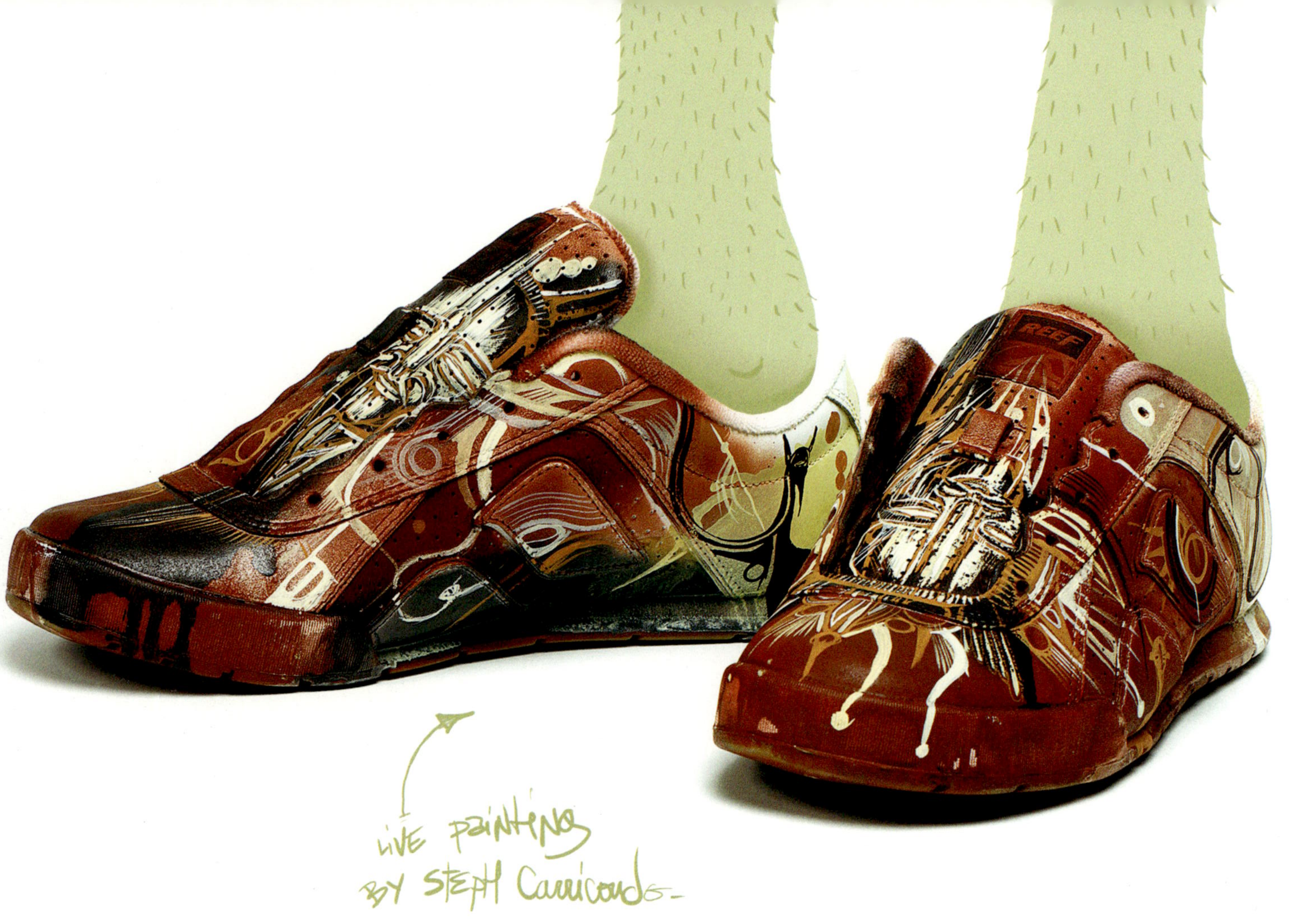

live painting
by STEFF Carricands-

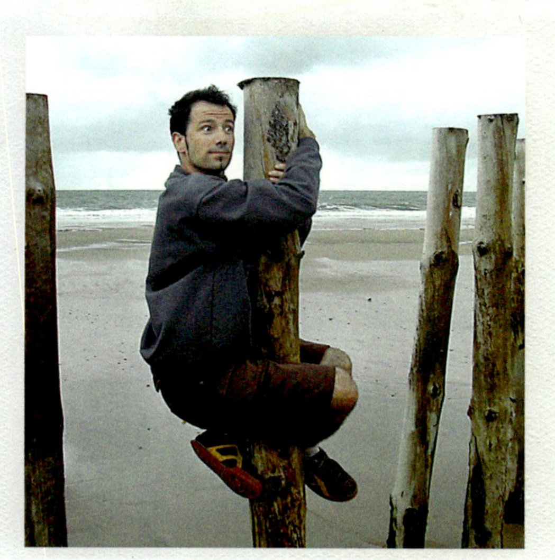

Following in his father's footsteps towards graphic exploration, Ned uses a brush, Indian ink, and acrylics in order to construct a bi-chromic world outlined by tribal shapes. The faces and symbols are superimposed and flow together. Shadows and colors make the atmosphere denser and it all fluctuates somewhere between a comic strip and the cinema. If covering a woman's body entirely with tattoos was his phantasm for a while, it was quickly replaced with a strong urge to create and publish his own comic book. "… see it in a shop, touch the cover, turn the pages." The 9ème Concept is the title of a comic he created when he was a kid. When he and his friends, Carricondo et Jerk, decided to found a collective, this is the name they chose.

Suivant les traces de son père vers l'exploration graphique, Ned utilise pinceau, encre de chine et acrylique pour construire un monde bi-chromique aux contours délimités par des formes tribales. Les visages et les symboles se superposent et se confondent. Les ombres et les couleurs rendent plus dense une ambiance qui oscille entre la bande dessinée et le cinéma. Si recouvrir intégralement le corps d'une femme de tatouage fut un temps son fantasme, ce dernier a été remplacé par l'idée de voir publiée une BD de sa conception. « …la voir en magasin, toucher la couverture et feuilleter les pages ». Le 9éme Concept est le titre d'une bande dessinée qu'il a créée gamin. Quand il décide, avec ses copains Carricondo et Jerk, de fonder un collectif, c'est ce nom qu'ils choisissent.

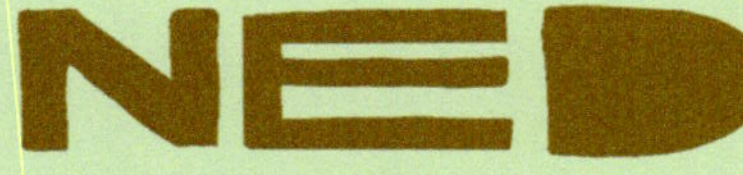

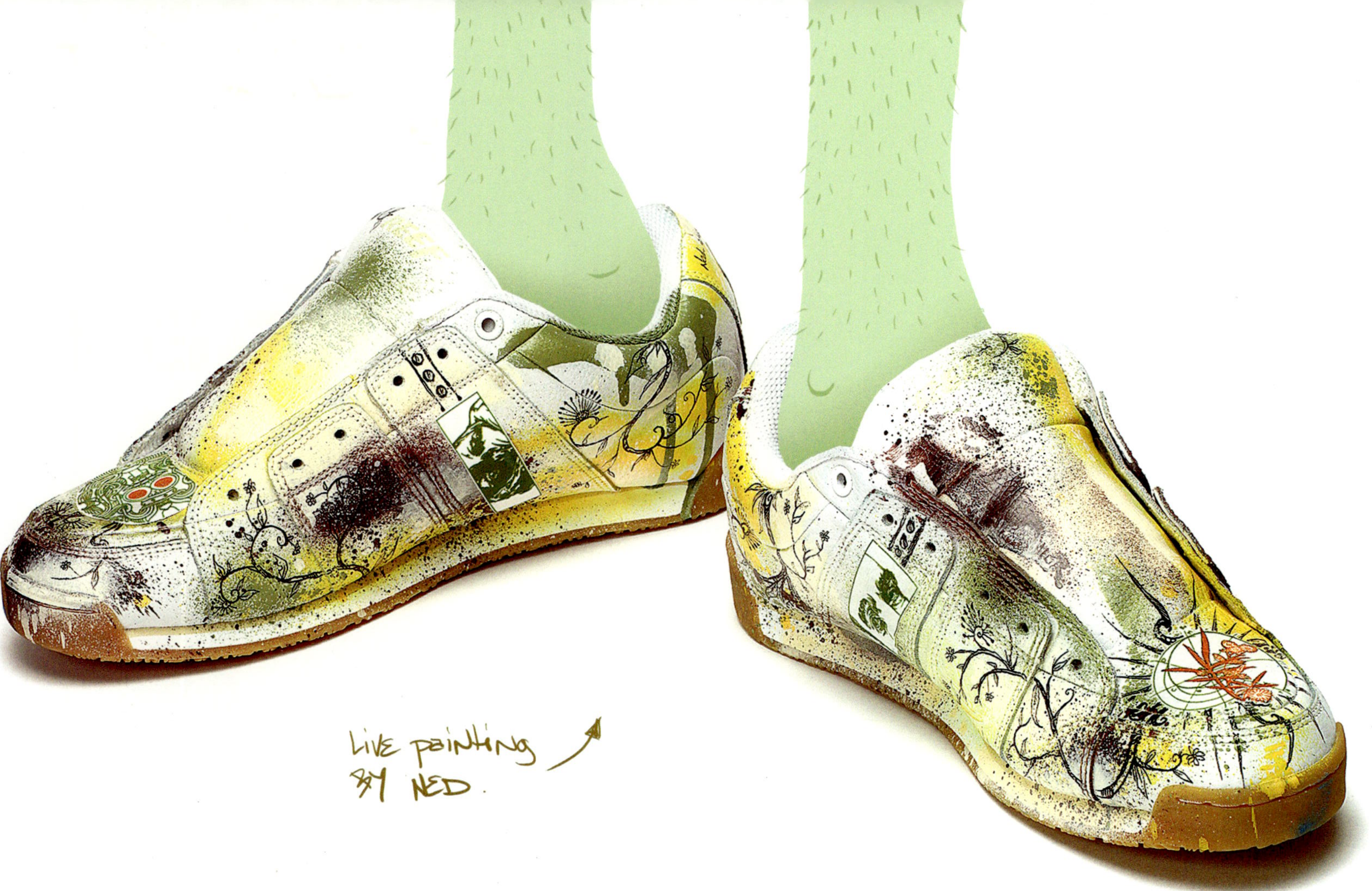
LIVE PAINTING
BY NED.

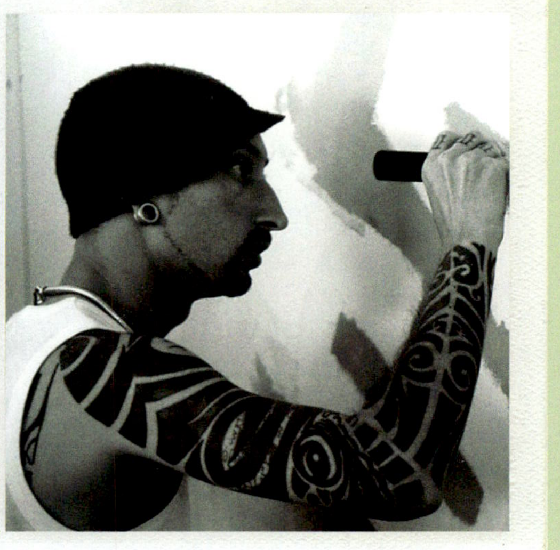

A passion for Comic Strips and scribbling with a pen on his school notebooks pushed Jerk into experimenting with more effective and finer instruments. He is a calm and reserved individual and is one of the three founders of the 9ème. It is his observation of objects from daily life and of urban and industrial development which is at the origin of his work composed of forms, slightly frightened characters and animals reminiscent of a sort of Asian festivity. "The 9ème is a group of friends who work together to create exhibitions and events, like Planet Reef, a source of multiple creations!"

Sa passion pour la BD et le gribouillage au stylo sur les cahiers de cours a poussé Jerk à s'essayer à des outils plus efficaces et plus fins. Individu calme et réservé, il fait partie du trio fondateur du 9ème. C'est son observation des objets de la vie quotidienne et du développement urbain et industriel qui est à l'origine d'un travail composé de volumes, de personnages et d'animaux un peu effrayés, rappelant une fête asiatique. « Le 9ème est un groupe d'amis qui travaillent ensemble pour réaliser des expos-événements, comme Planet Reef, une source de créations multiples ! »

JERK45

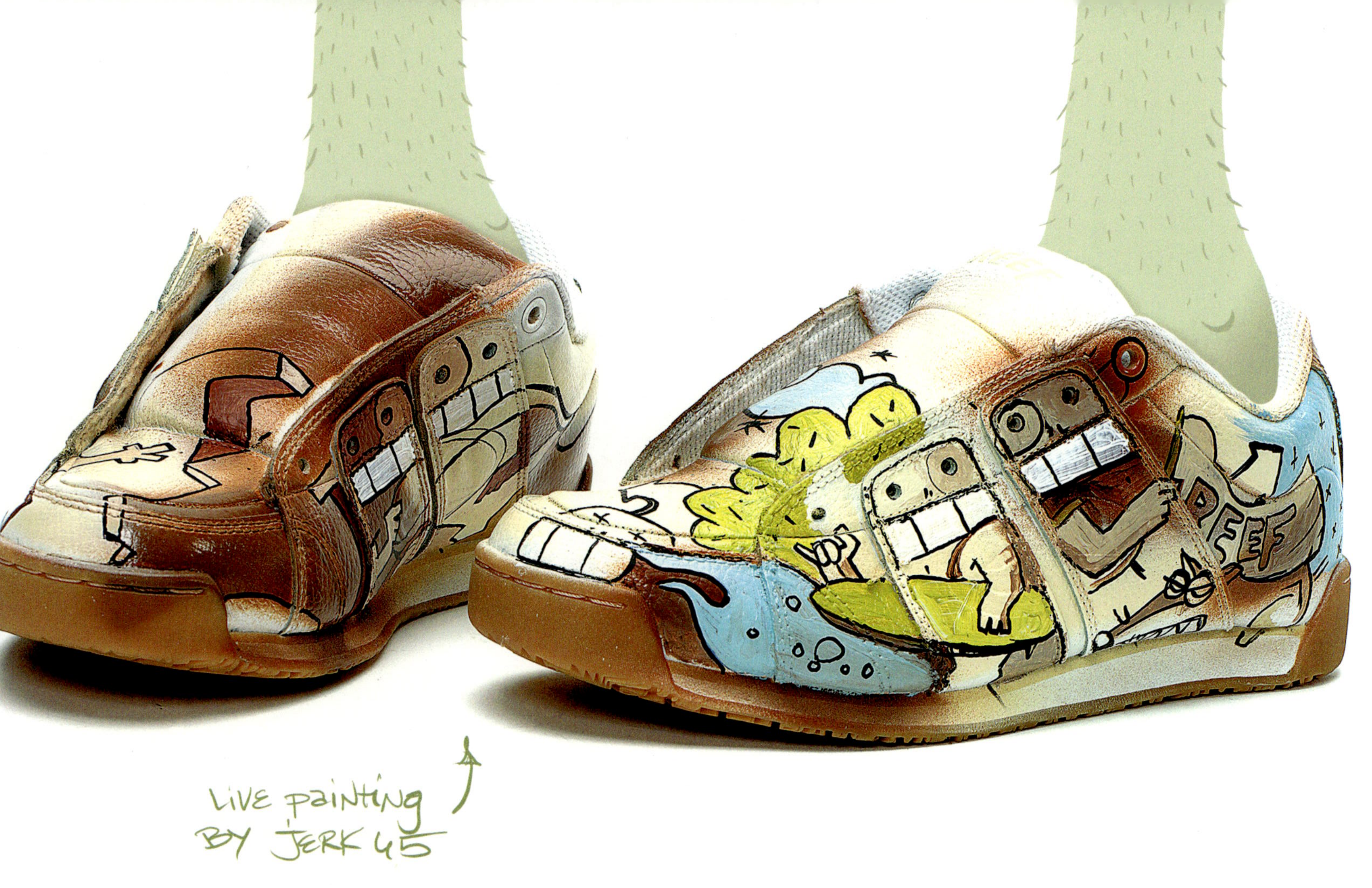

live painting
by Jerk 45

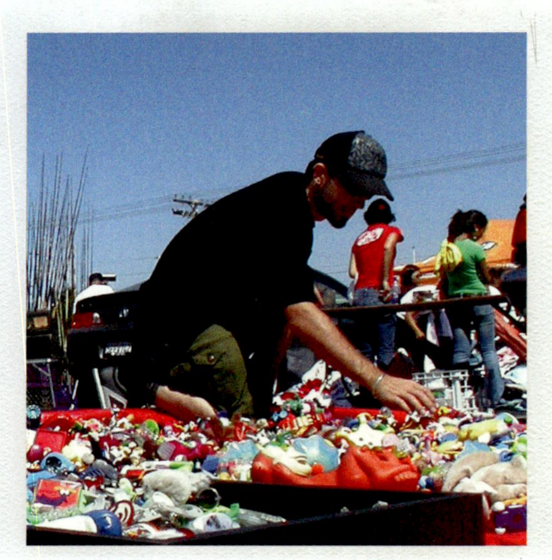

The result of spending hours in front of his computer and a fantastic collection of toys, Big Jul's painting is rejuvenating. Portraits of characters with touching and lively expressions and the slick traits of plastic dolls cohabit in vast brightly lit space. In front of an army of mannequins and mass market playthings, Big Jul proclaims without concession: " The 9ème Concept is the leading group in graphic art in France today."

Fruit de nombreuses heures passées devant son ordinateur et sa passionnante collection de jouets, la peinture de Big Jul vous rajeunit. Dans ses toiles, les portraits de personnages aux expressions touchantes et bien vivantes et les traits lisses des poupées en plastique cohabitent dans de vastes espaces fortement illuminés. Devant son armée de mannequins et de produits ludiques de grande consommation, Big Jul proclame sans concession : « Le 9ème est le groupe, chef de file, des arts graphiques en France aujourd'hui ».

BiG JUL

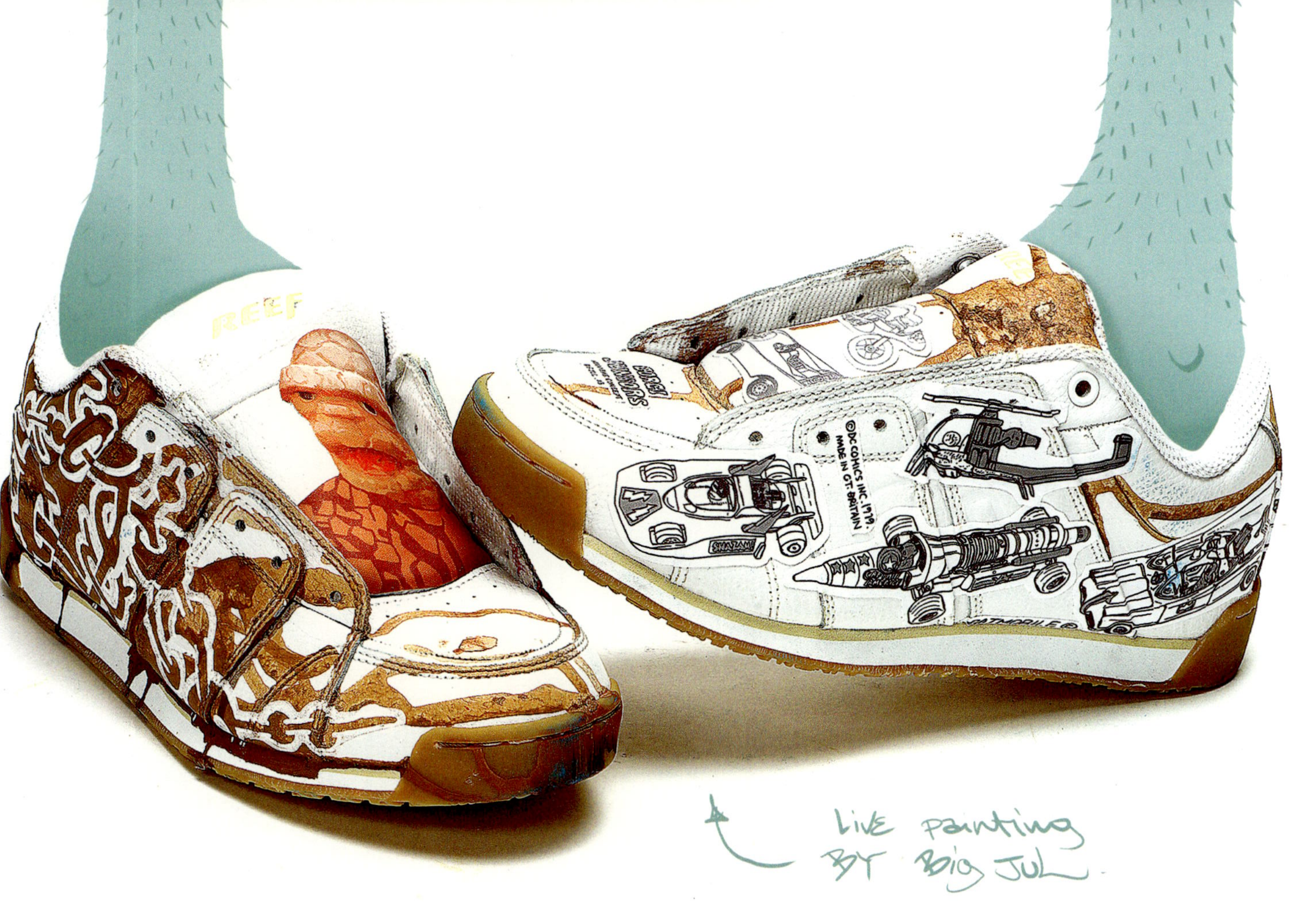

Live painting BY BIG JUL.

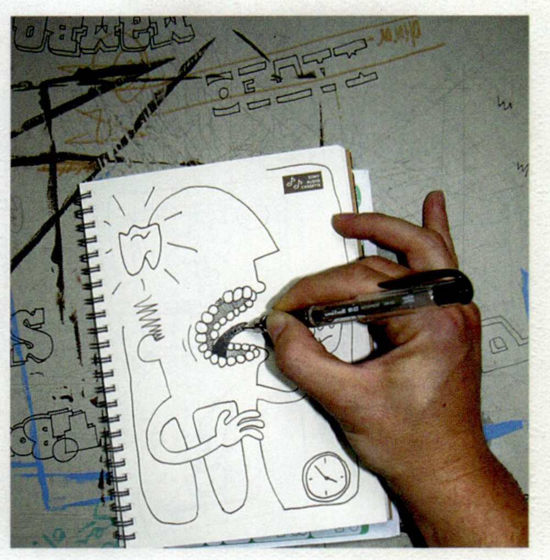

Mambo evolves in a universe full of symbols, icons, and sign posts. His past experience as a graffiti artist influences his current creations: a concentration of messages, signs and caustic humor, creating a powerful visual effect. As a world traveler, he has created works on walls wherever he has been: India, Senegal, the USA, Japan, Brazil, Mexico, and Spain. Mambo attacks any kind of material (media, material, Hertzian or commercial) and radically transforms any kind of surface. He surprises his public with an ever evolving technique. He doesn't confine himself to a category but develops his drawing however he likes.

Mambo évolue dans un univers de symboles, d'icônes et de panneaux indicateurs. Son passé de graffeur influence ses créations actuelles : un concentré de messages, de signes et d'humour caust que créant un effet visuel puissant. Grand voyageur, il crée des œuvres sur les murs partout où il passe : l'Inde, le Sénégal, les U.S.A., le Japon, le Brésil, le Mexique, l'Espagne. Il s'attaque à tous les supports (médiatiques, physiques, hertziens ou commerciaux) et transforme de manière radicale toutes les surfaces. Mambo surprend son public en faisant évoluer ses techniques. Il ne se cantonne pas à un genre mais fait évoluer son trait, au gré de ses envies.

MAMBO

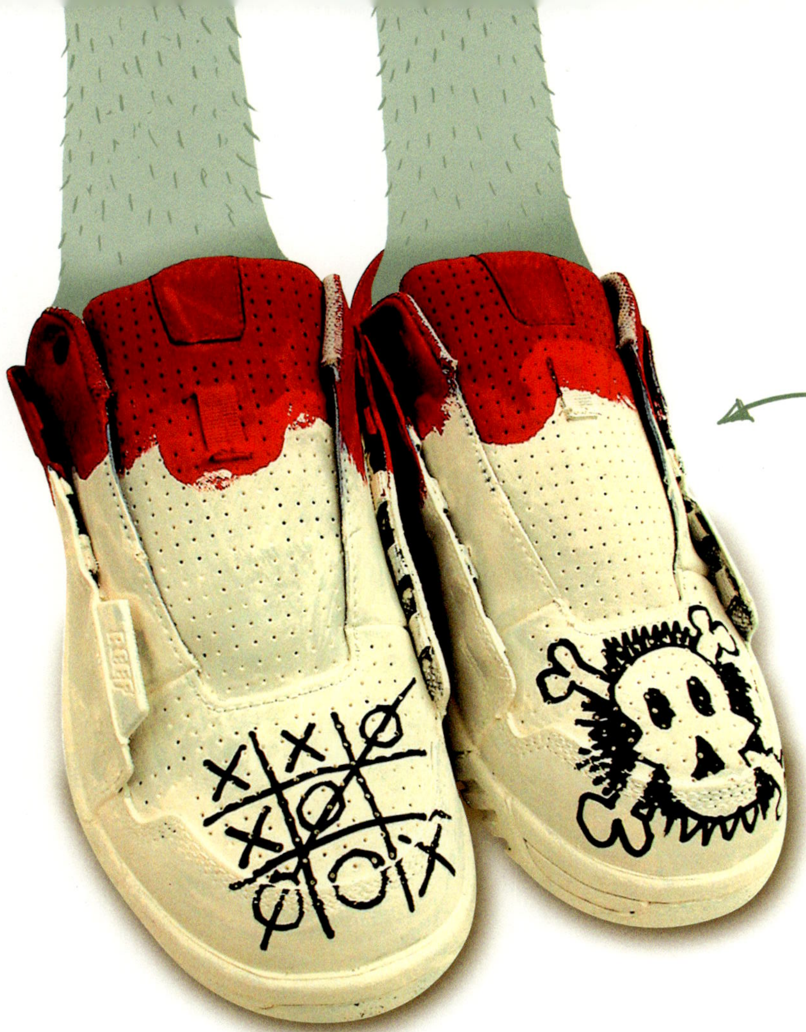

live painting by Mambo.

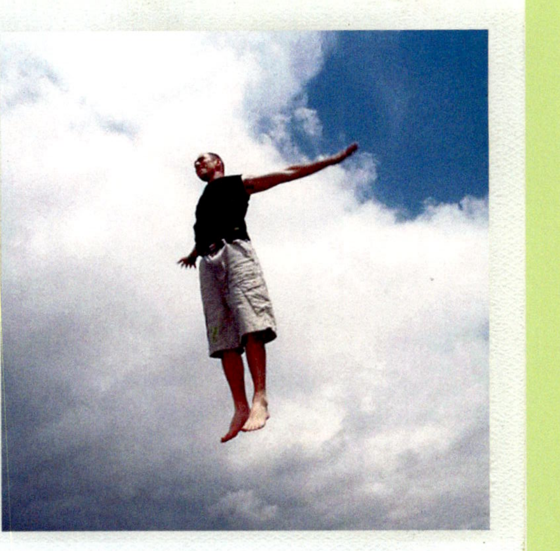

Ankh began to do graffiti at the beginning of the 90's on the walls of his home town, snuggled up to the Alps. It is this means of expression which led him to attend a graphic arts school. Having assimilated more institutional techniques, he continues to utilize aerosol bombs and acrylics to compose and place his characters, both realistic and humoristic, in strange situations. His main source of inspiration remains the street. " The 9ème Concept is the most beautiful adventure I've ever known. I am always happy when there are people capable of organizing projects like Planet Reef. They take our work seriously. When I see the impact... I only hope that this is just the beginning ! "

Ankh a commencé au début des années '90 à faire du graffiti sur les murs de sa ville natale, blottie aux pieds des Alpes. C'est ce mode d'expression qui l'a conduit sur les bancs d'une école de graphisme. Fort de techniques plus institutionnelles, il continue à utiliser des bombes aérosols et de l'acrylique pour composer et placer ses personnages réalistes et humoristiques dans des situations bizarres. Sa principale source d'inspiration reste la rue. « Le 9ème Concept est la plus belle aventure que j'ai connue jusqu'a présent. Je suis toujours content qu'il y ait des gens pour organiser des projets comme Planet reef. C'est vraiment prendre notre boulot au sérieux. Quand je vois l'impact… j'espère que ça n'est que le début ! »

ANKHONE

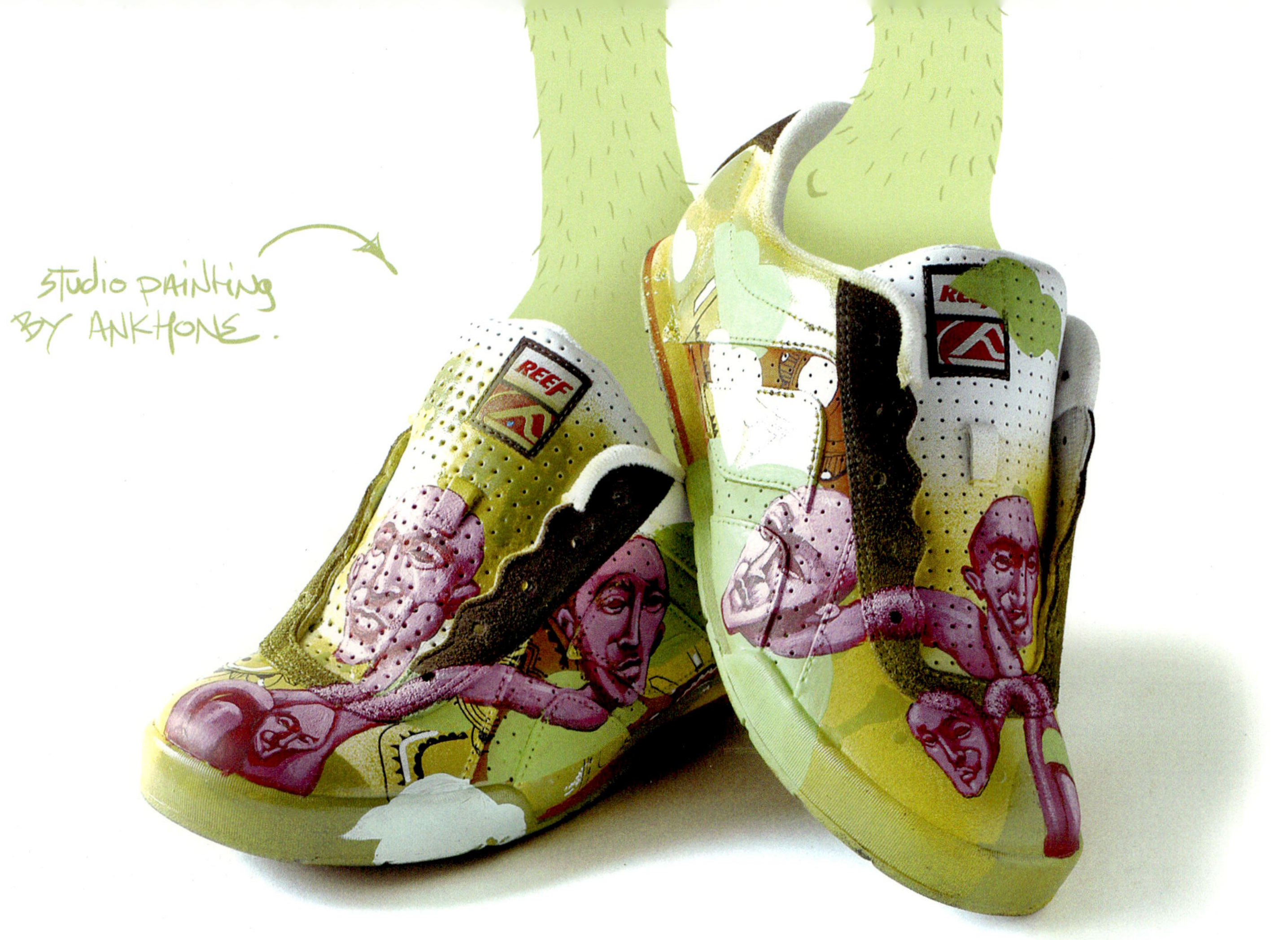

studio painting
BY ANKHONE.
REEF
REEF

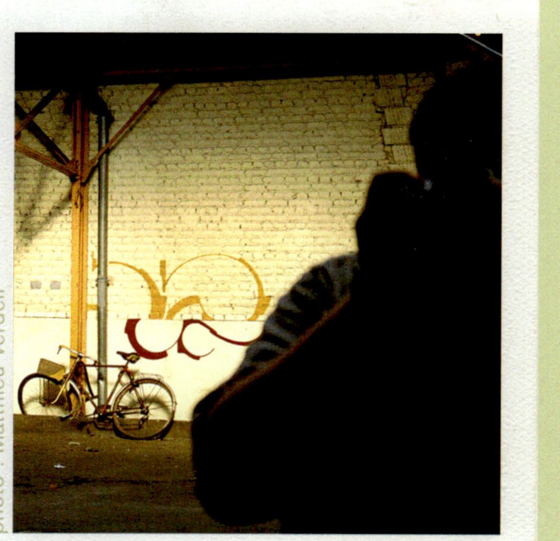

photo : Matthieu Verdeil

As a kid, Alëxone was already at ease with a pencil in his hand. It is graffiti which convinced him to abandon the rigorous forms of numbers in favor of tracing arabesques, a passion which has remained ever since. Alëxone loves to draw on walls, and they do him justice. He has developed his style on their bricks and they display his characters reminiscent of comic strip characters with exuberant behavior and a profusion of surrealistic detail. His messages attract the attention of passersby and captivate them with their beauty. This is the very essence of street art: to render a work instantly accessible to the largest number of people. "Almost all of my travels have left a mark on me, whether they were to Nantes or to the Island of the Reunion. Besides, it isn't necessarily traveling to the most remote places which impresses me the most. It is sufficient to take off with the simple urge to discover."

Petit, Alëxone était déjà à l'aise un crayon à la main. C'est le graffiti qui l'a décidé à abandonner la forme rigoureuse des chiffres pour tracer des arabesques, une passion qui ne le quittera plus. Alëxone adore dessiner sur les murs. Ils le lui rendent bien. Il a bâti son style sur leurs briques et ils arborent ses personnages à résonance de bandes dessinées aux comportements exubérants, truffés de détails surréalistes. Ses messages attirent le regard des passants et séduisent par leur beauté. C'est l'essence même du street-art : rendre accessible de façon instantanée une œuvre d'art au plus grand nombre. « Presque tous mes voyages ont été marquants. Ceux de Nantes à l'île de la Réunion ! D'ailleurs ce ne sont pas toujours les voyages dans des pays lointains qui m'ont le plus marqué ! Il suffit de partir avec la simple envie de découvrir ! »

ALËXONE

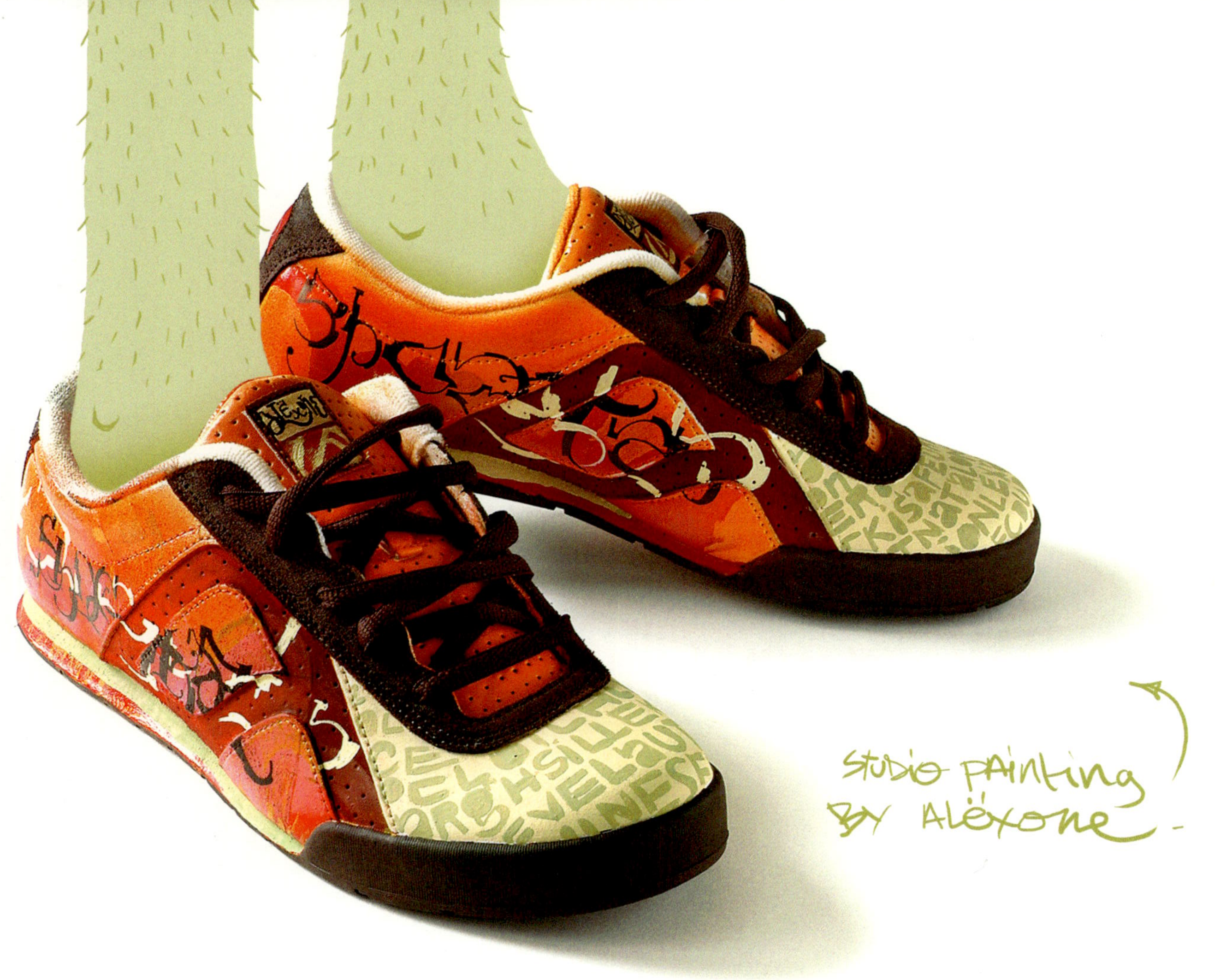

19

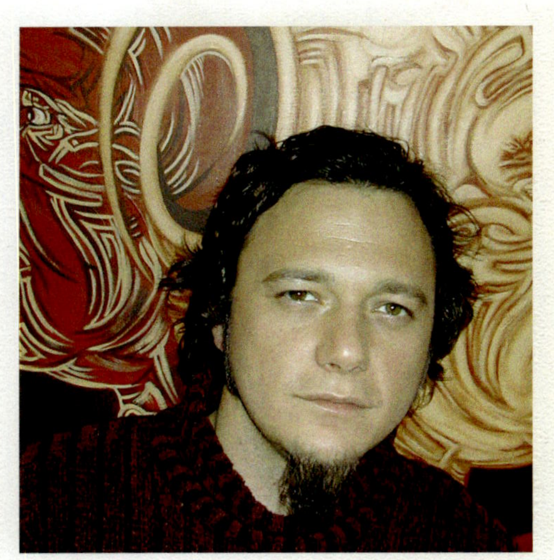

Counterfeit apprentice, he has replaced the sheets of false currency with penciled drawings tone on tone. Cyrf attracts attention by playing somewhere on the boundary between reality and the unreal. Comics, Primitive Art, horror cinema and tribal writing are the inspiration for his portraits steeped in mysticism. His vision of the collective: "A school, a family, a collection of exchanges between very different personalities to do a coherent job. By going forward together, each one advances as an individual ! It is a rich adventure about which the final word hasn't been said."

Apprenti faux monnayeur, il a remplacé la planche à billets par le dessin ton sur ton au crayon. Cyrf attire le regard en jouant à la frontière du réel et de l'irréel. La BD, l'art primitif, le cinéma d'épouvante et les écritures tribales lui inspirent ses portraits empreints de mysticisme. Sa vision du collectif : « Une école, une famille, un ensemble d'échanges et de personnalités différentes, pour un travail cohérent ! En avançant ensemble, on avance individuellement ! C'est une riche aventure qui n'a pas dit son dernier mot ! ».

CYRIL FRITSCH

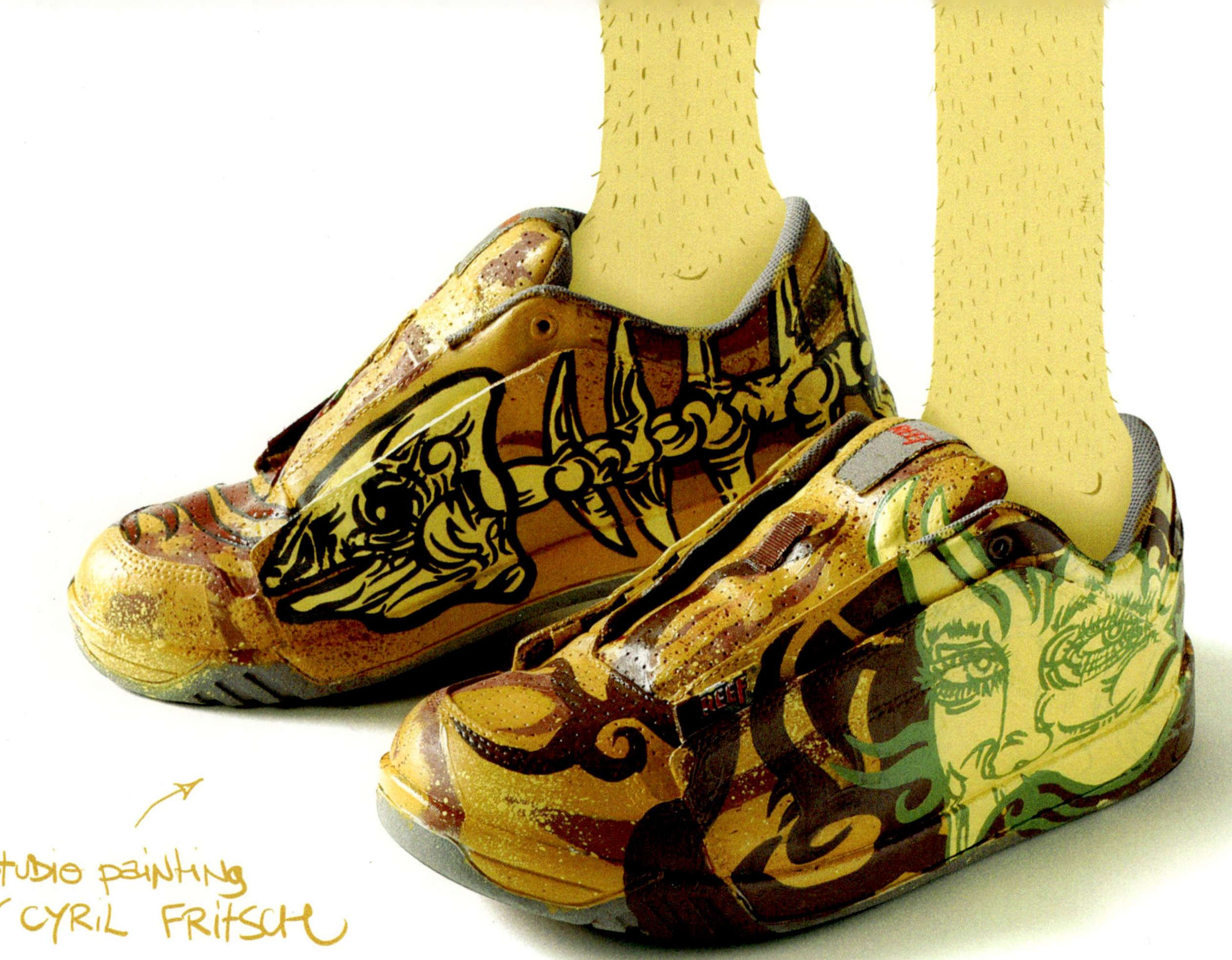

studio painting
by Cyril Fritsch

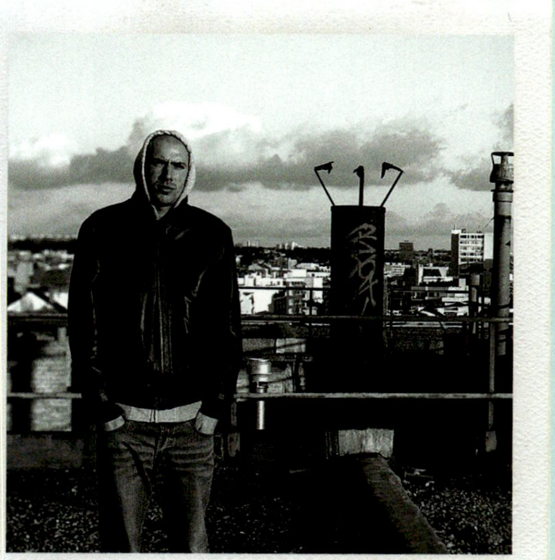

Veenom is one of these creative types for whom drawing is as natural an act as breathing and who uses anything he can get his hands on to leave his mark. His work results from an exploration of his unconscious, but he produces very clean precise images. Eggs always occupy a place in his paintings which are charged with powerful symbols. He claims various inspirations : post-war American artists and above all illustrators and creators of posters. "It is the individuality of each one which creates the collective force!"

Veenom est un de ces types créatifs pour qui dessiner est aussi naturel que de respirer et qui utilise tous les supports à sa portée pour laisser sa marque. Son travail résulte de l'exploration de son inconscient, mais il produit des images nettes. Les œufs trouvent toujours une place sur ses toiles composées de forts symboles. Il revendique diverses inspirations : les artistes américains de l'après guerre, mais surtout les illustrateurs et concepteurs de posters. « C'est l'individualité de chacun qui fait la force collective ! ».

VEENOM

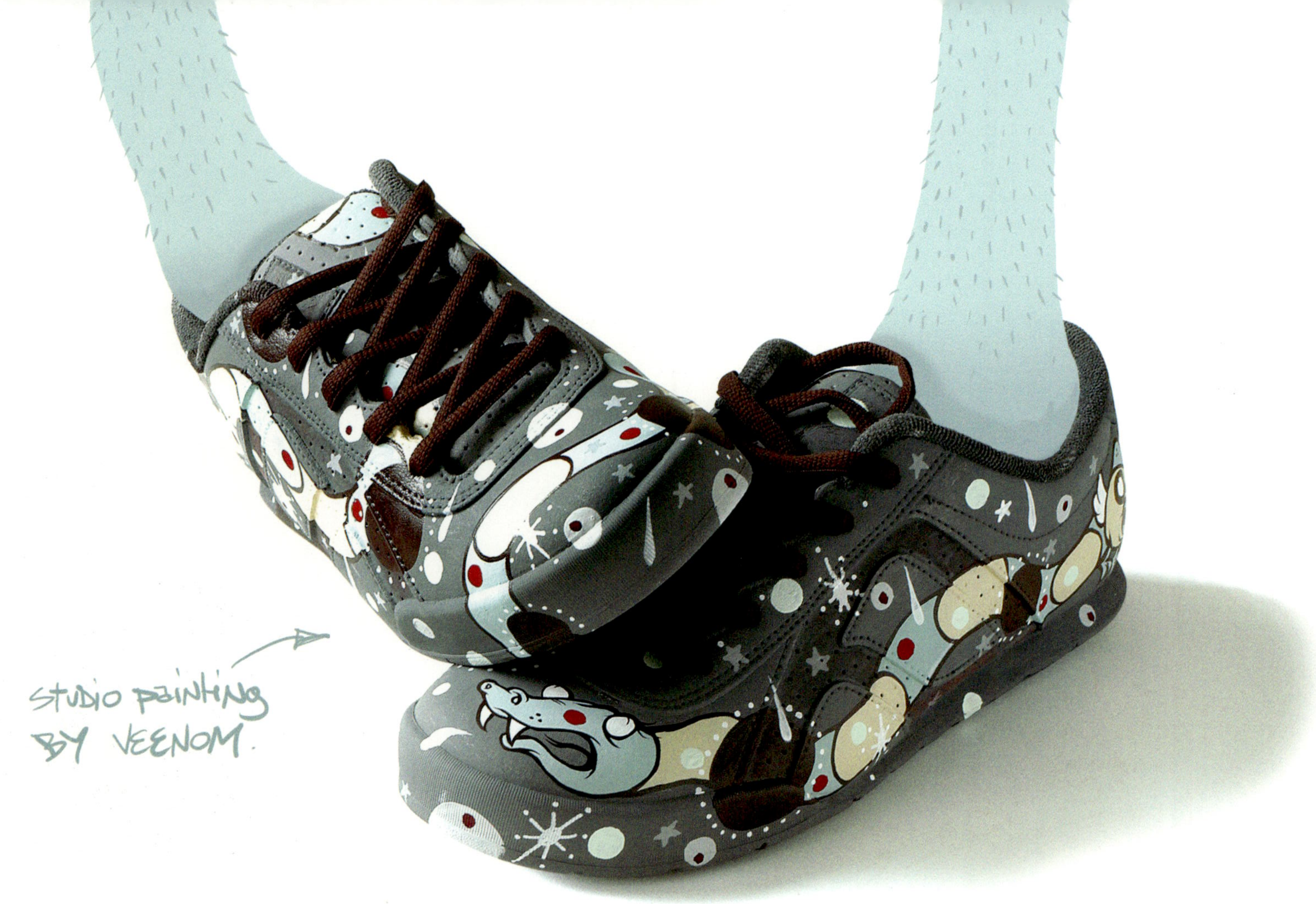

STUDIO PAINTING
BY VEENOM.

ROMAIN FROQUET

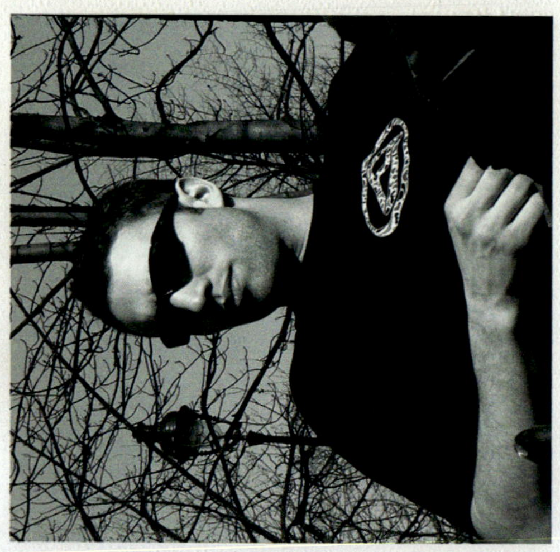

His work is made of assemblages and superimpositions. "When I paint, I really have the impression that the earth stops rotating. I am in a protective cocoon and I feel good." His paintings combine characters composed of geometric figures and words, and texts which are evocative of the subjectivity of our perception and interpretations. His symbol is a closed door, and when it is open, represents "an opened mind. An obstacle which anyone can surmount; it suffices to have the key, to not be afraid to go beyond obstacles and appearances".

Son travail est fait de mélanges, de superpositions. « Lorsque je peint, j'ai vraiment l'impression que la terre s'est arrêtée de tourner, je suis dans ma bulle et je suis bien ». Ses toiles mélangent des personnages composés de pièces géométriques et des mots, des textes qui évoquent la subjectivité de notre perception, de nos interprétations. Son symbole est une double porte fermée et ouverte qui représente « l'ouverture d'esprit. Un obstacle que chacun peut surmonter, il suffit d'avoir les clefs, de ne pas avoir peur d'aller au-delà des obstacles et des apparences ».

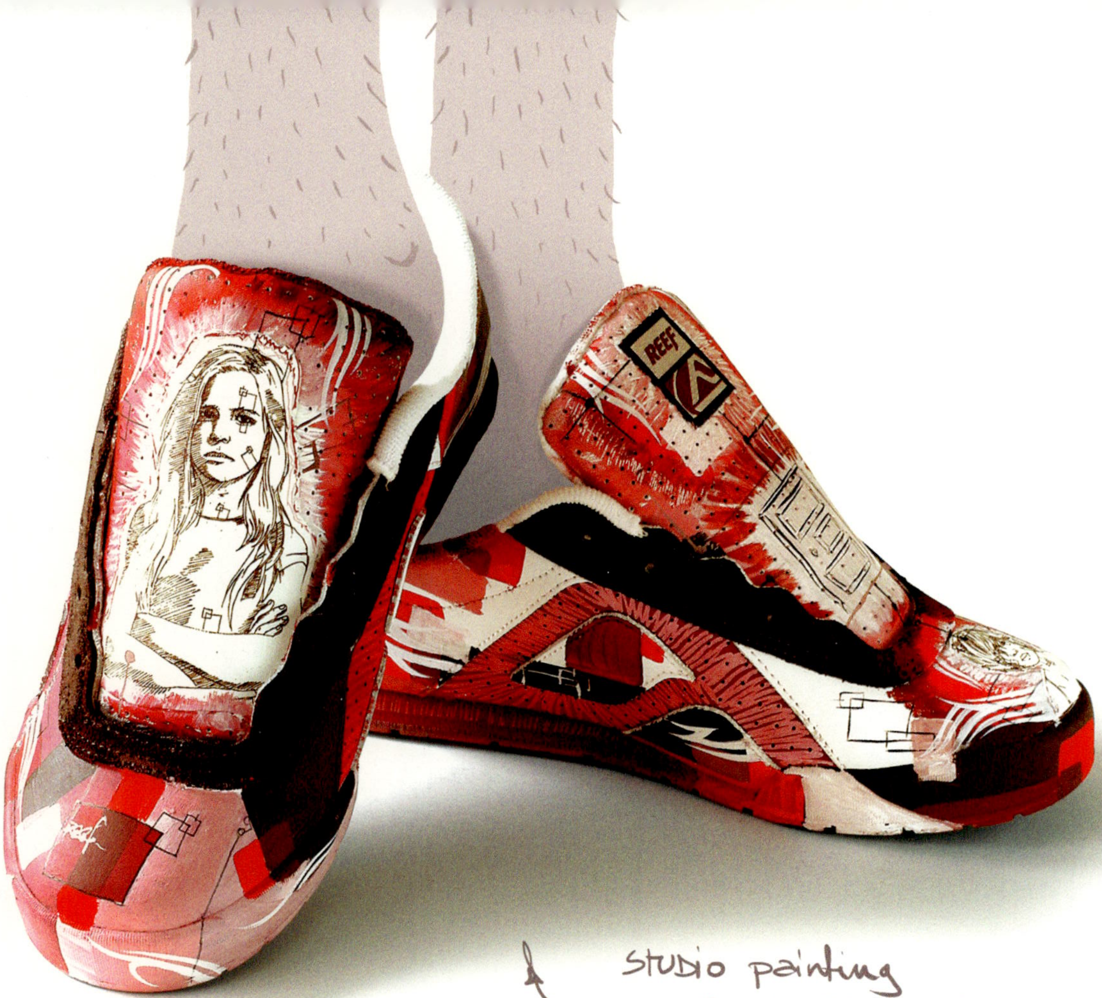

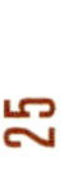

studio painting
BY Romain Froquet.

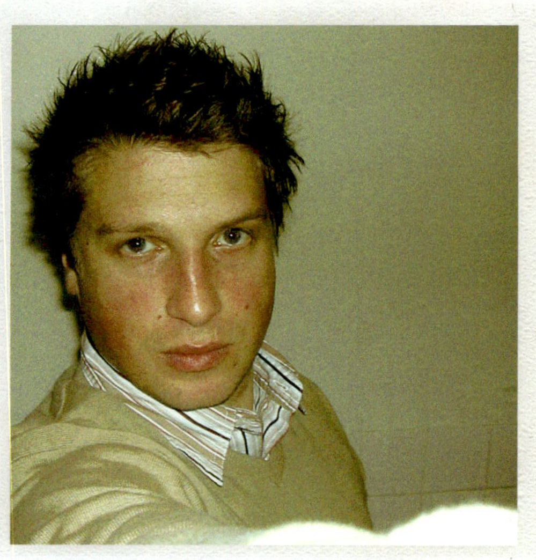

JEROME MOLARD

Jey is a veritable "rider", an artist in every sense of the term. He creates graphic works on any kind of support (canvas, wall, human body). As a talented graphic and tattoo artist, he is passionately involved in and strongly asserts his belonging to a tribe while having an exaggerated taste for tattoos, nature and traveling, all elements of which make for the particularity of surf sports.

Jey est un véritable « rider », un artiste au sens plein du terme. Ses créations graphiques s'épancuissent sur tous les supports (toile, mur, corps humain). Tatoueur et graphiste de talent, c'est un passionné qui revendique son appartenance à une tribu et un goût immodéré pour le tatouage, la nature et les voyages… des éléments qui font la particularité des sports de glisse.

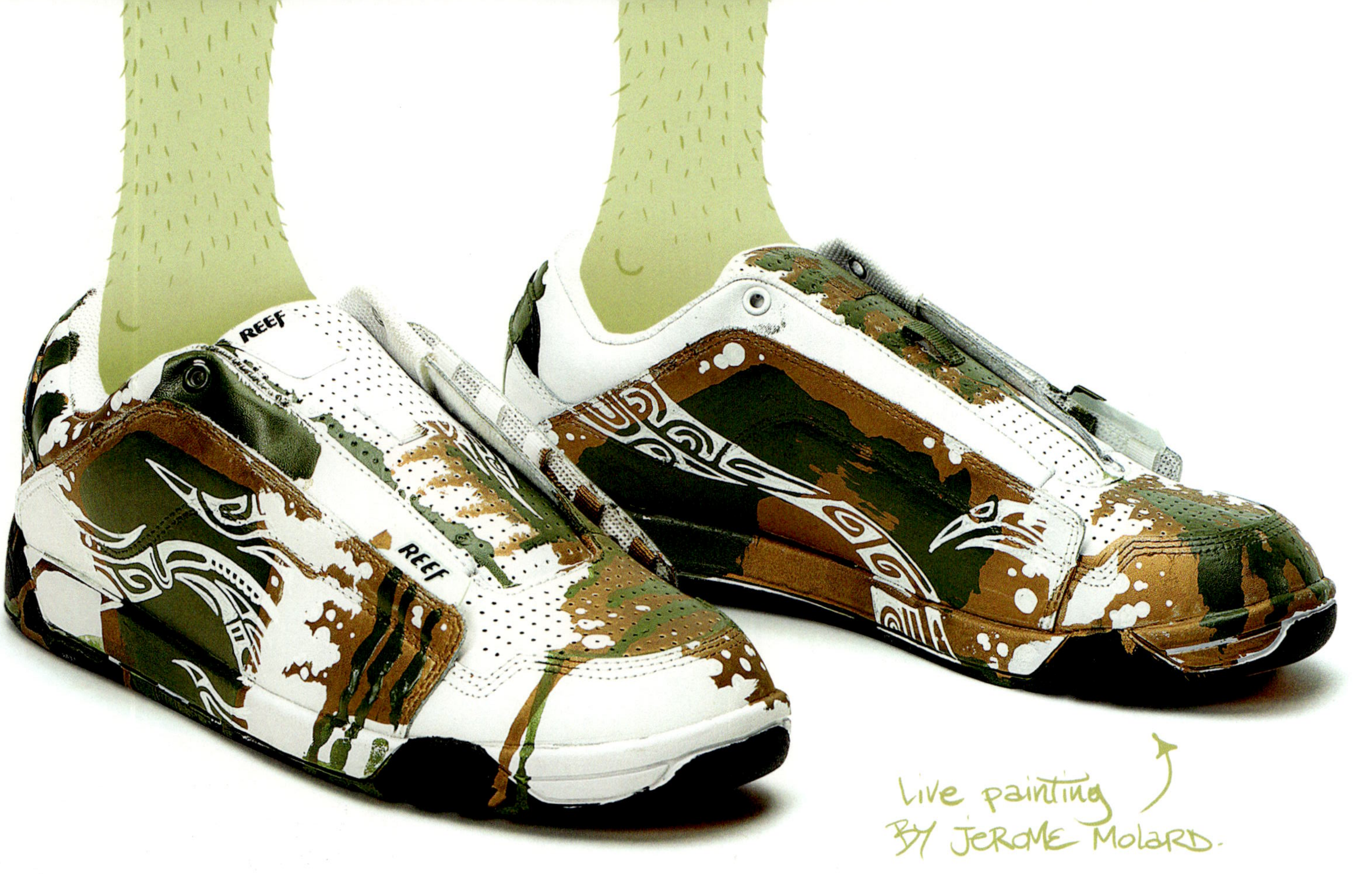

Live painting
by Jerome Molard.

Clément's "vibe" is calligraphic, traced in Indian ink or simply a pencil. Clement Laurentin gives a central role to people and faces. His backgrounds are urban and the framework is metallic. However, Clement talks about nature and his childhood as the fountains of his inspiration. Planet Reef? "One more bridge thrown down between art and surf." The 9ème Concept? "A unique art school." Perhaps his diploma will lead him to accomplishing "a living painting with trees growing, wind blowing, and birds singing".

Avec une « vibe » calligraphique, tracée à l'encre de chine ou simplement au crayon, Clement Laurentin donne un rôle central aux personnes et aux visages. Les fonds sont urbains, les cadres métalliques. Pourtant, Clément cite la nature et l'enfance comme fontaines de son inspiration. Le Planet Reef ? « Un pont de plus jeté entre l'art et le culte de la glisse ». Le 9ème Concept ? « Une école d'art unique en son genre ». Son diplôme le conduira peut-être à réaliser « une toile vivante avec des arbres qui poussent, du vent qui souffle et des oiseaux qui chantent ».

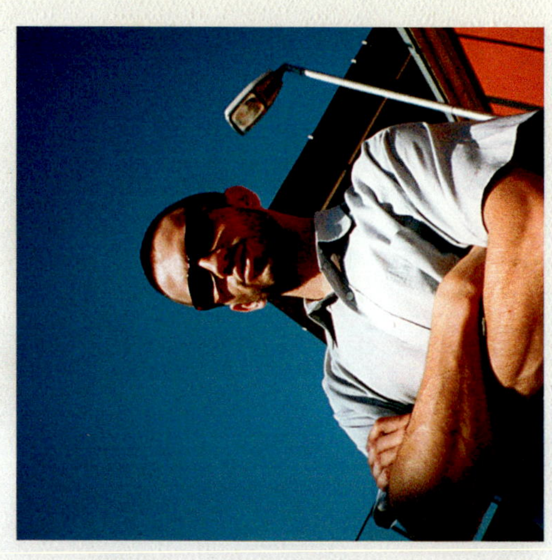

CLEMENT LAURENTIN

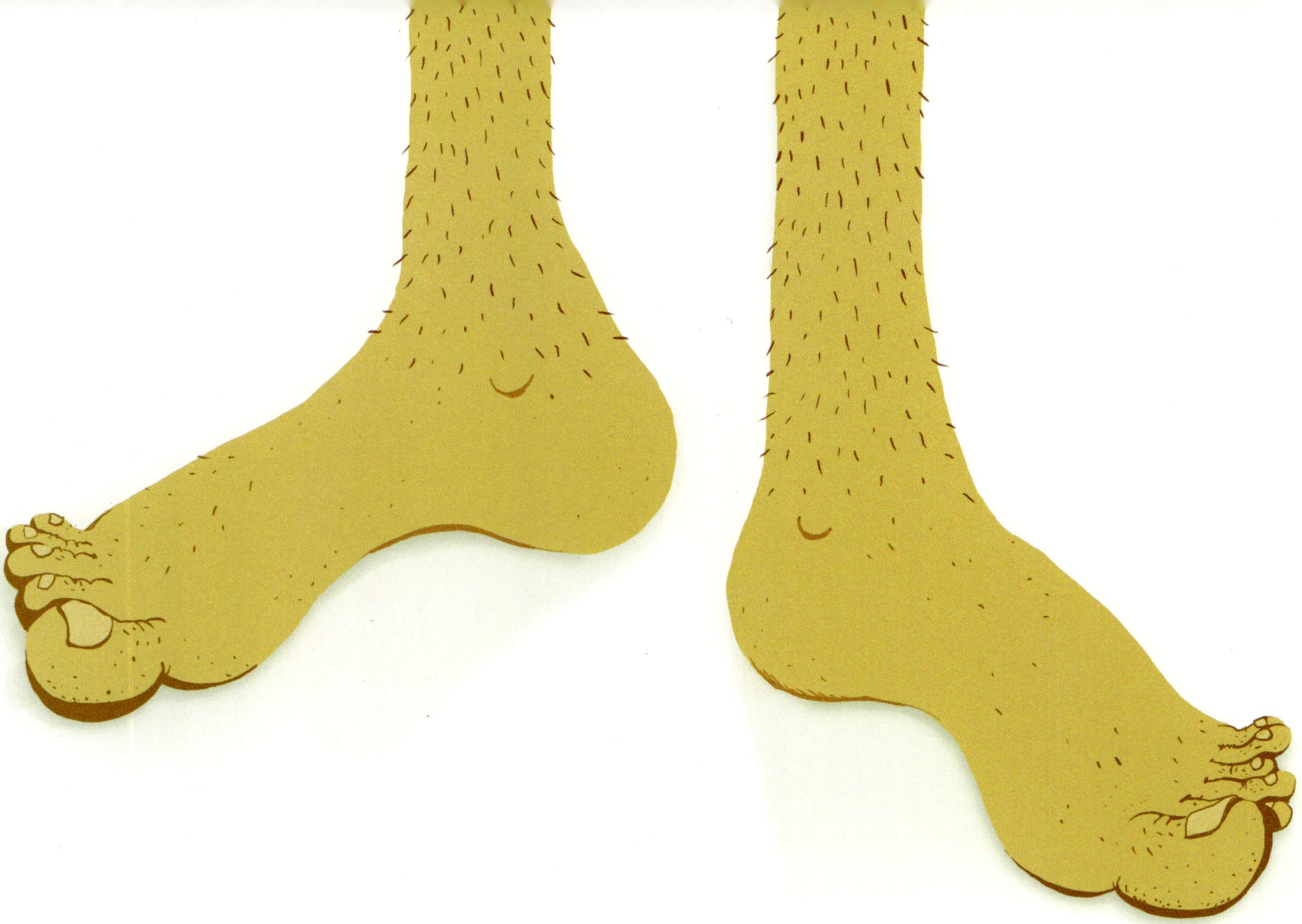

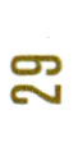

'LiSBON July 2003—

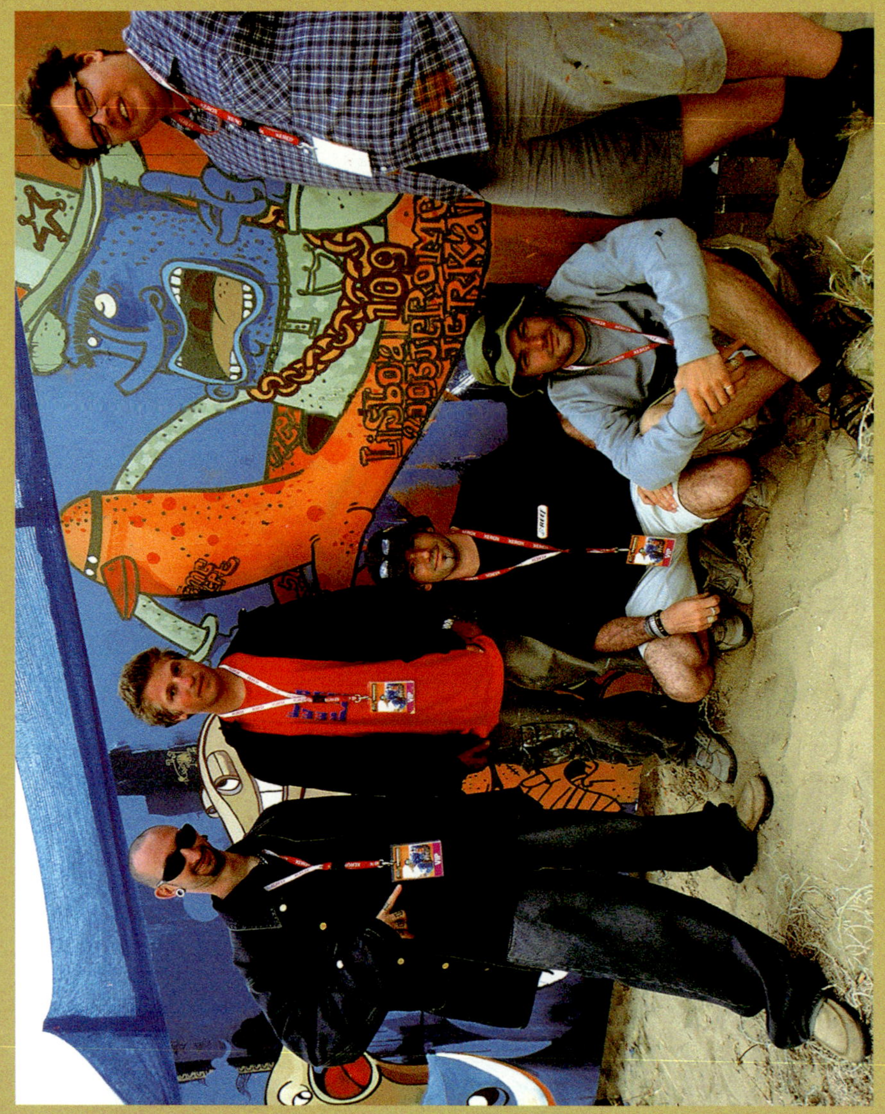

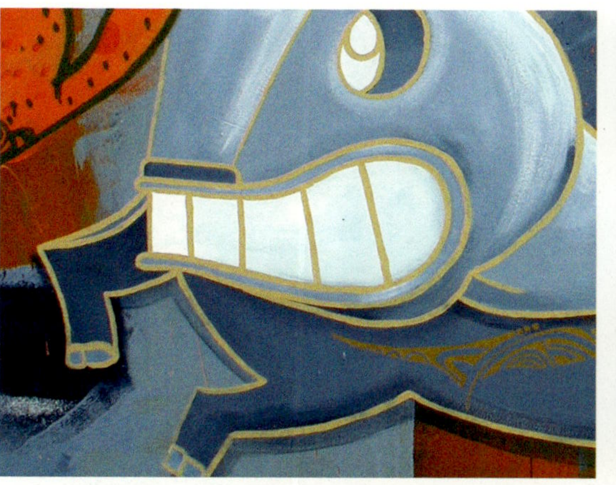

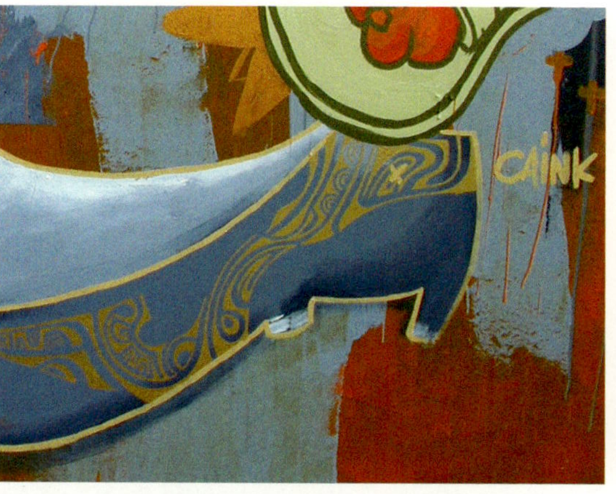

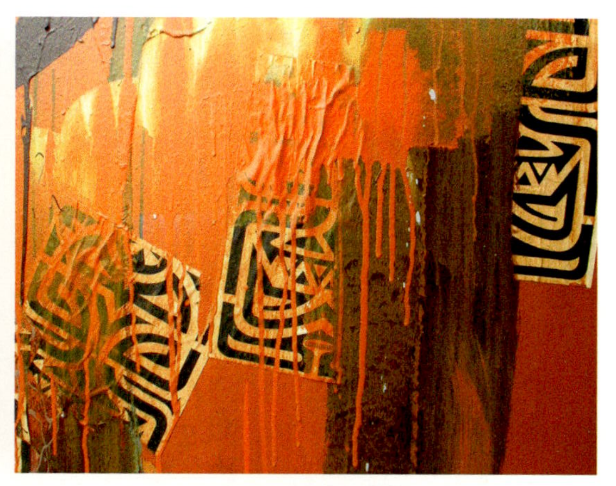

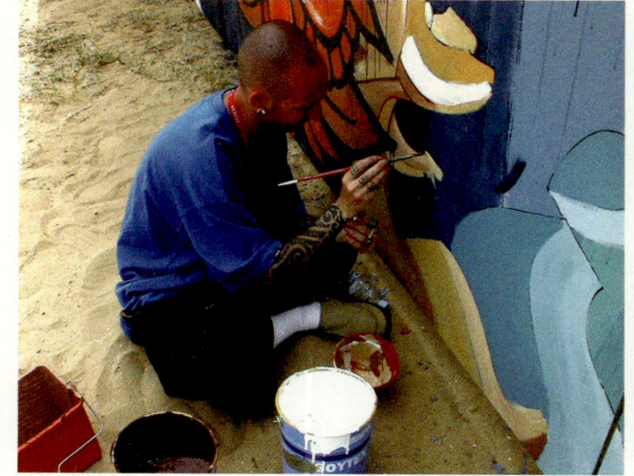

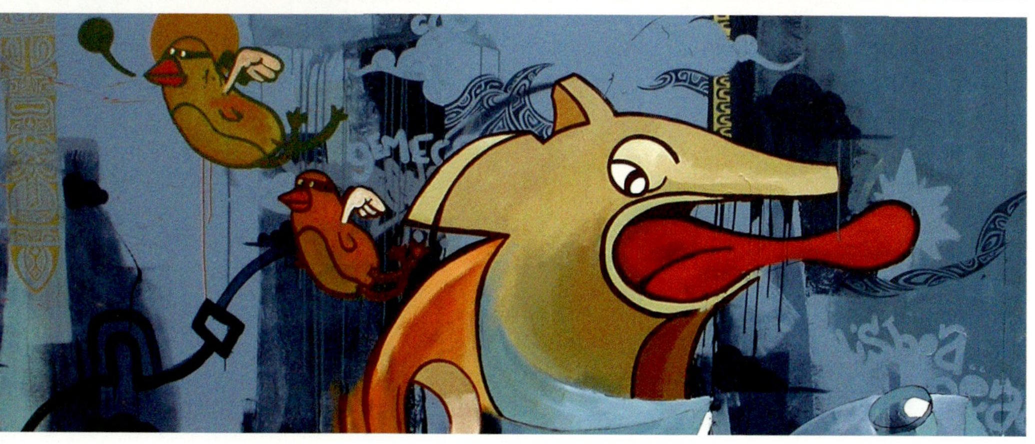

LiSBON

Live painting by Alëxone, Jérome Molard and Jerk 45

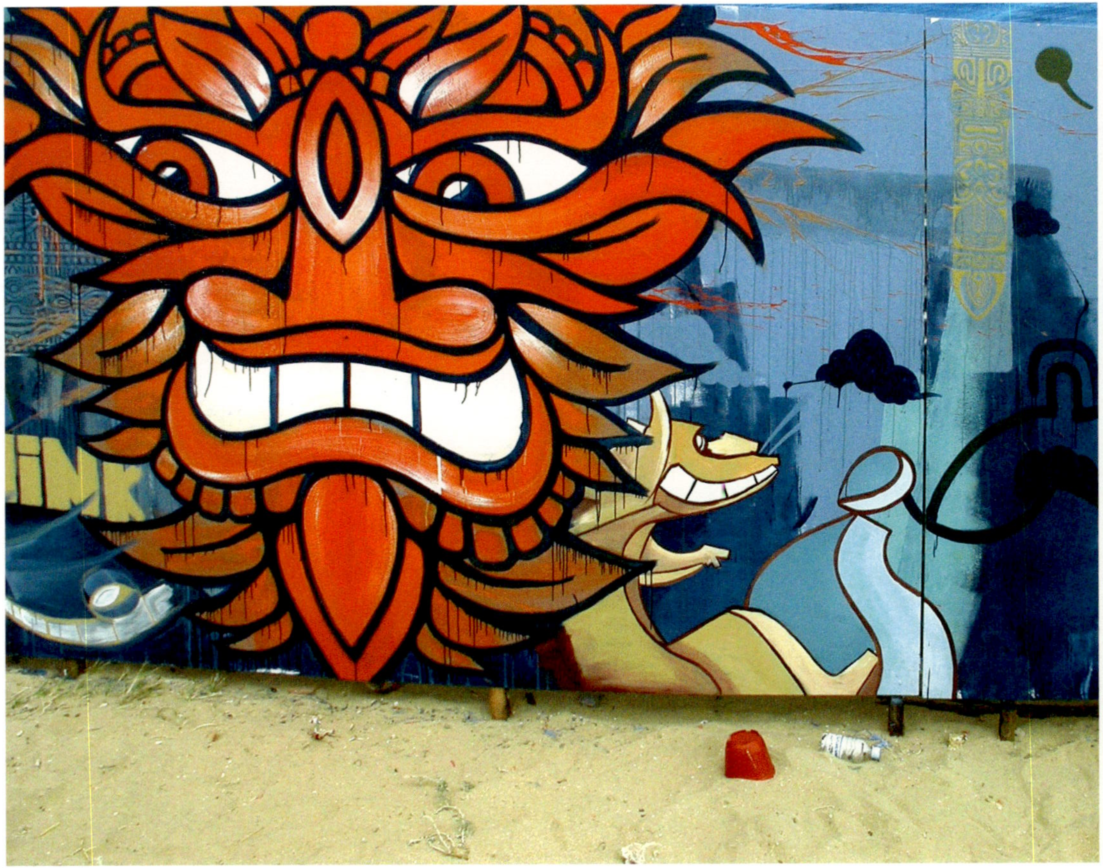

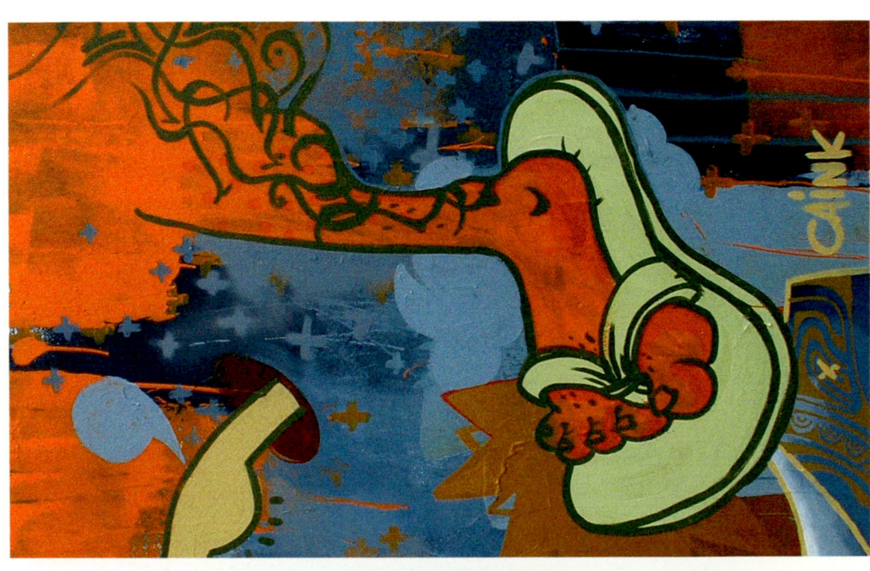

live painting on the beach, acrylic paint on wood, 20m in 3 days

LiSBON

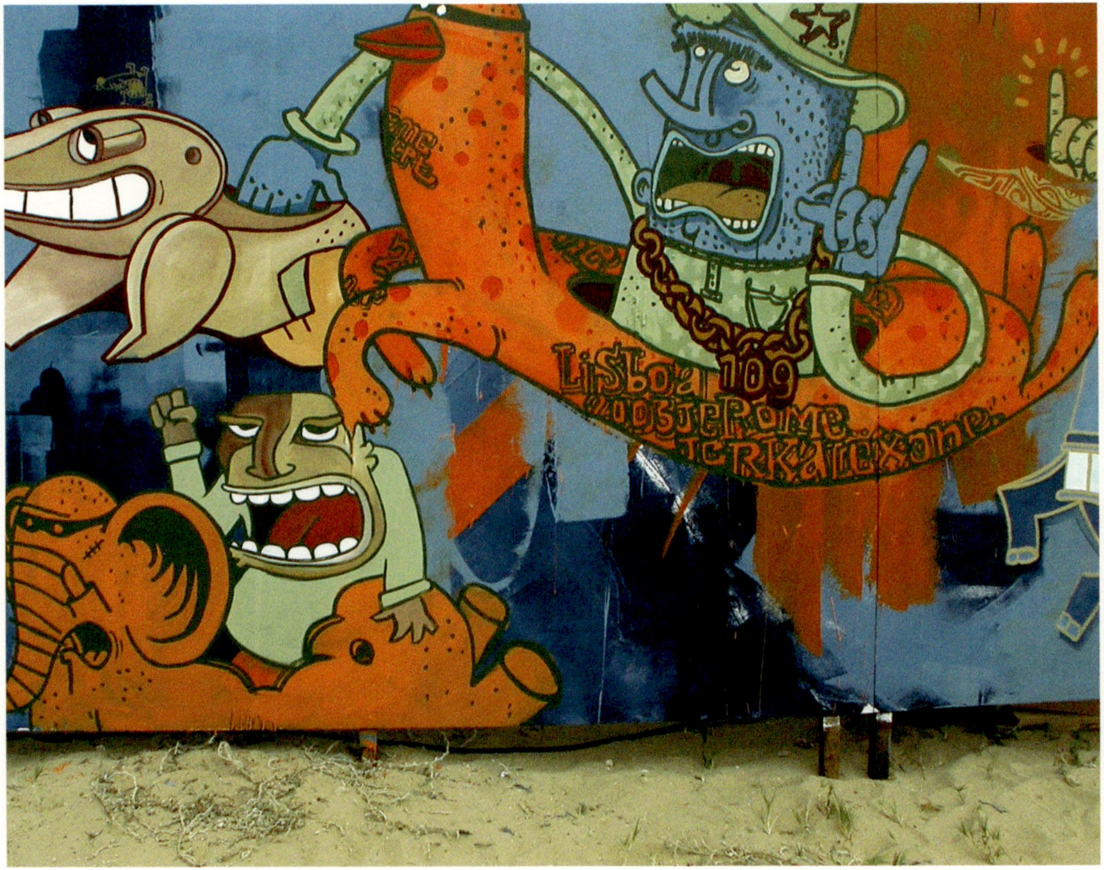

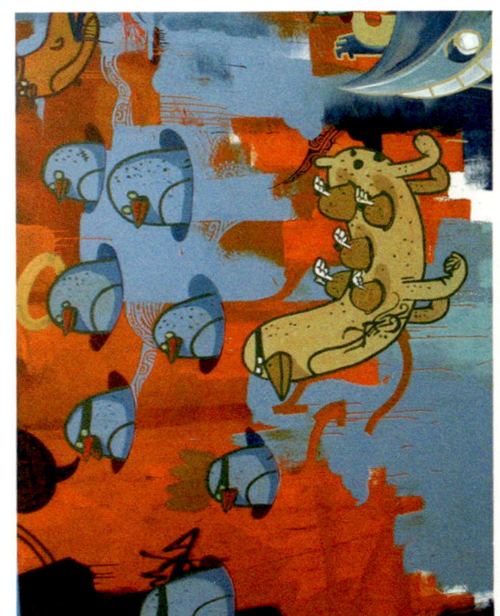
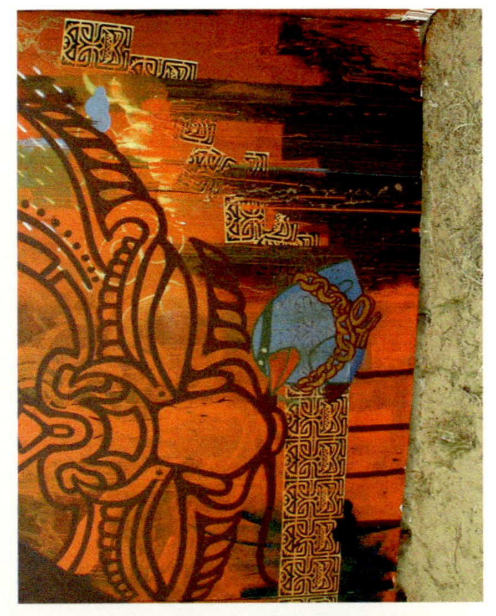

LiSBON

Alëxone, Jérome Molard and Jerk 45

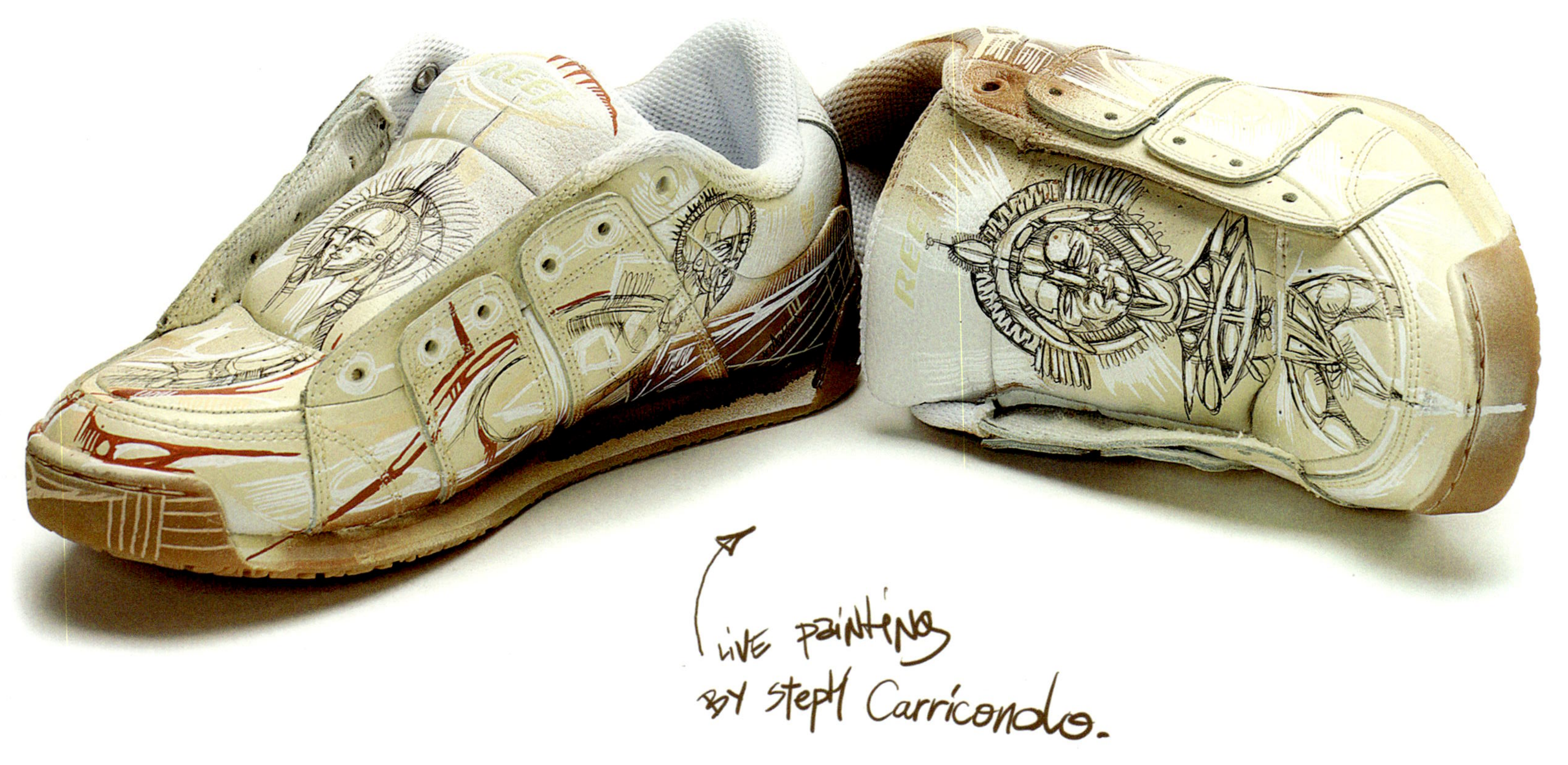

Live painting by Steph Carricondo.

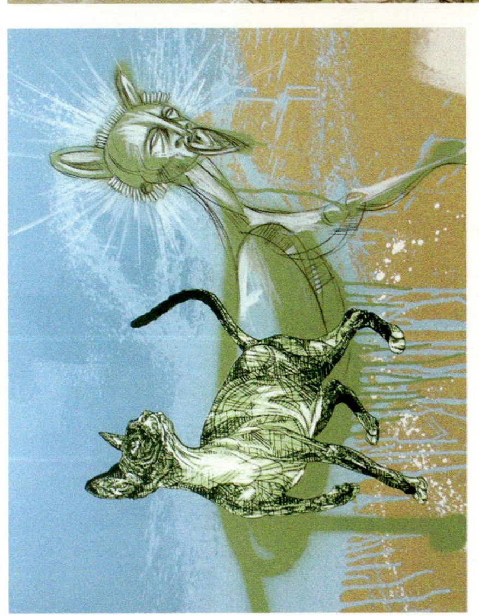
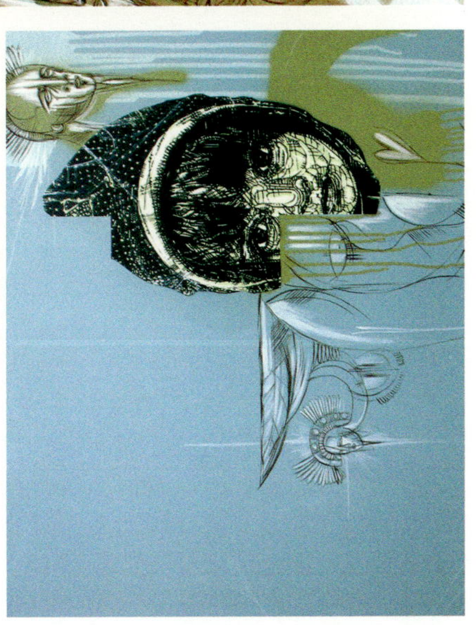

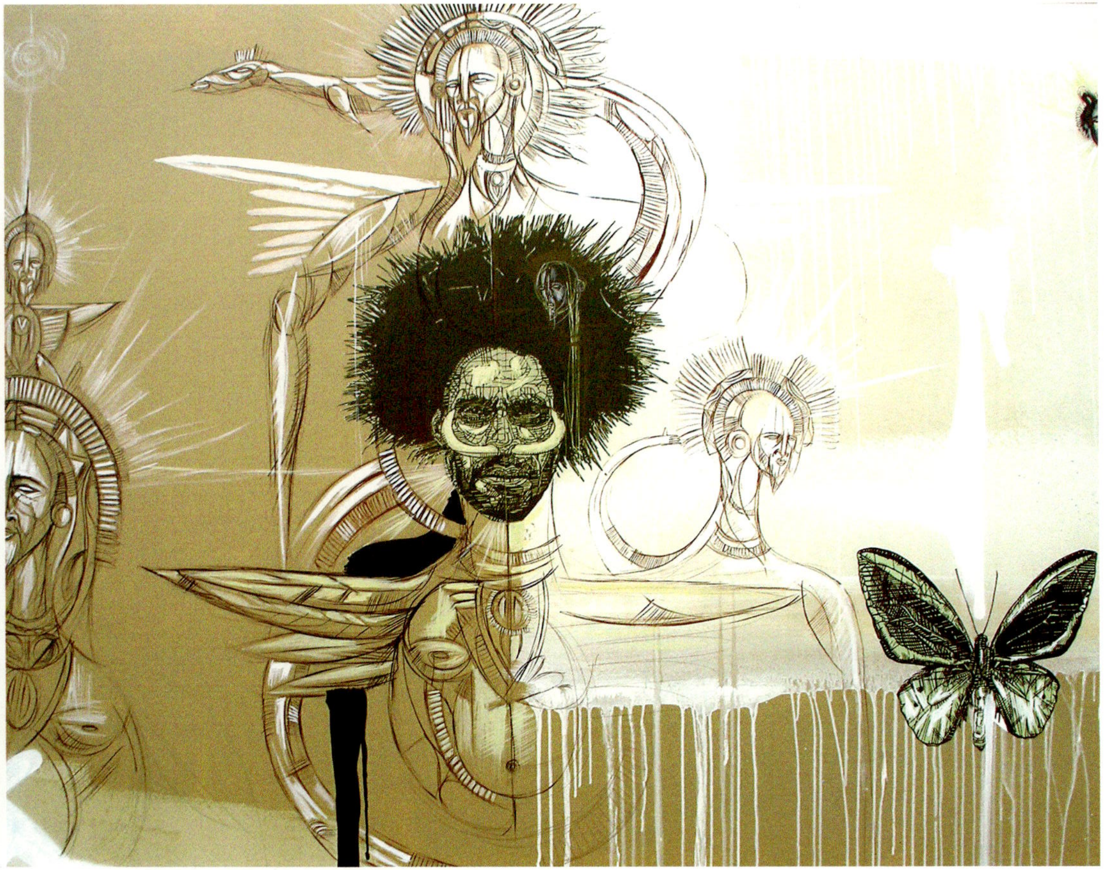

LiSBON

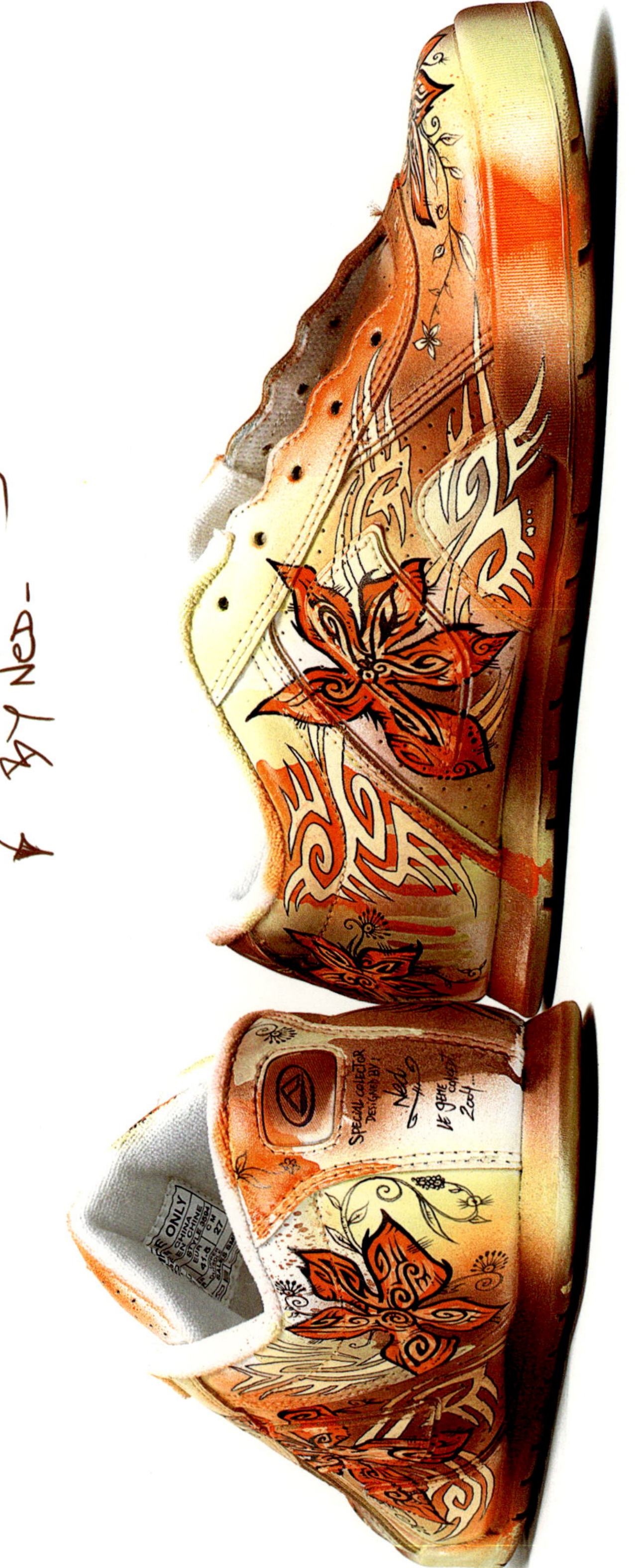
live painting
BY NED-

REEF
REEF
REEF
ALWAYS ON
ALWAYS ON
ALWAYS ON
NO SWAYLV

WORL
USA GUYS
USA GIRLS
EUROPE
UK
JAPAN

REEF
ALWAYS ON
ALWAYS ON

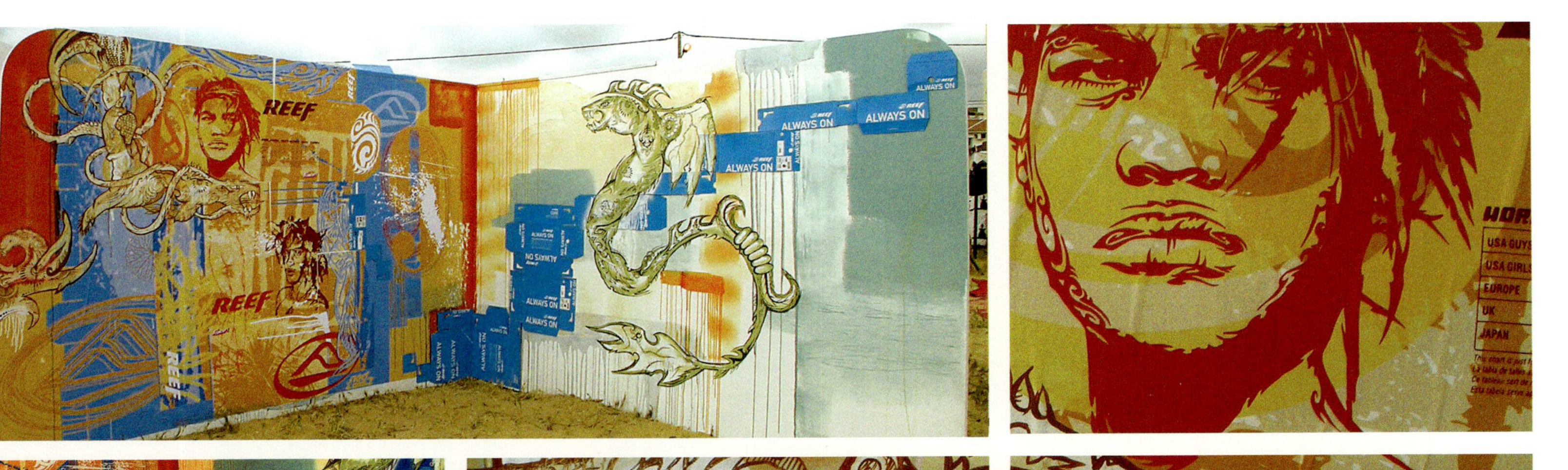

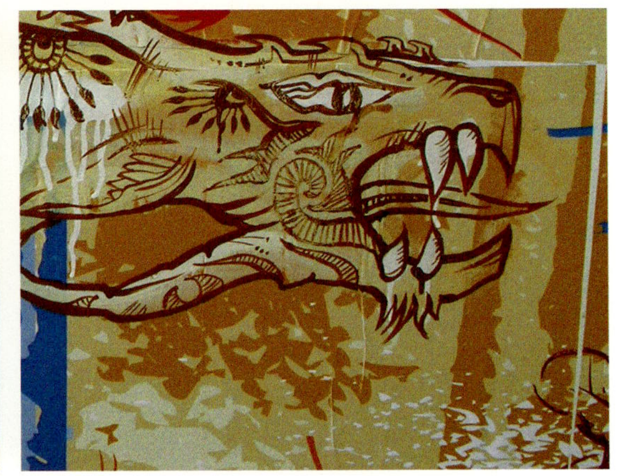

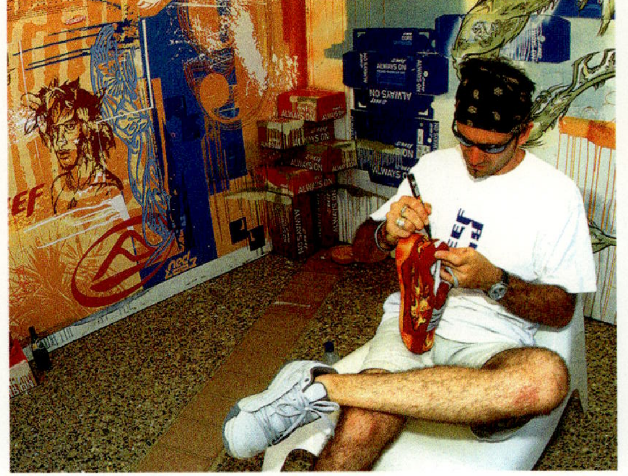

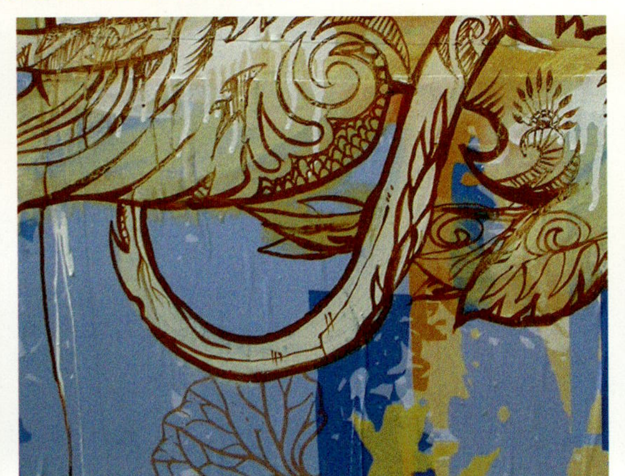

LiSBON

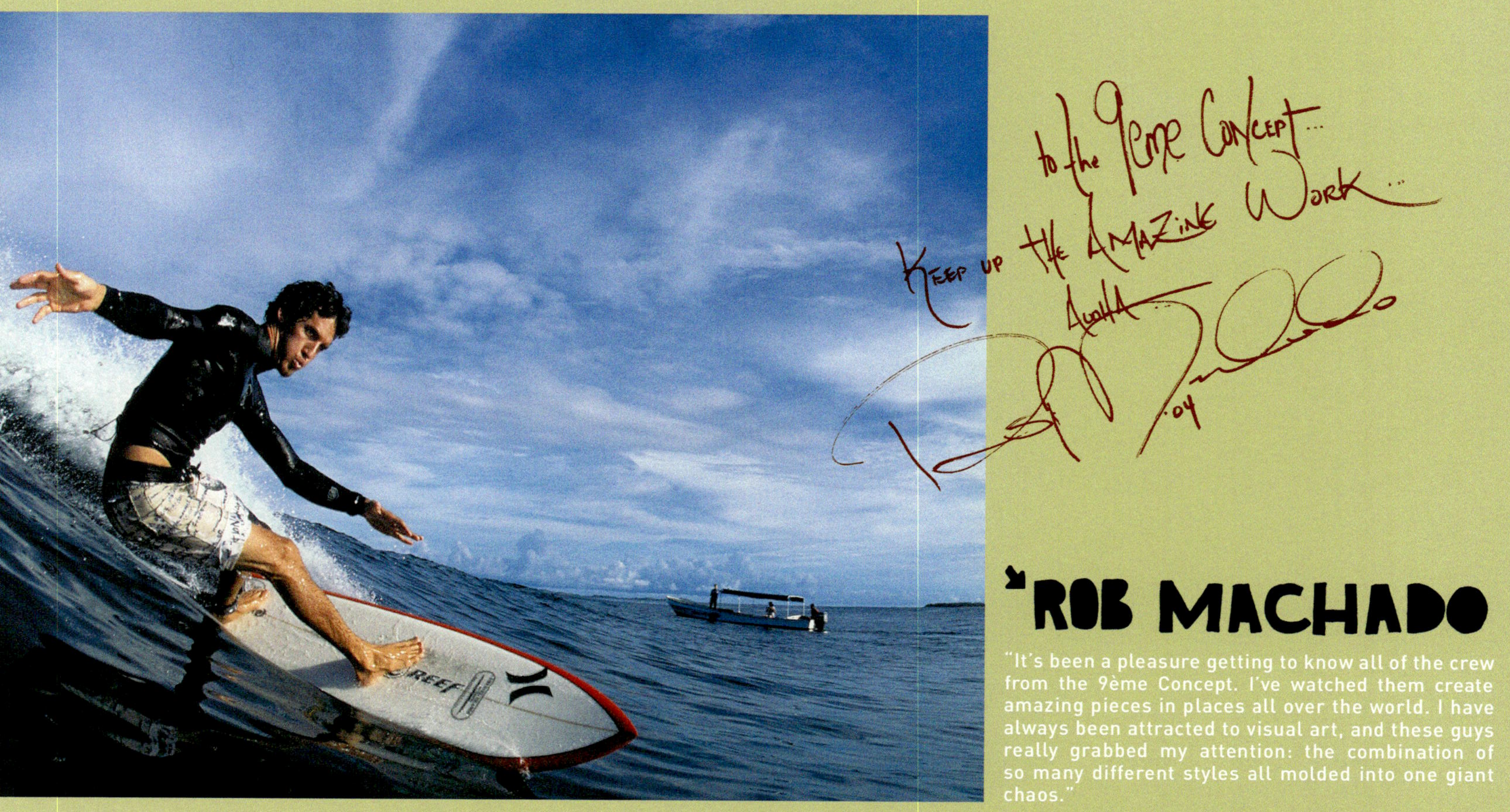

›ROB MACHADO

"It's been a pleasure getting to know all of the crew from the 9ème Concept. I've watched them create amazing pieces in places all over the world. I have always been attracted to visual art, and these guys really grabbed my attention: the combination of so many different styles all molded into one giant chaos."

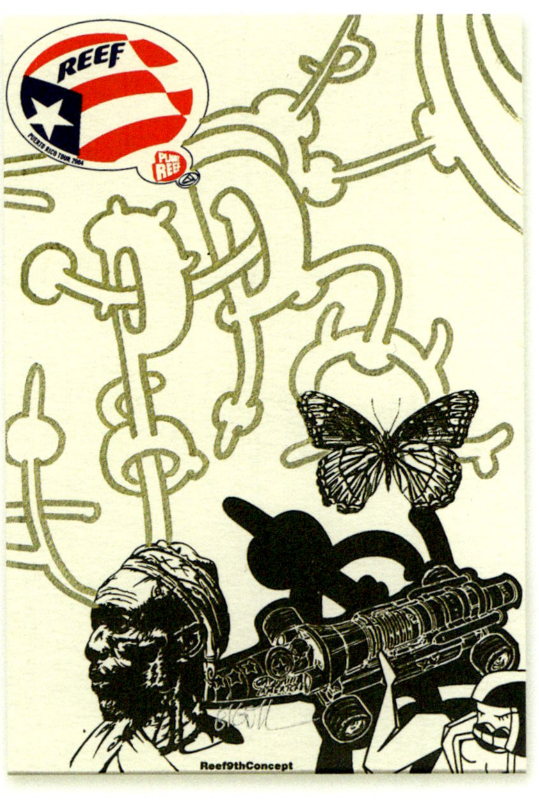

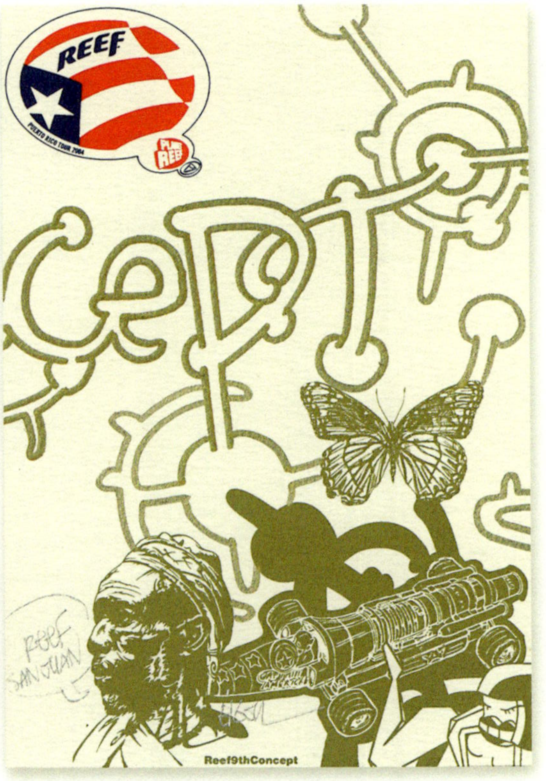

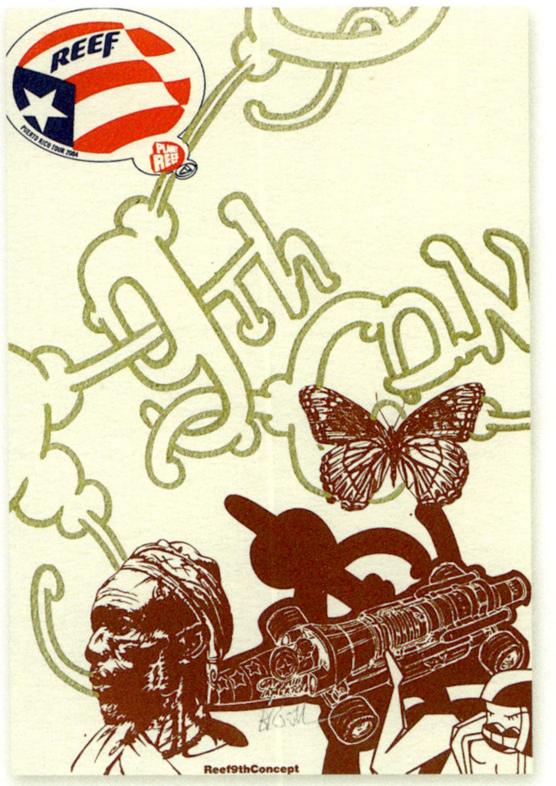

Drawings on silk screen cards by Big Jul

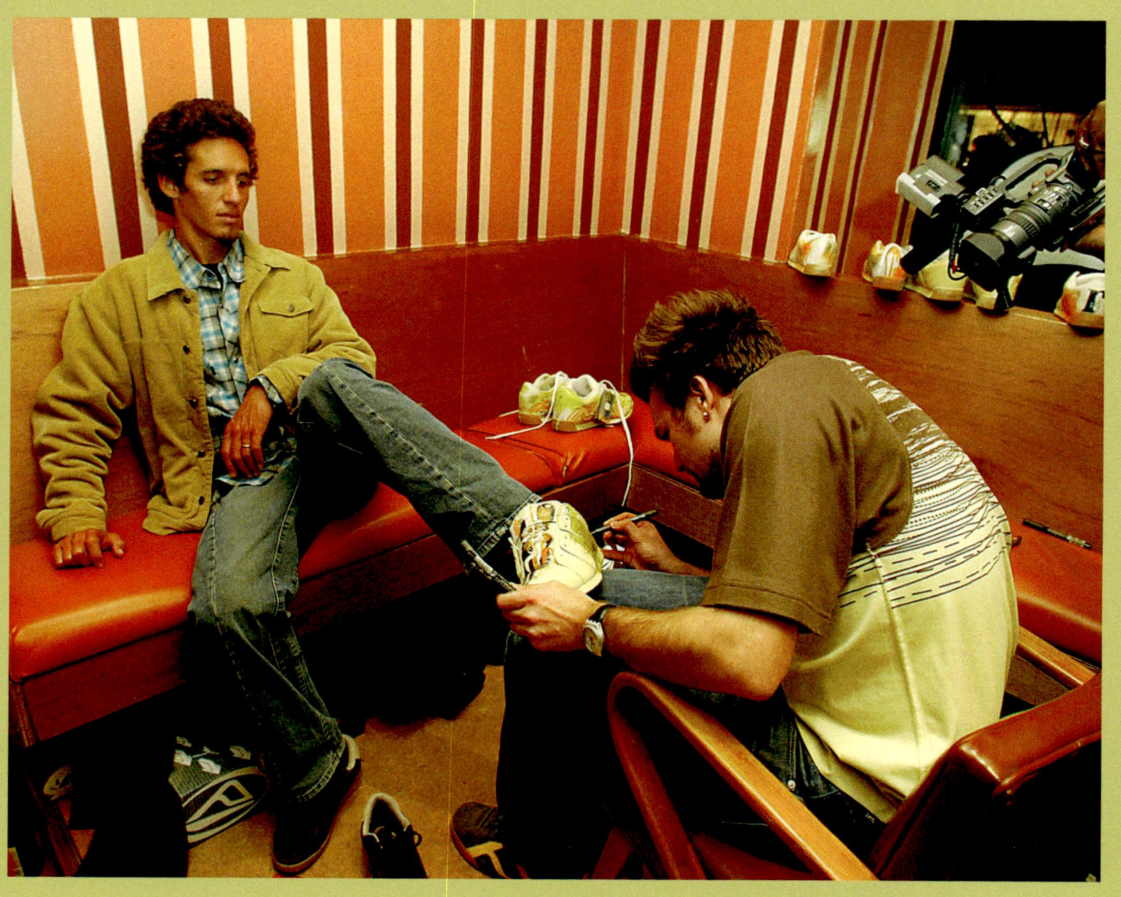

*HOLLYWOOD
february 2004 —

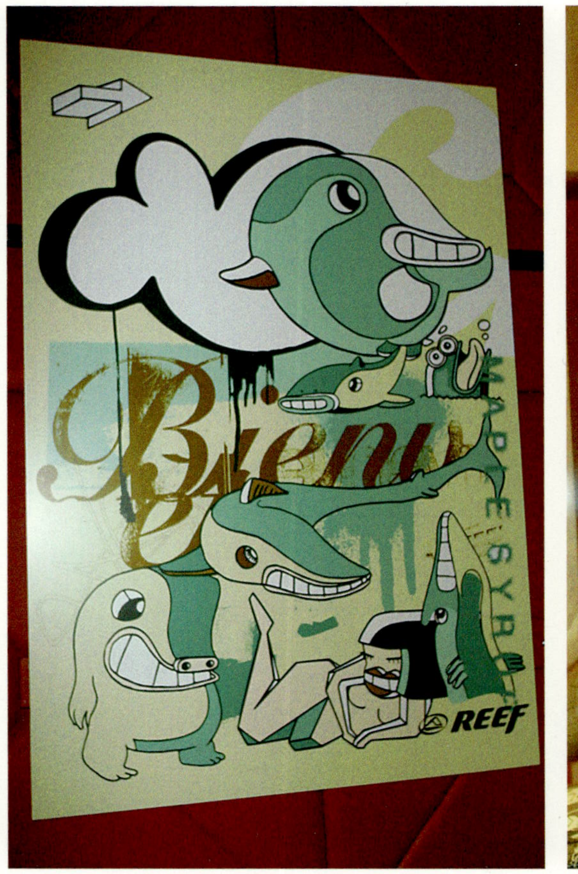

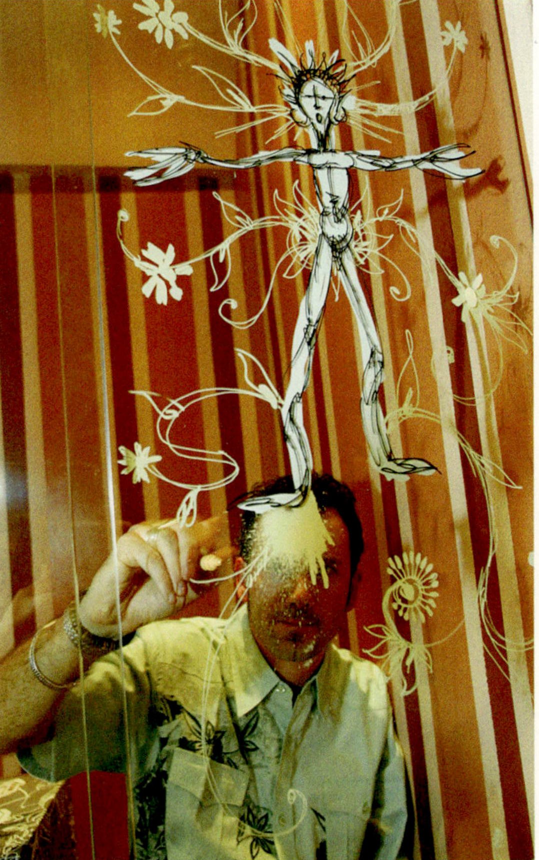

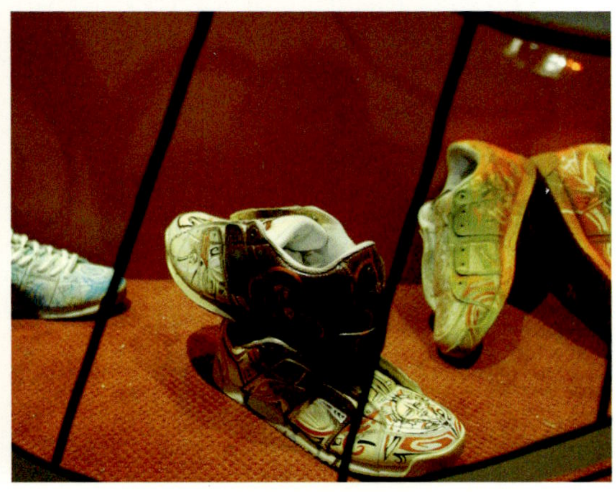

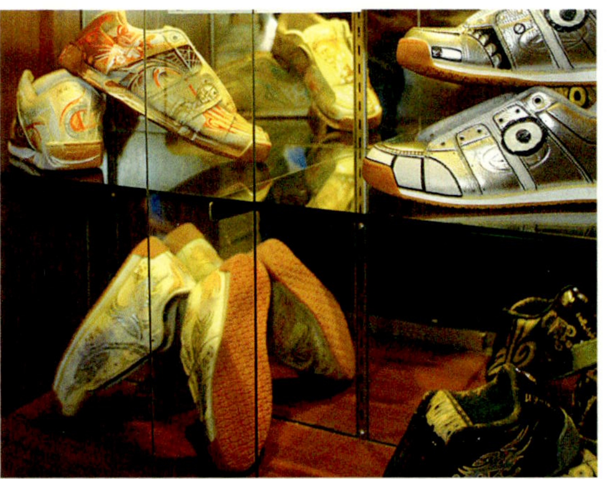

HOLLYWOOD

Ned live painting

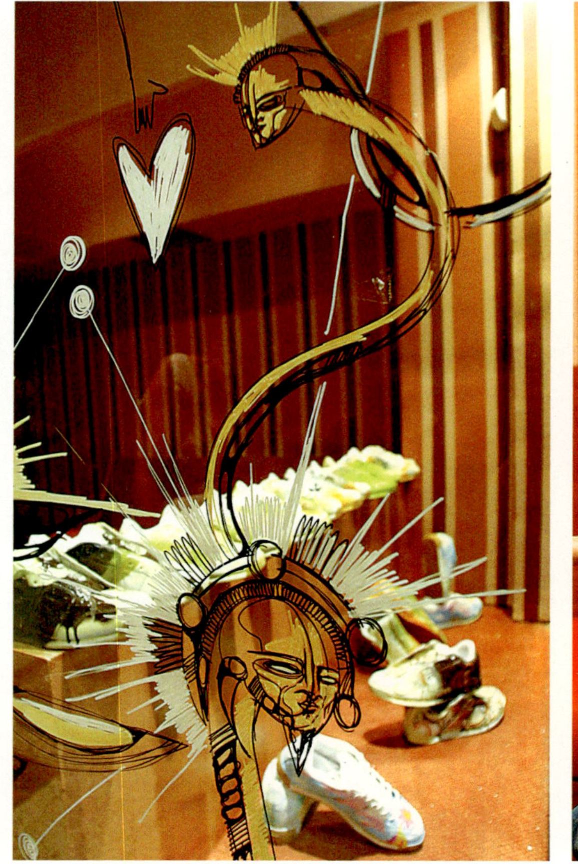

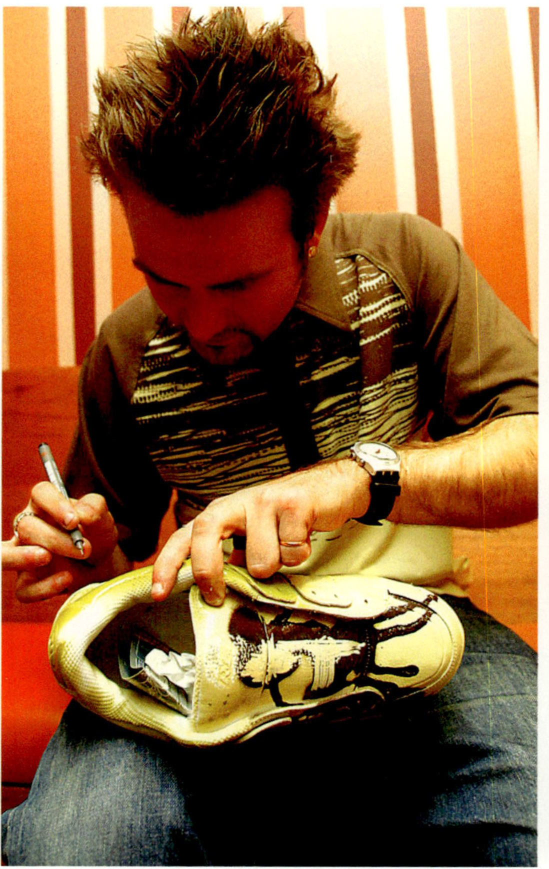

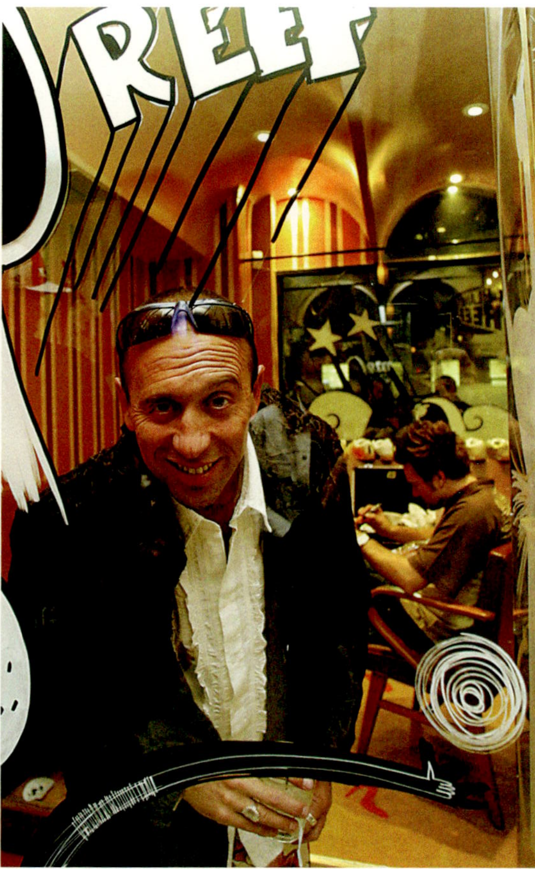

Steph Carricondo customizing Reef shoes

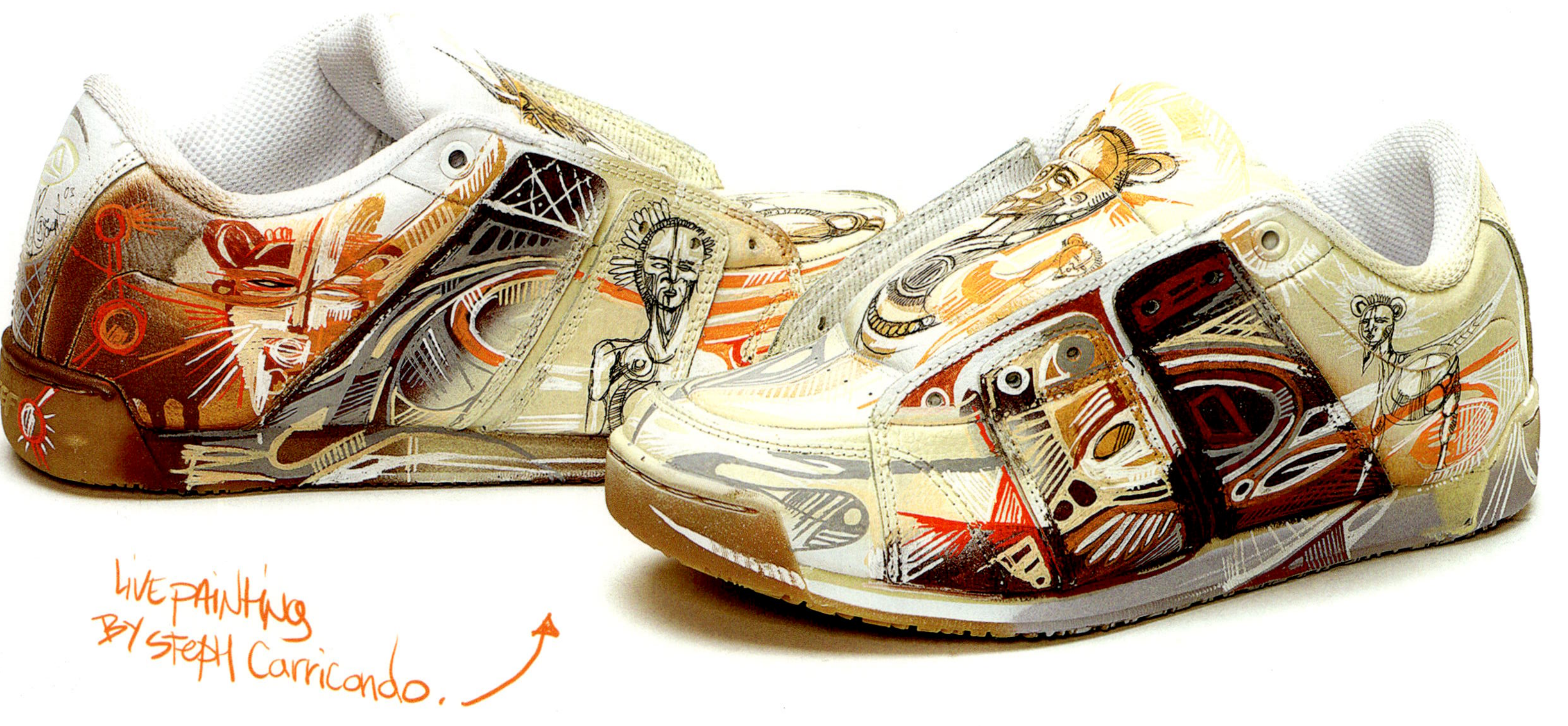
LIVE PAINTING
BY STEPH Carricondo.

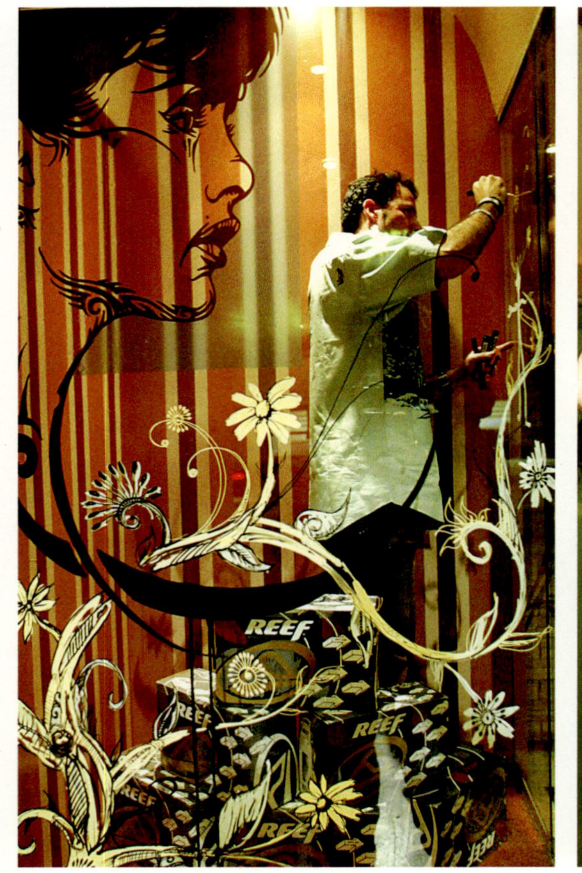

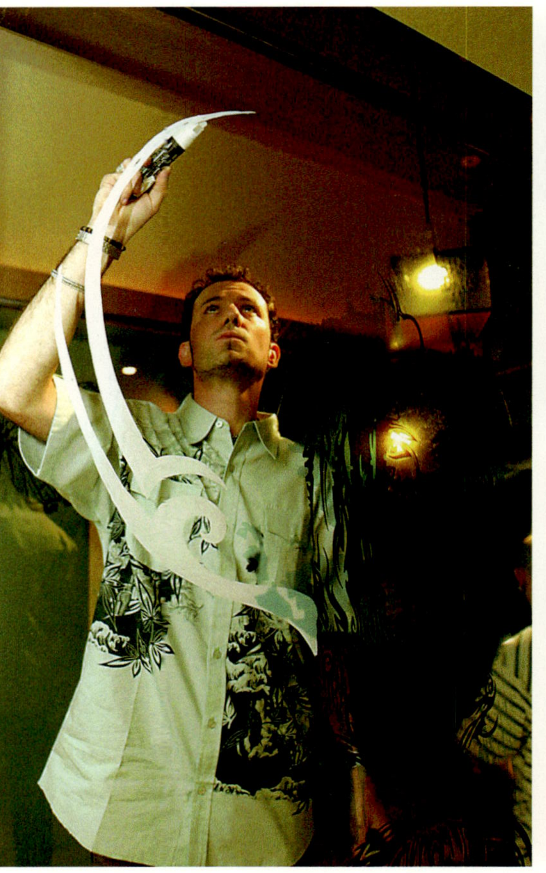

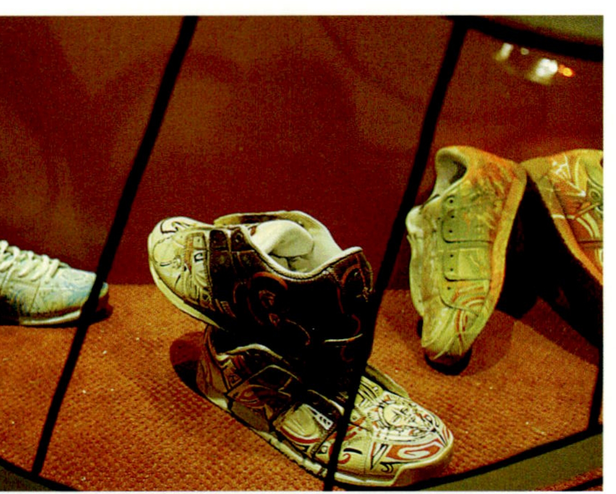

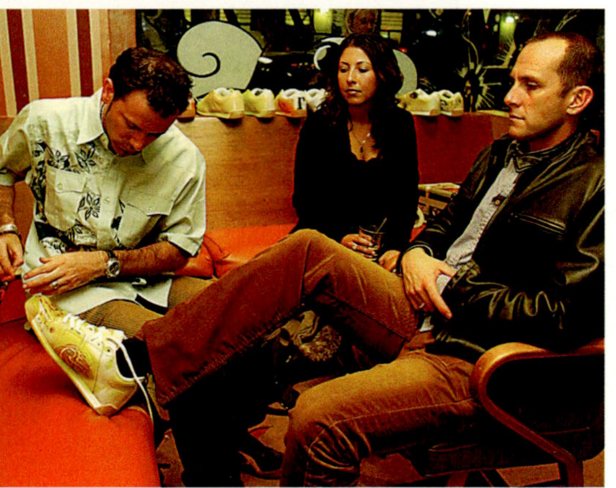

HOLLYWOOD

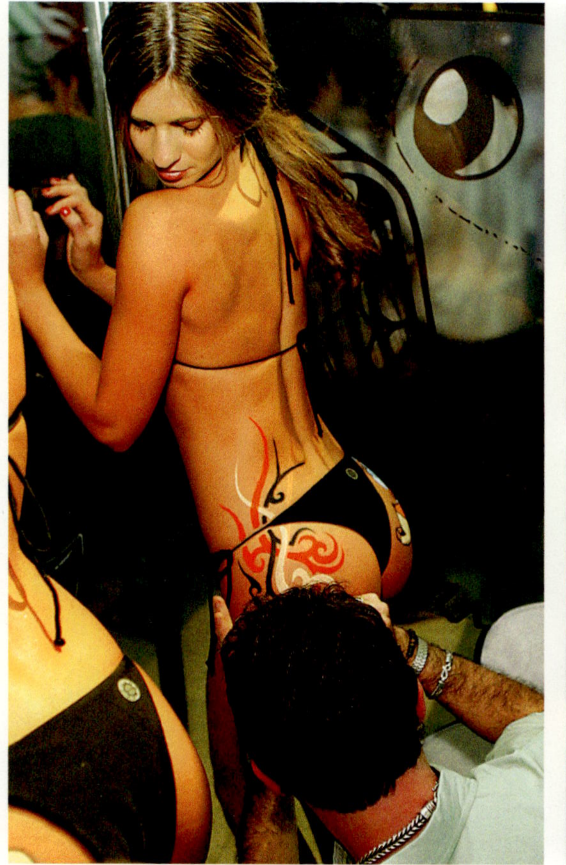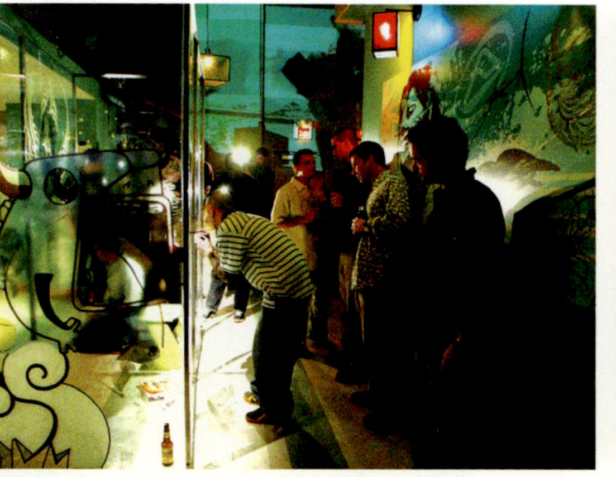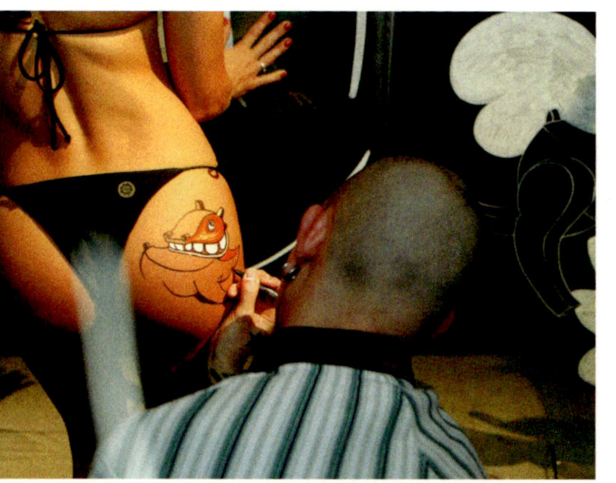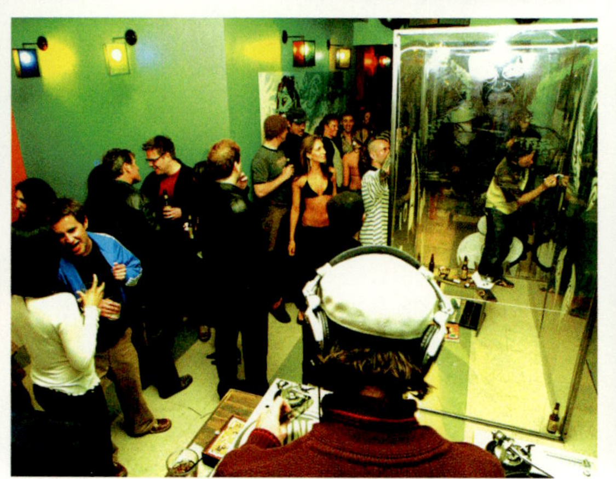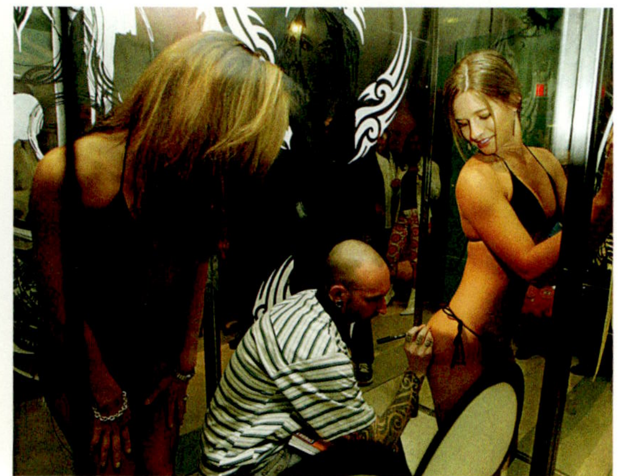

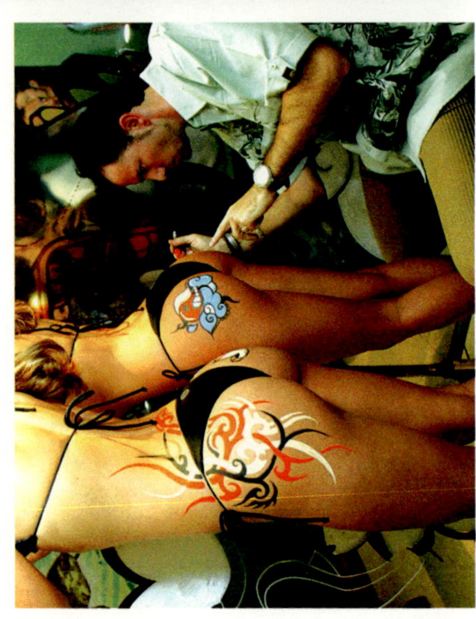

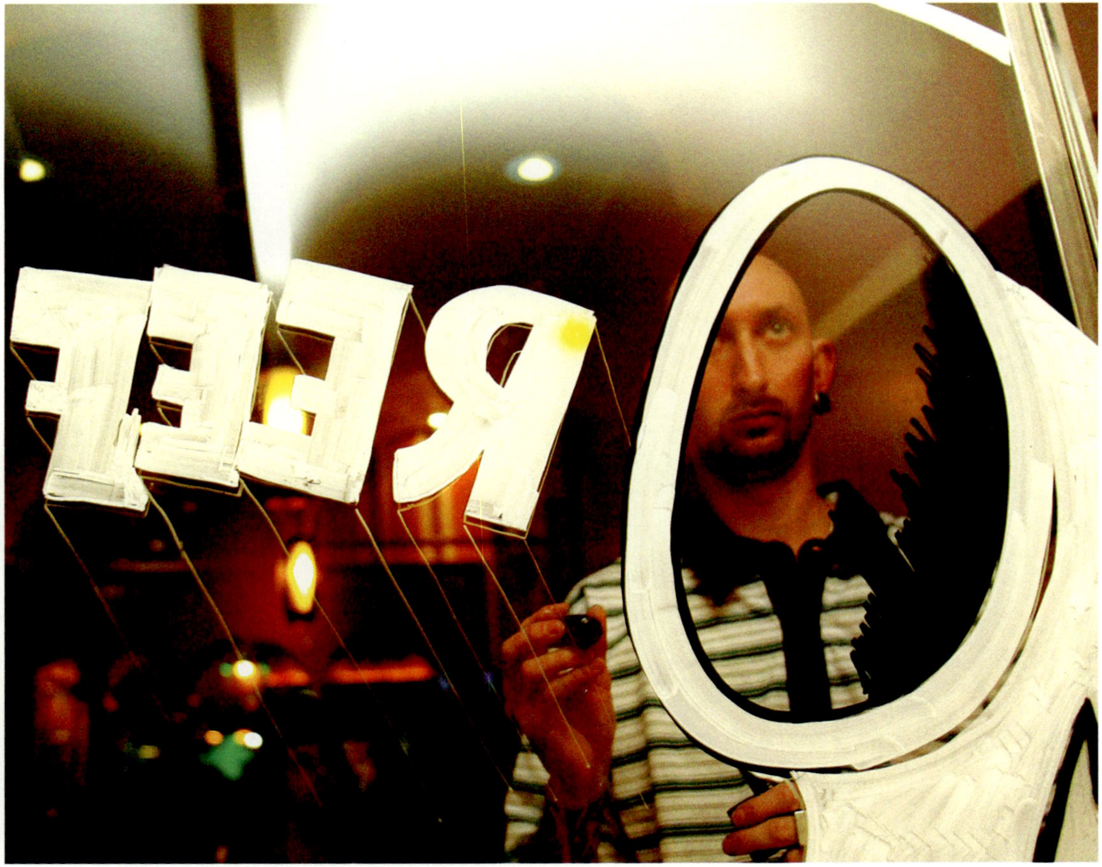

KEEF

HOLLYWOOD

studio painting
BY STEPH Carricondo/JERK 45/Ned

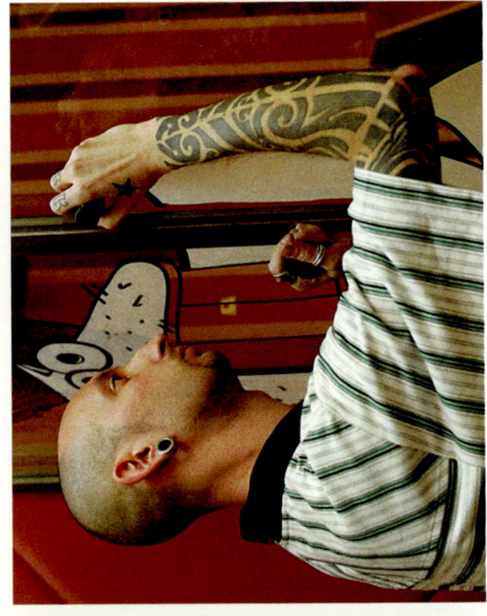

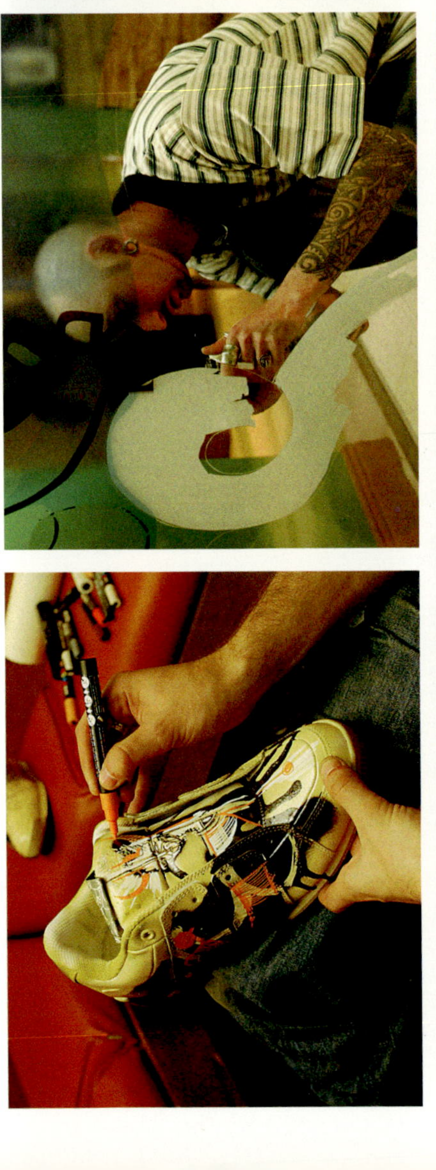

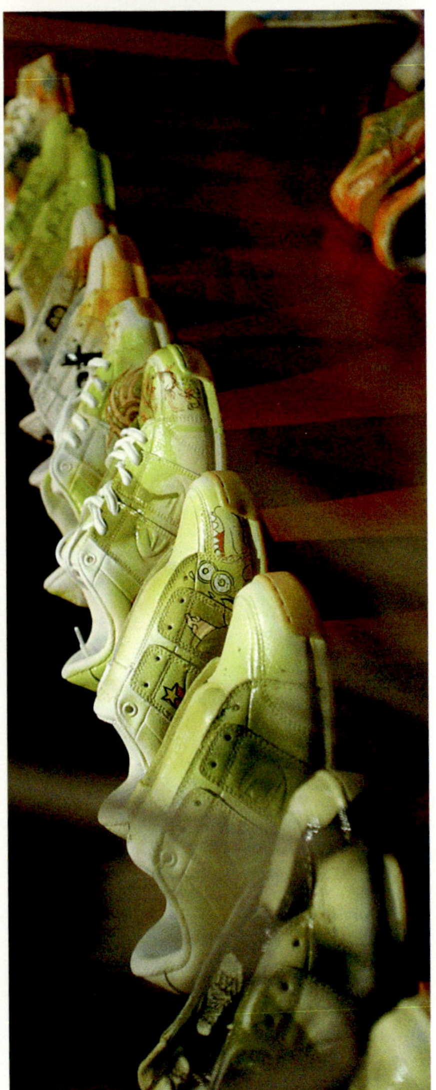

HOLLYWOOD

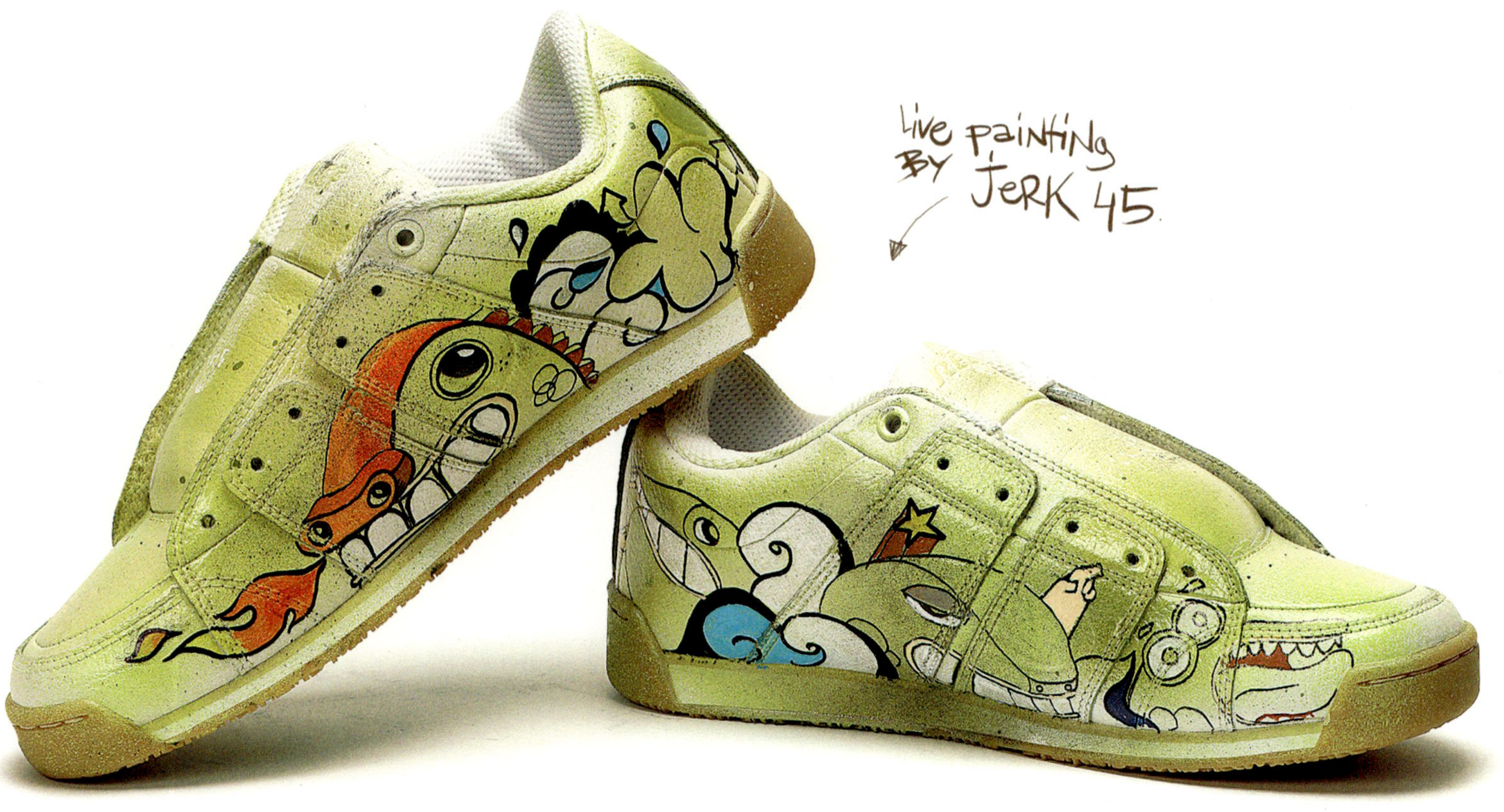

live painting
by JERK 45

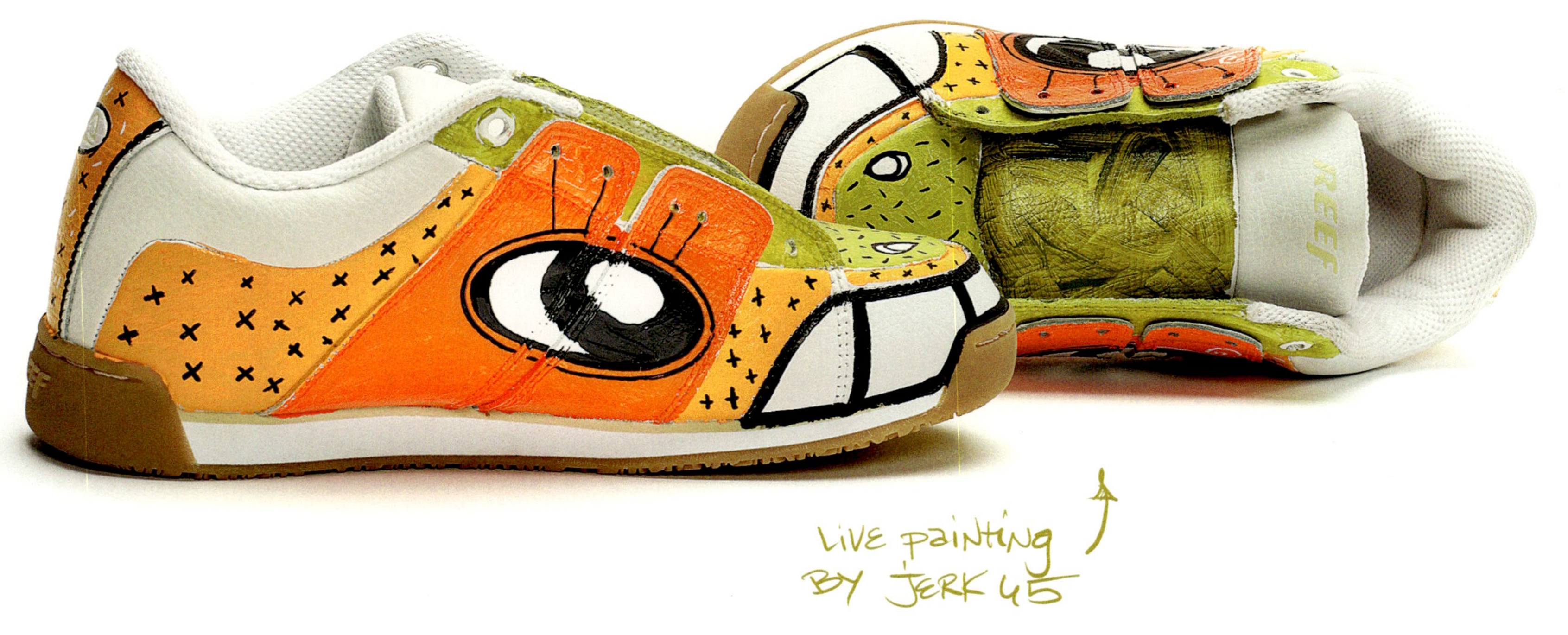
REEF
Live painting
by Jerk 45

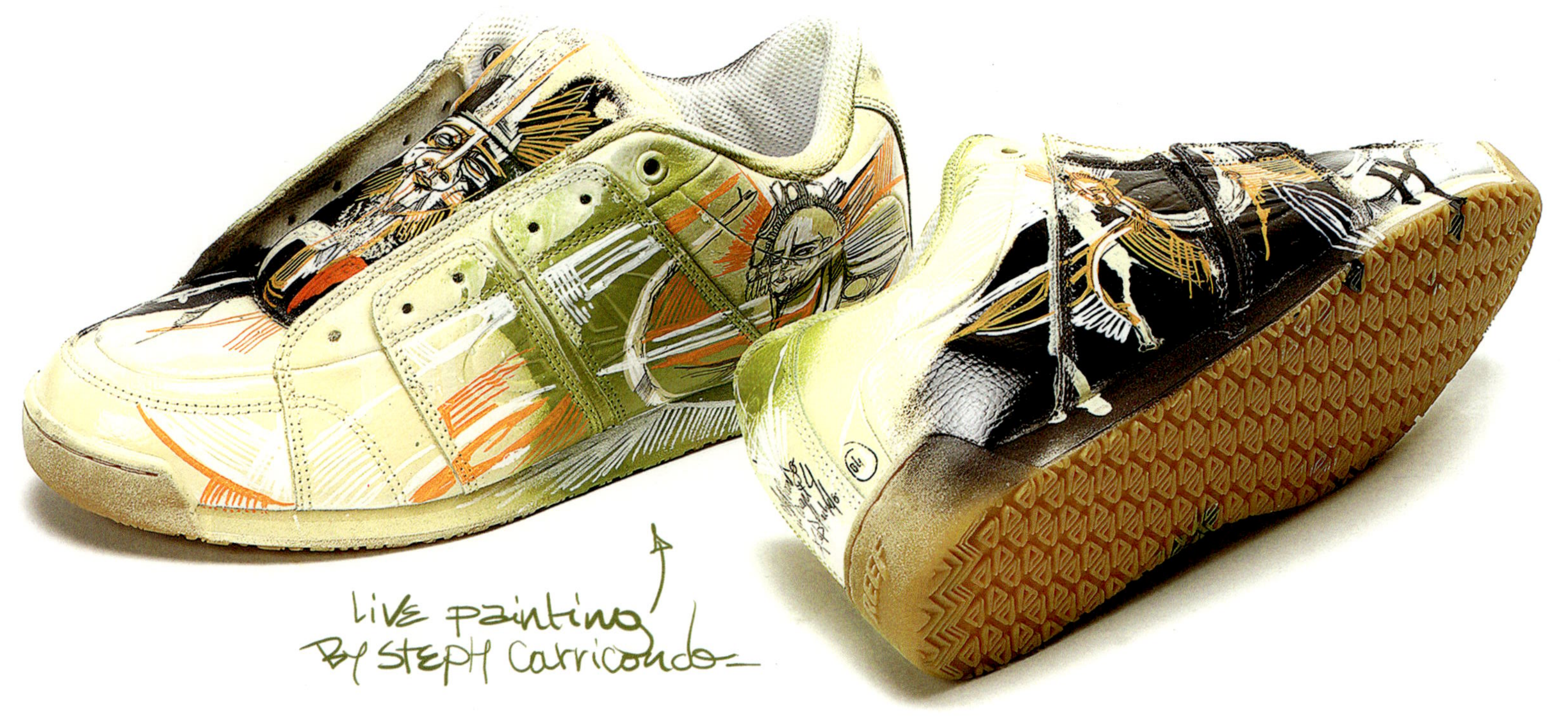
Live Painting
By Steph Carricondo

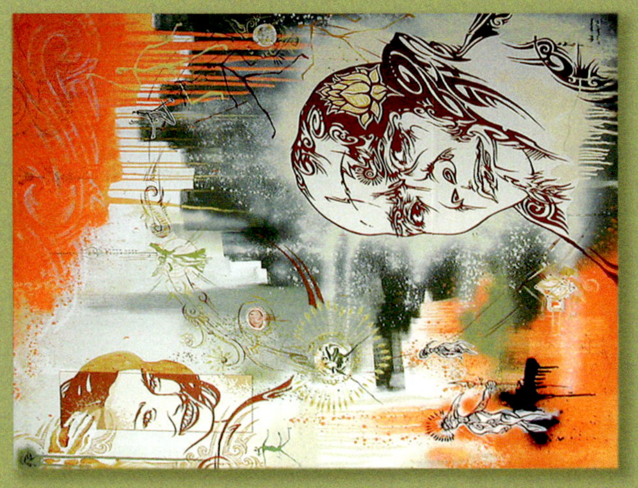

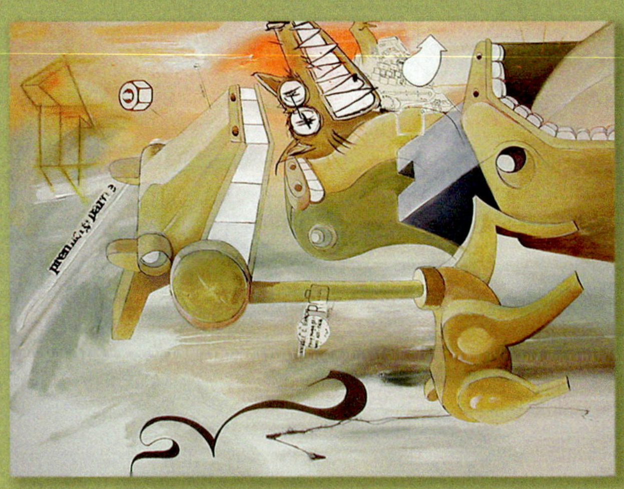

'MUNICH *february 2004*

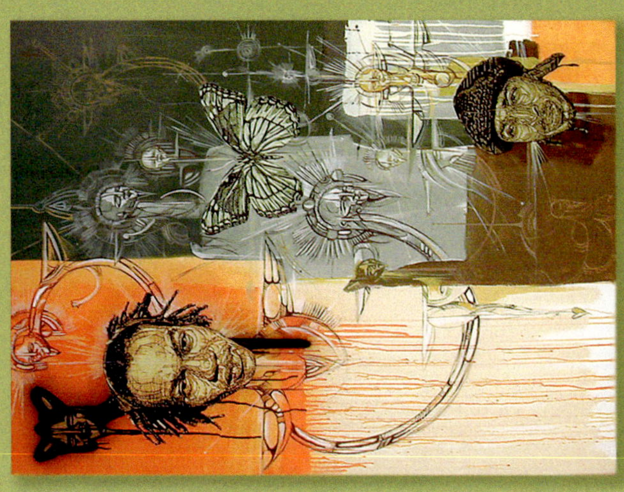

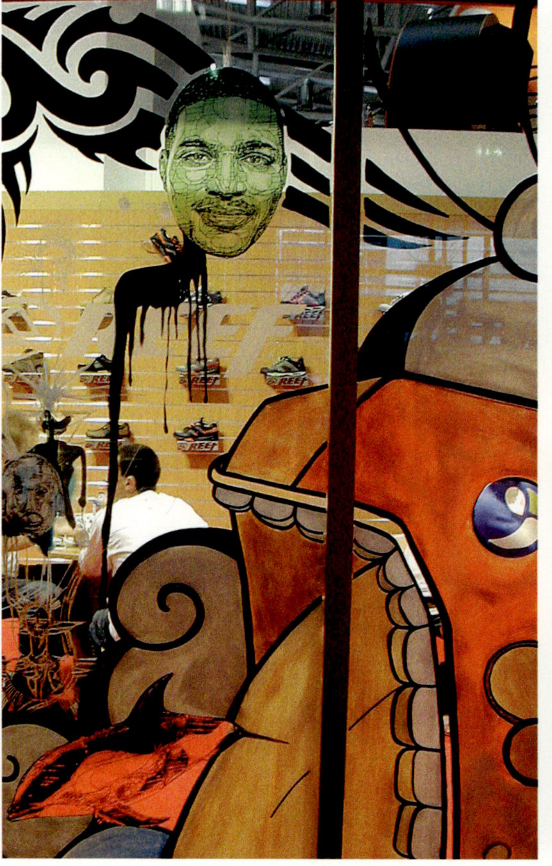
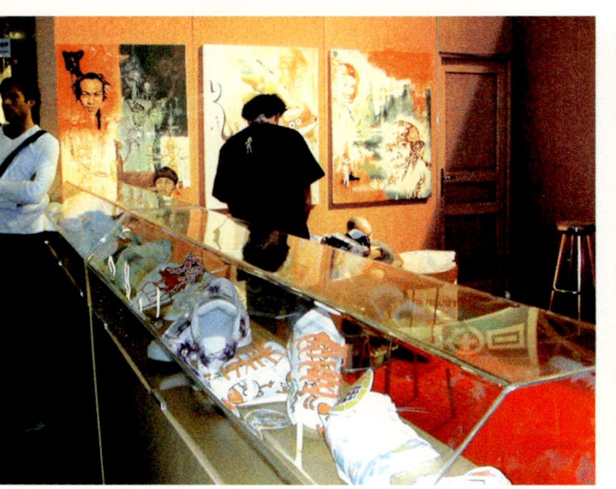
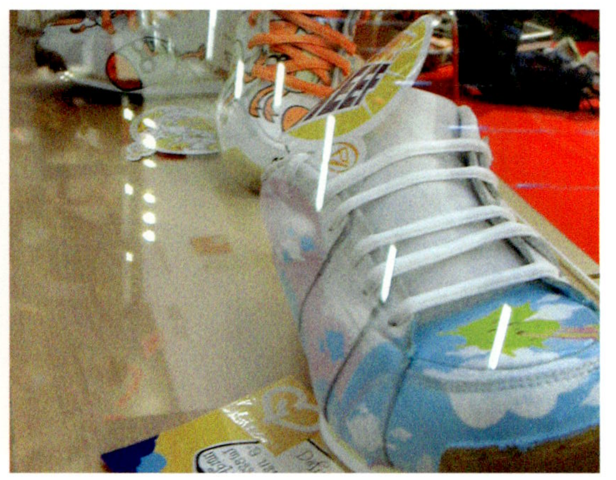
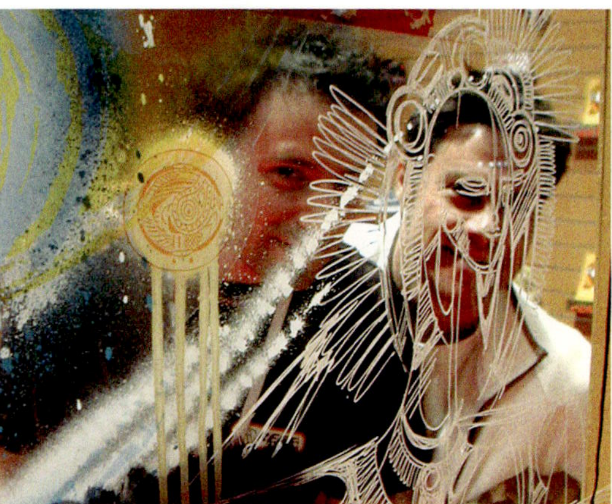
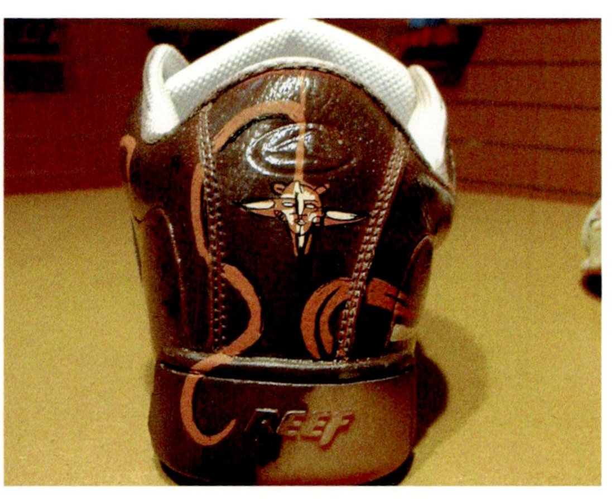

MUNiCH

53

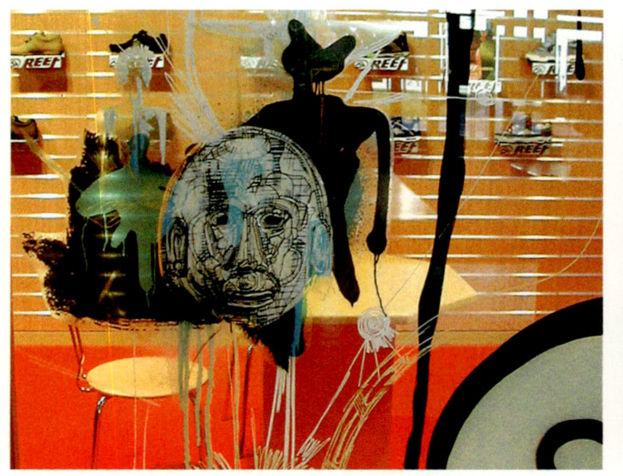
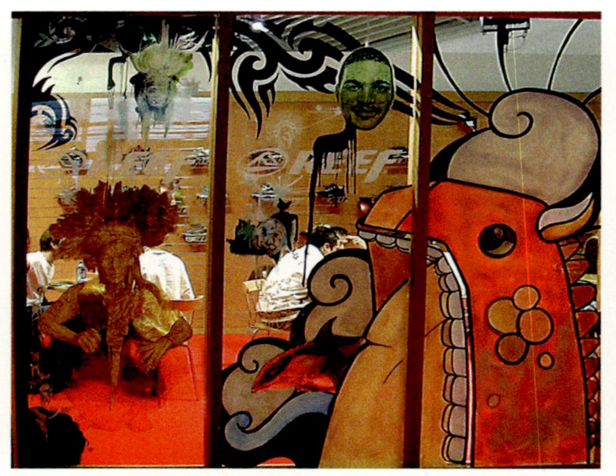
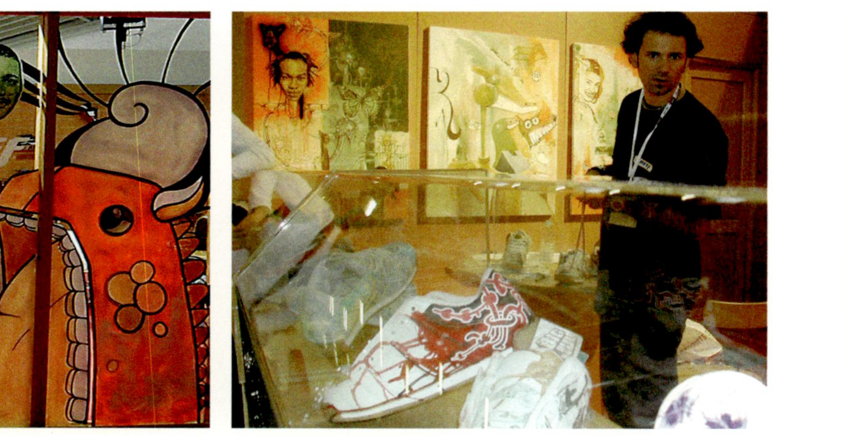
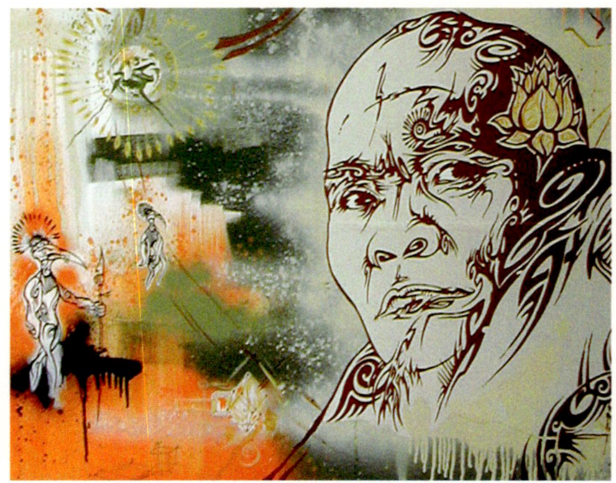
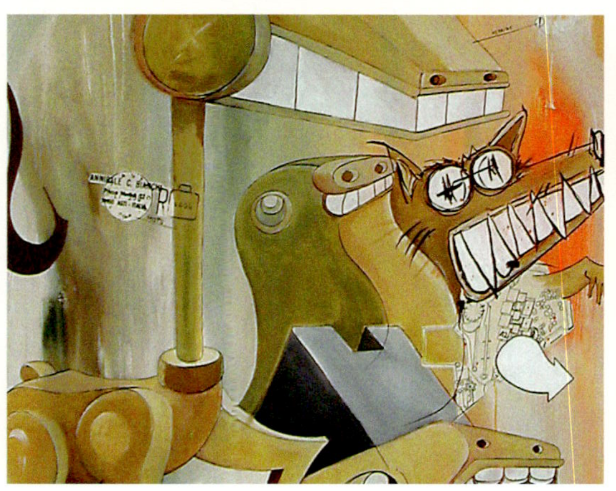
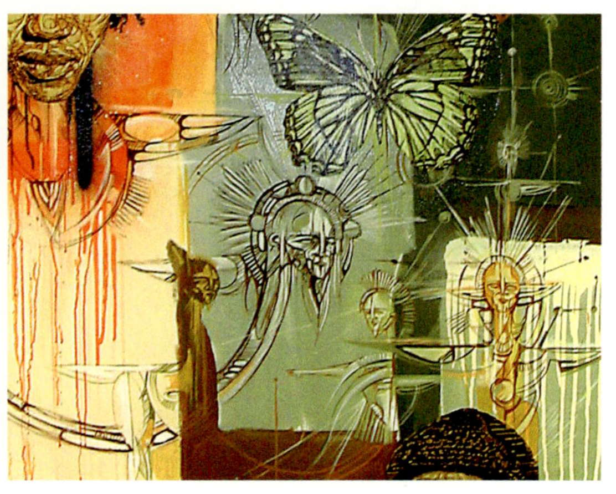

MUNiCH

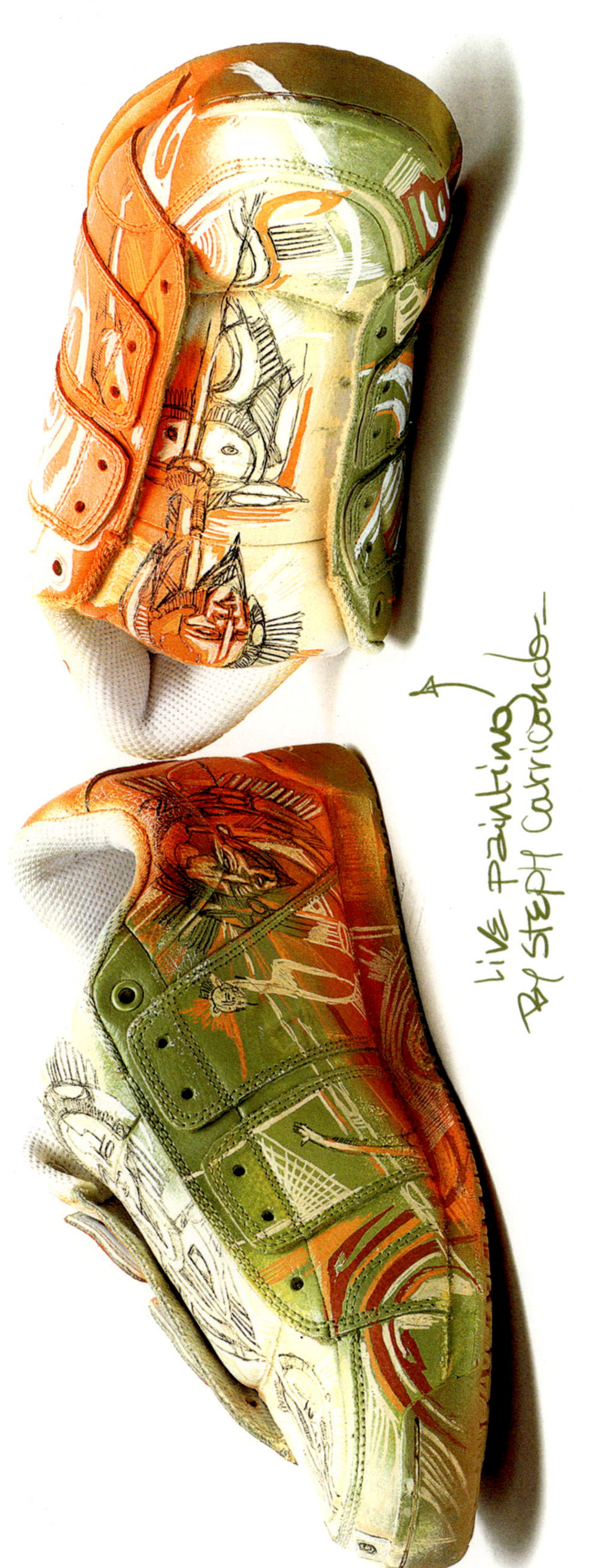

Live painting
by Steph Carricondo

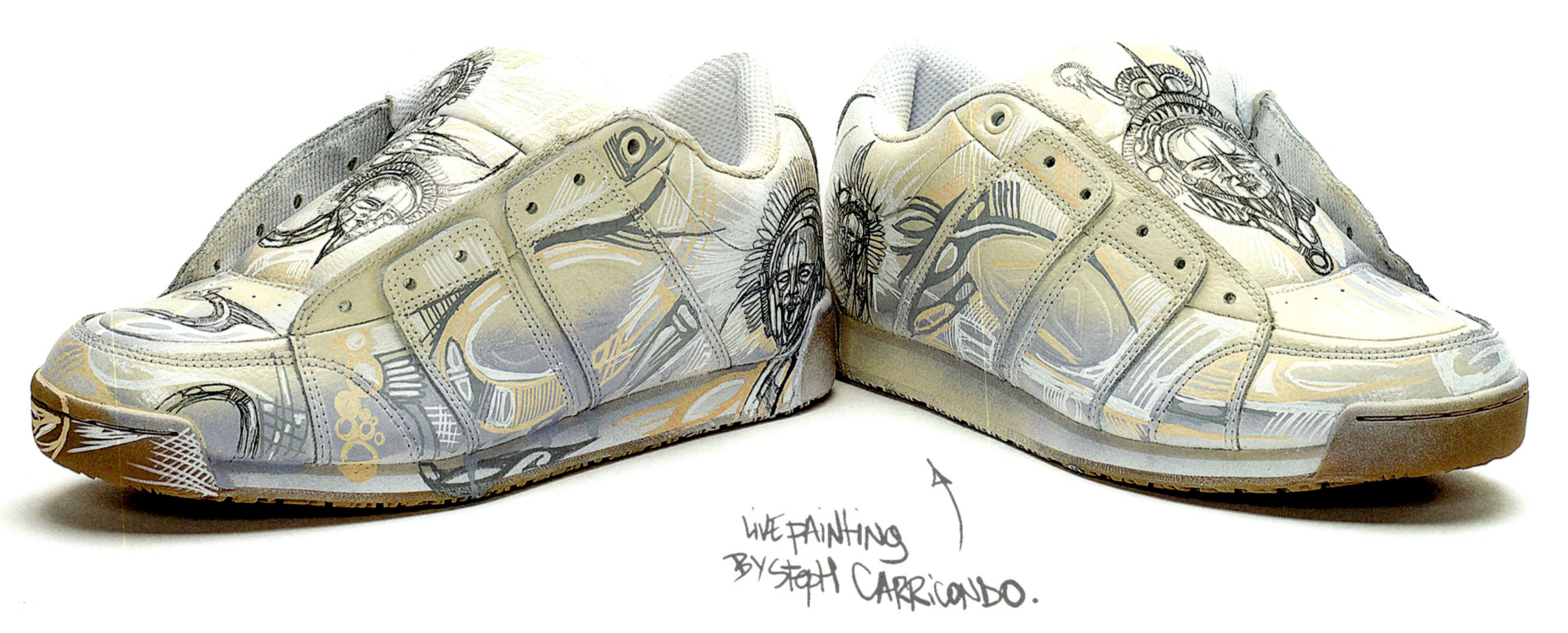

LIVE PAINTING
BY STEPH CARRICONDO.

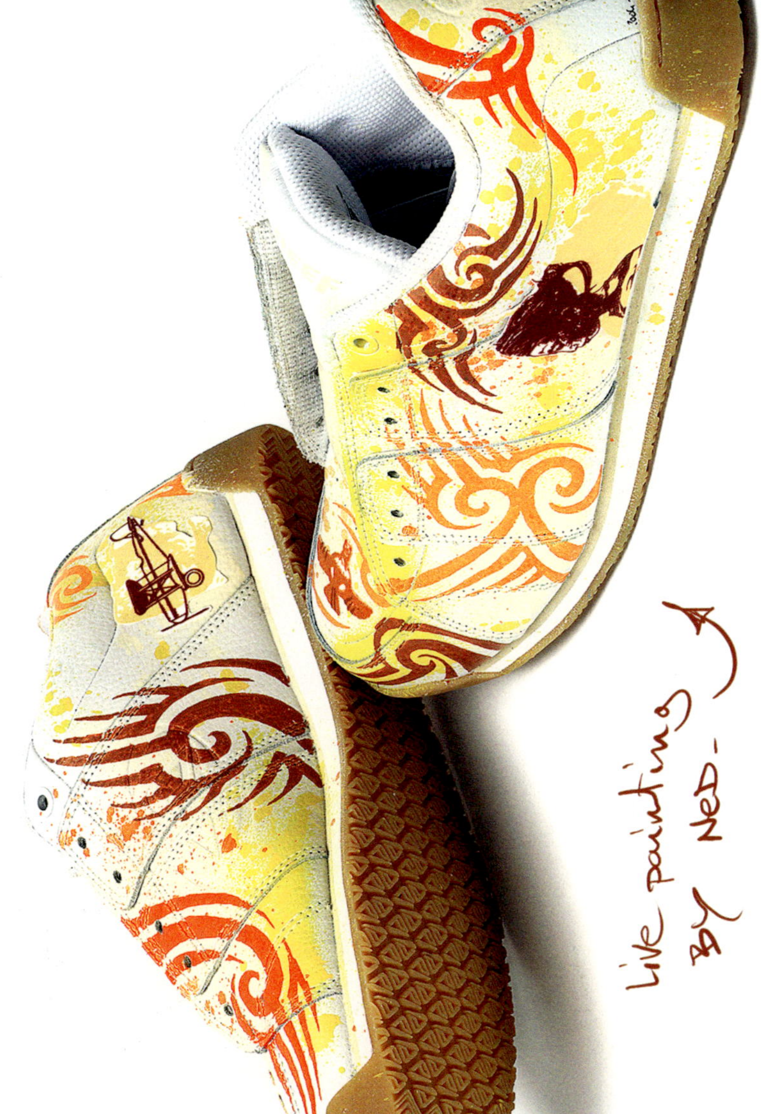
Live painting
BY NED.

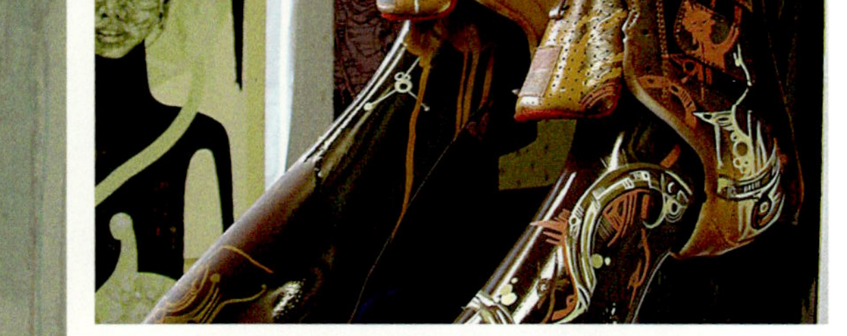
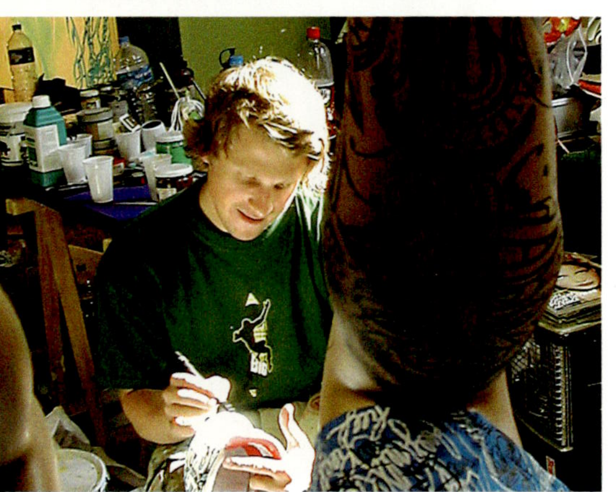
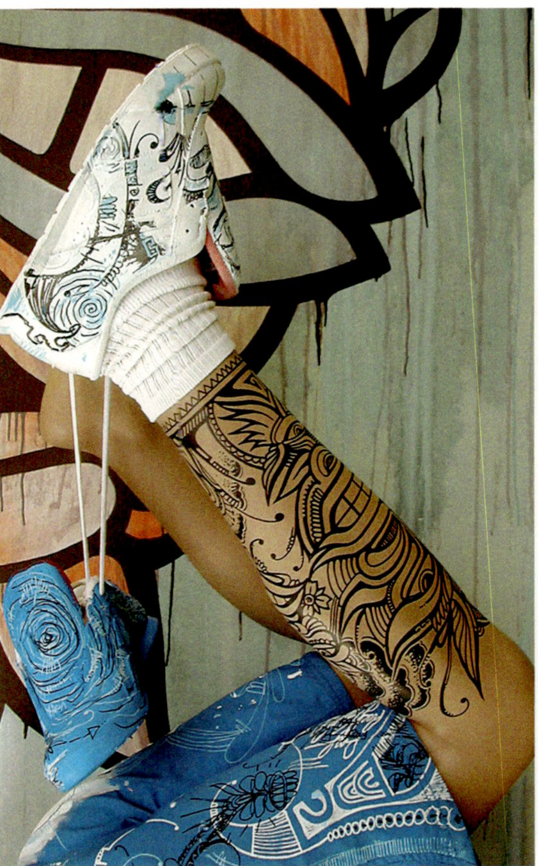
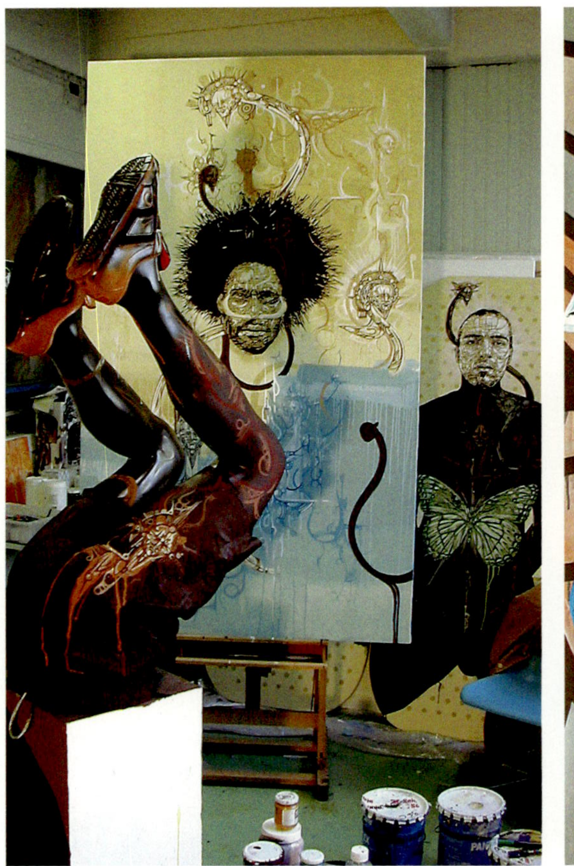

Steph Carricondo and Jérome Molard painting in the 9ème concept studio

STUDIO PAINTING

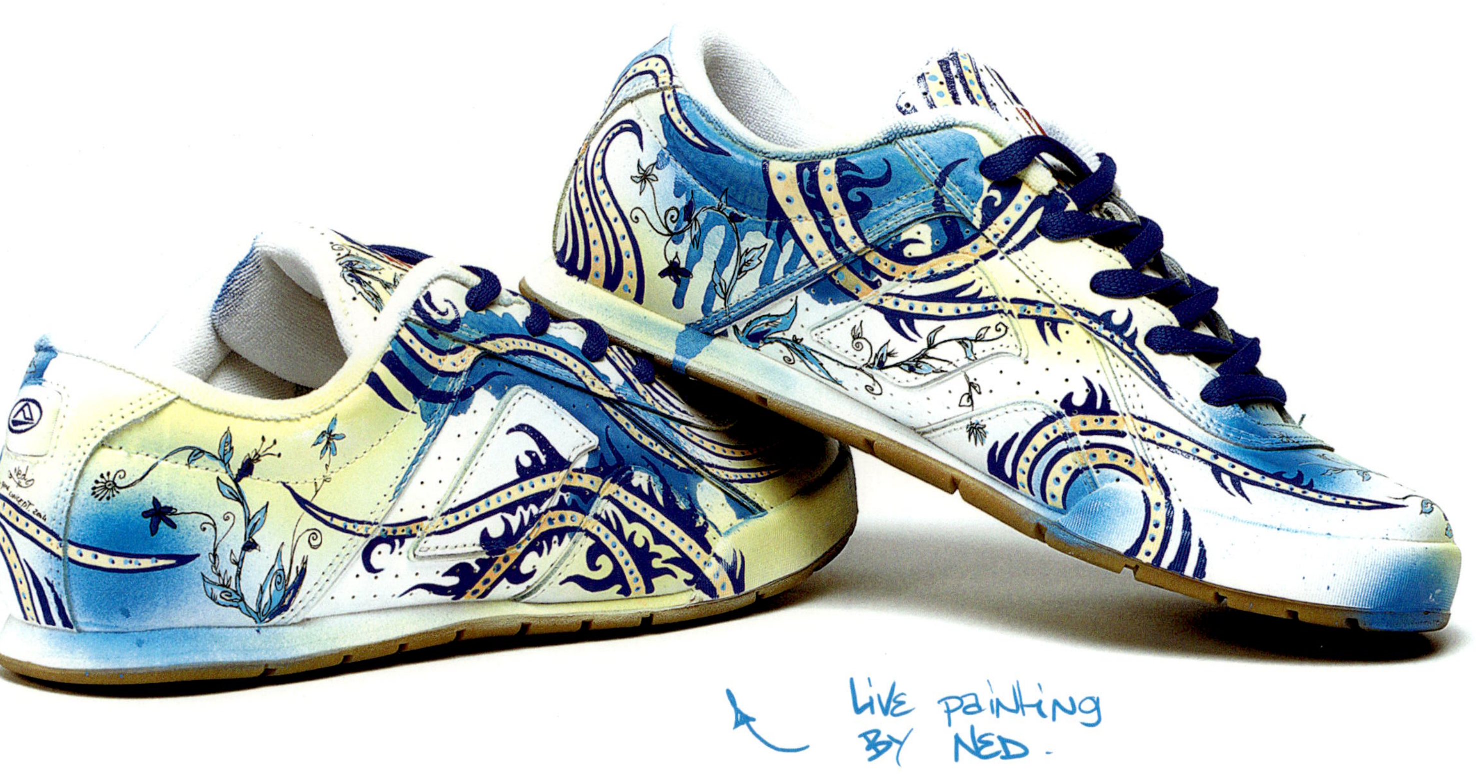
LIVE PAINTING
BY NED.

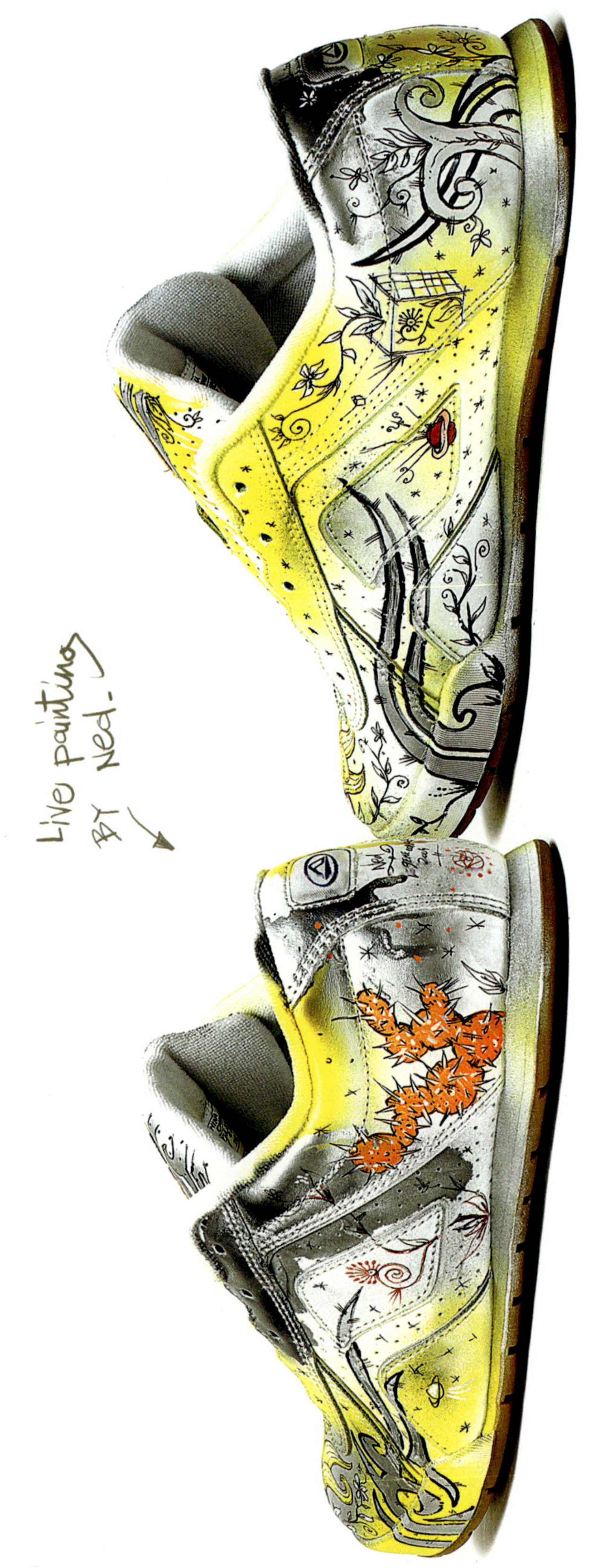

Live painting
BY Ned.

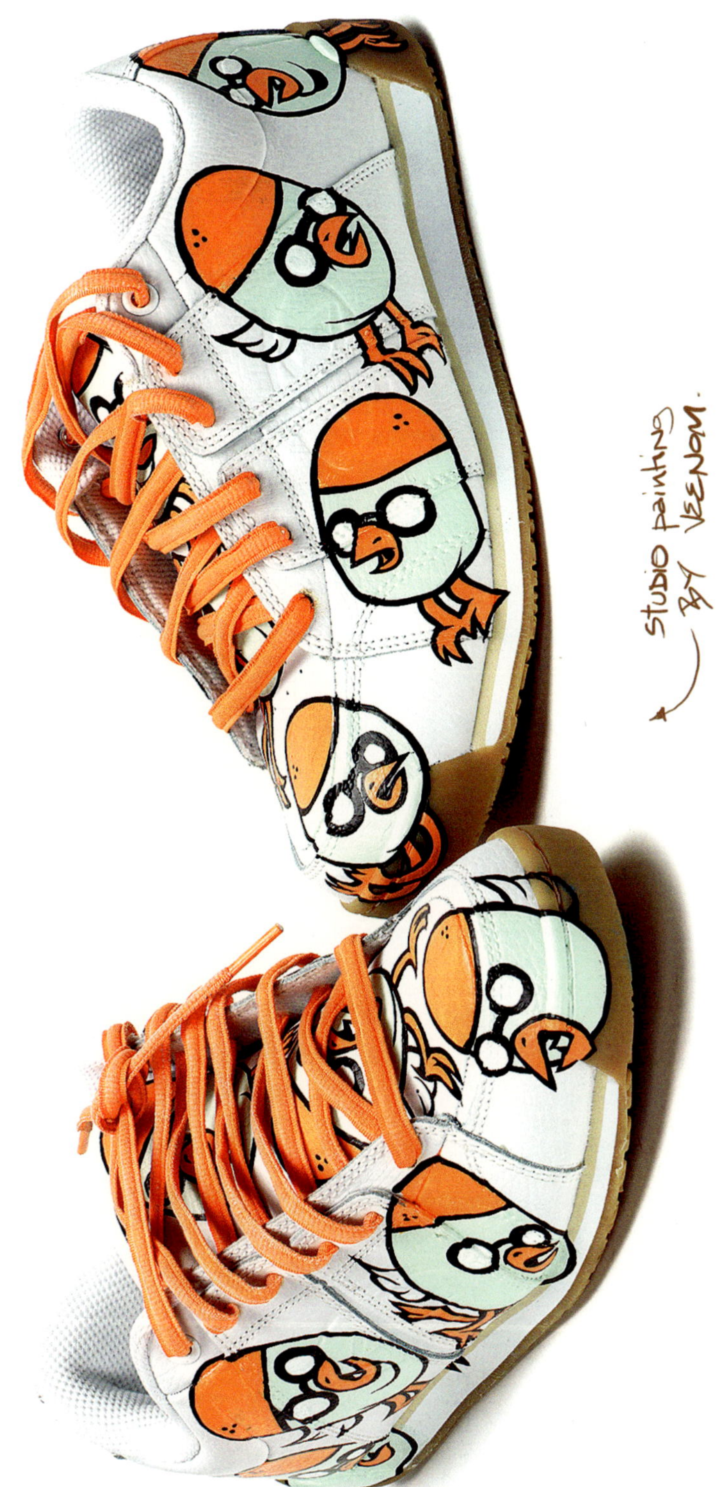

STUDIO painting
BY VEENOM.

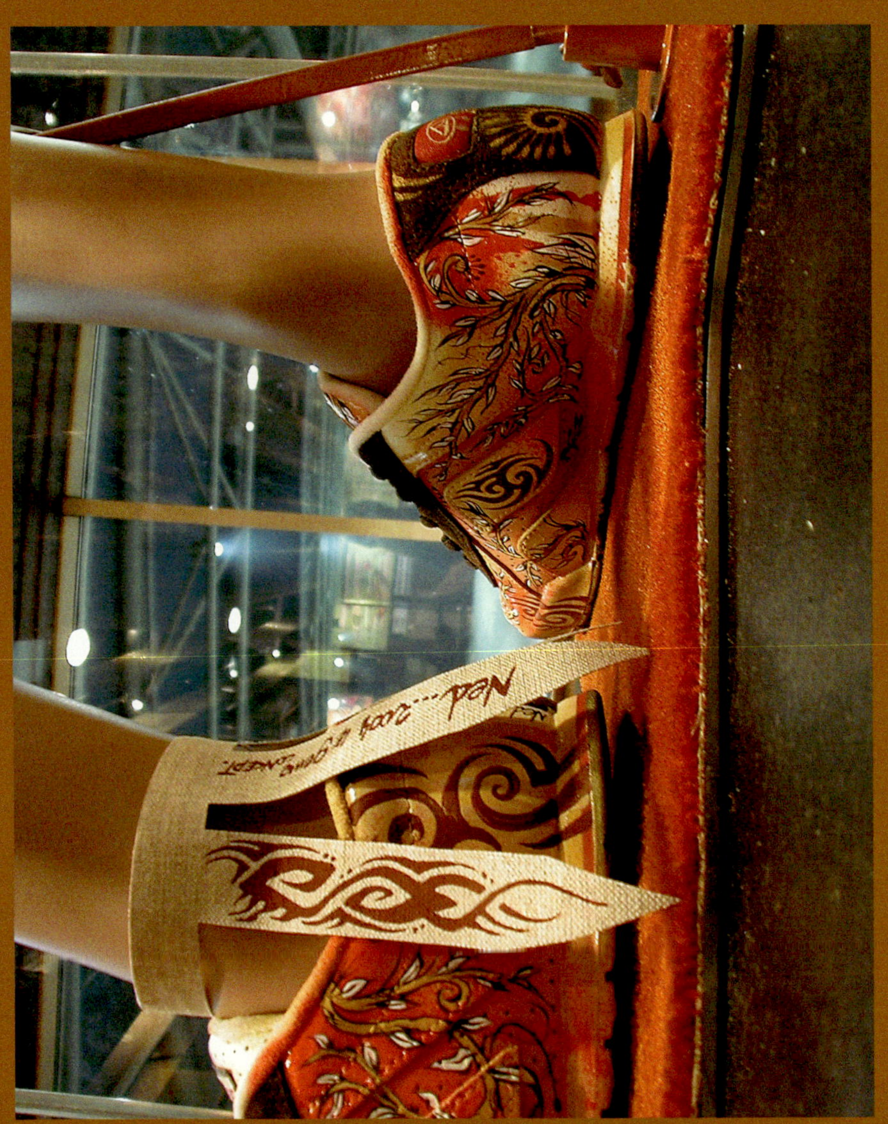

'MADRID
June 2004—

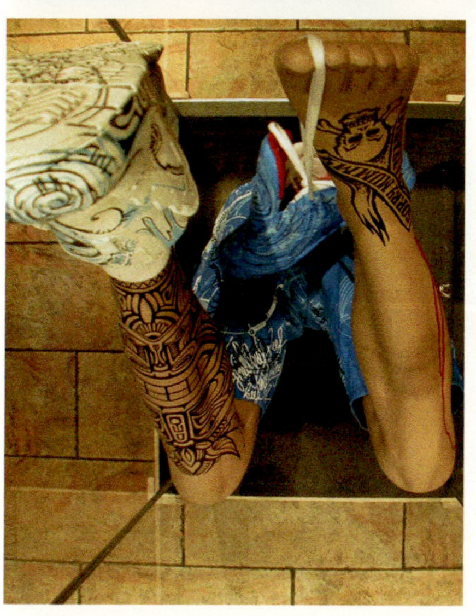

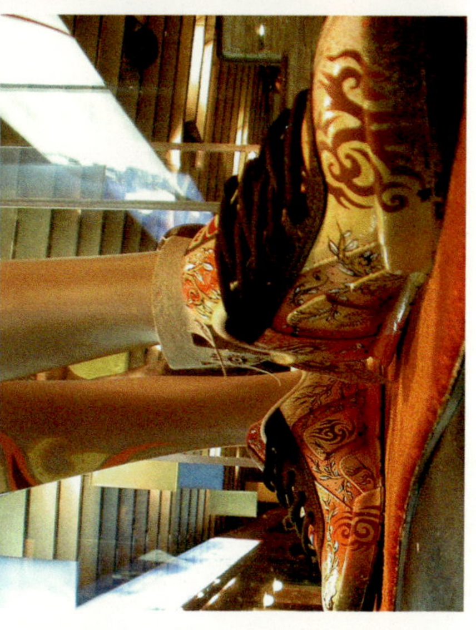

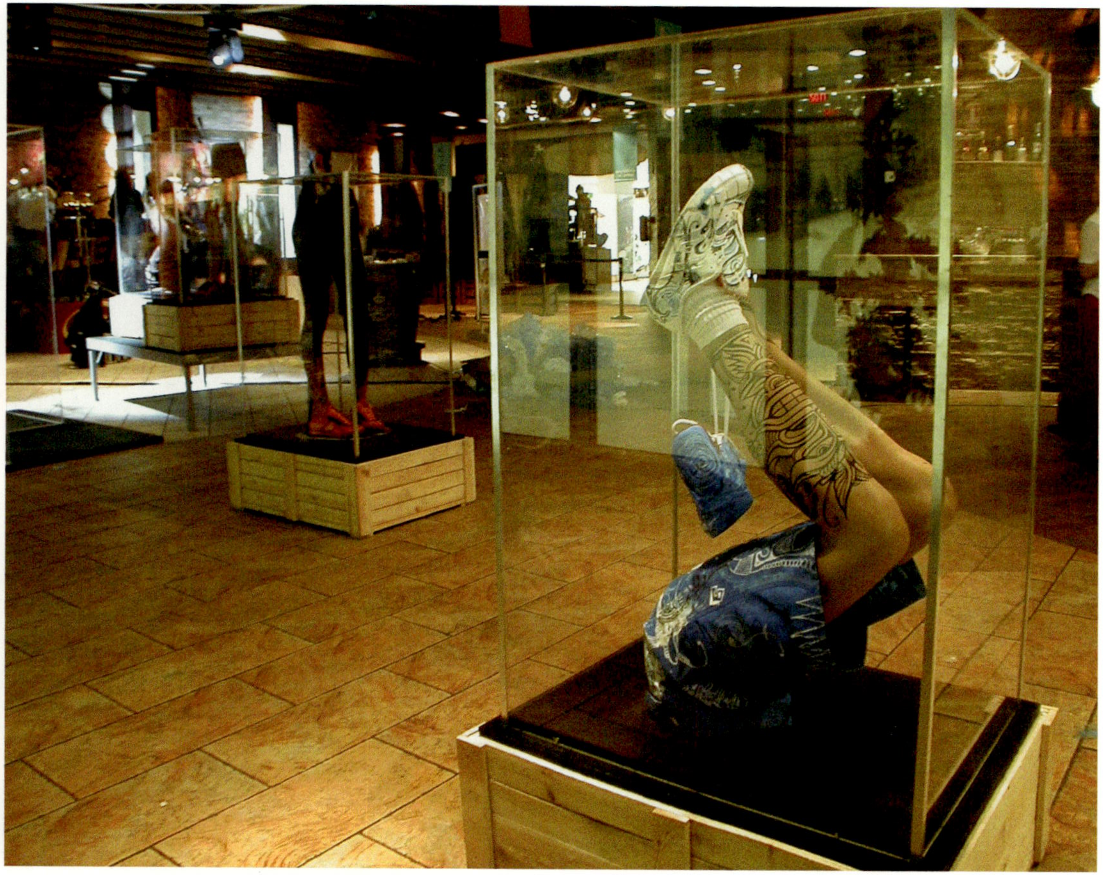

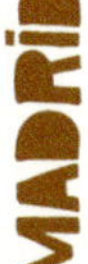

MADRID

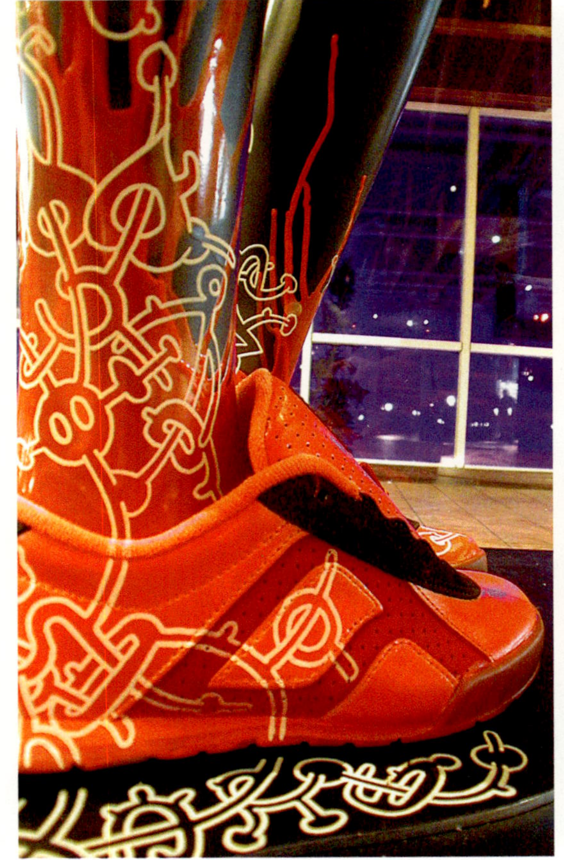
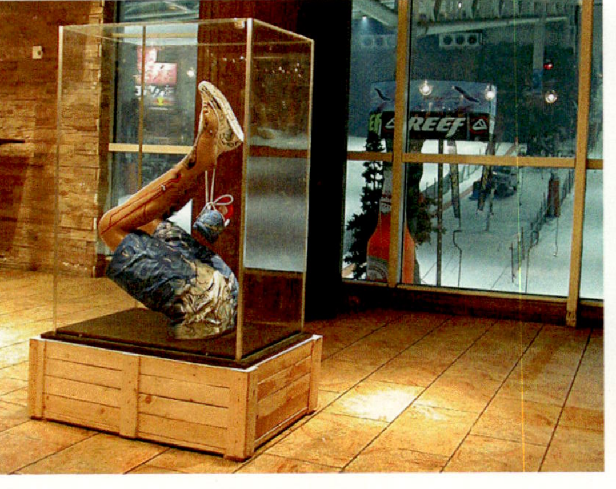
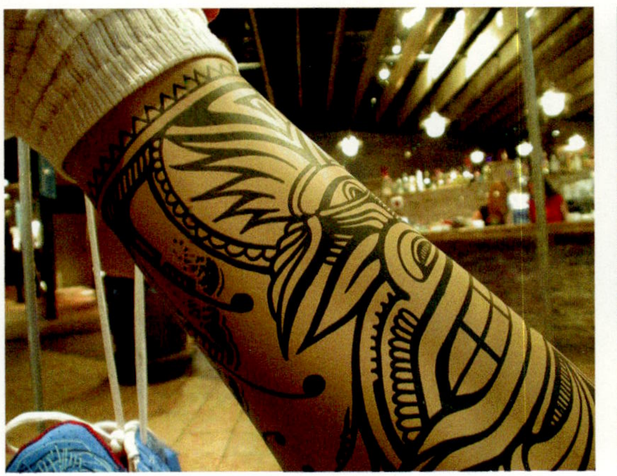
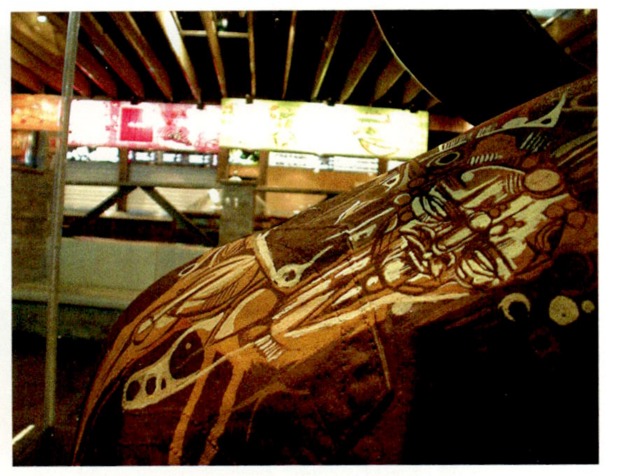
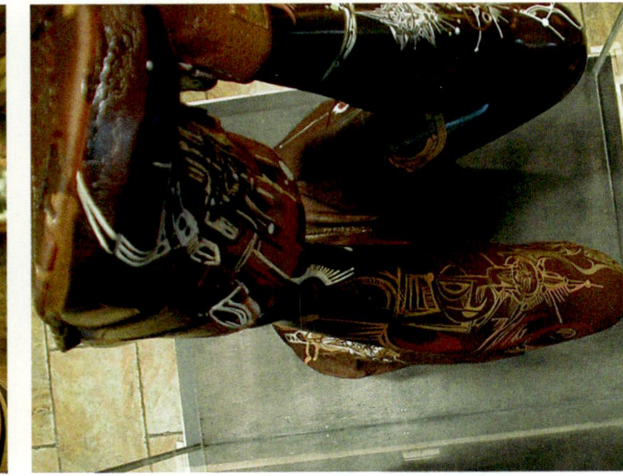

MADRID   Big Jul   Jerome Molard   Steph Carricondo

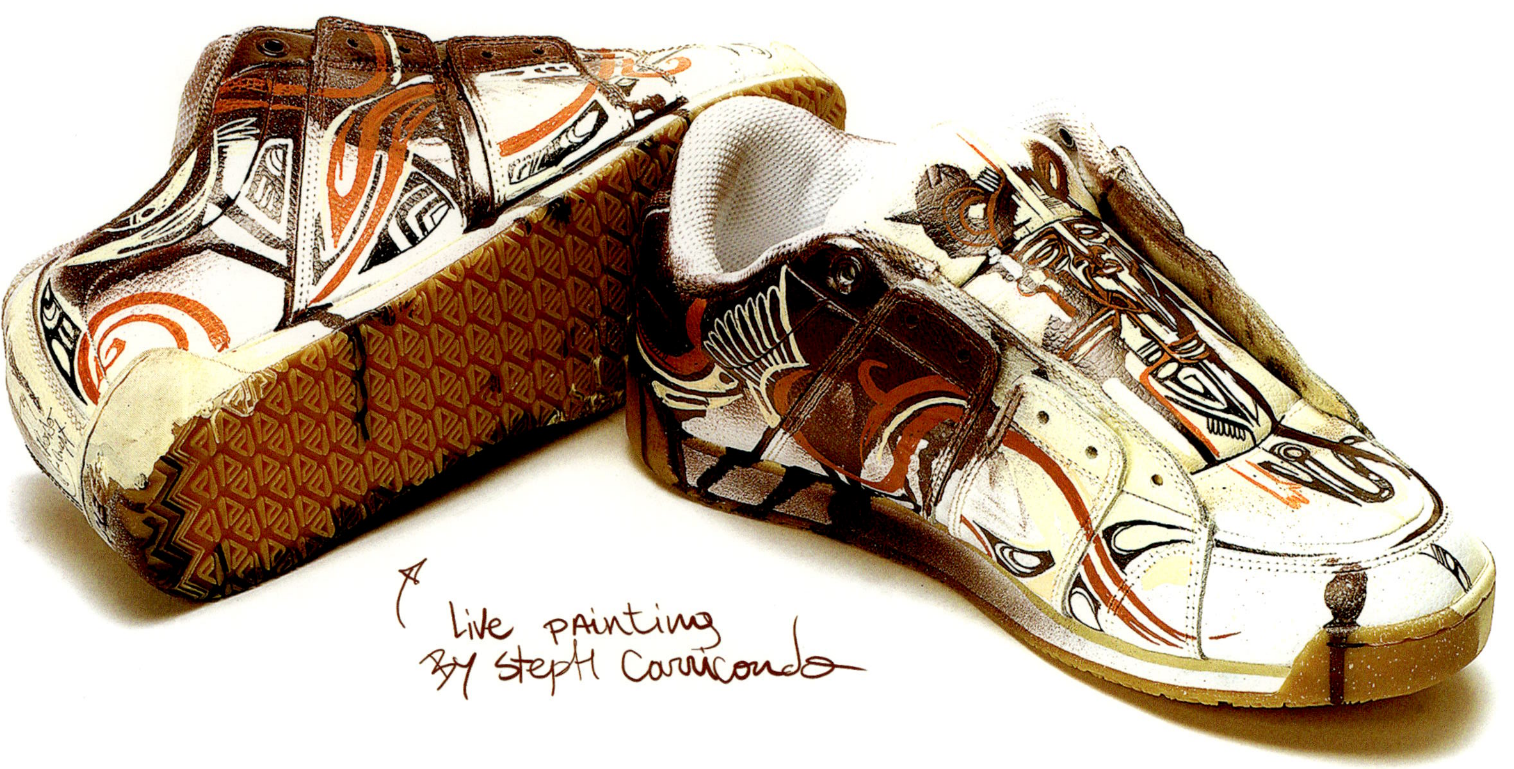

A live painting
By Steph Carriconda

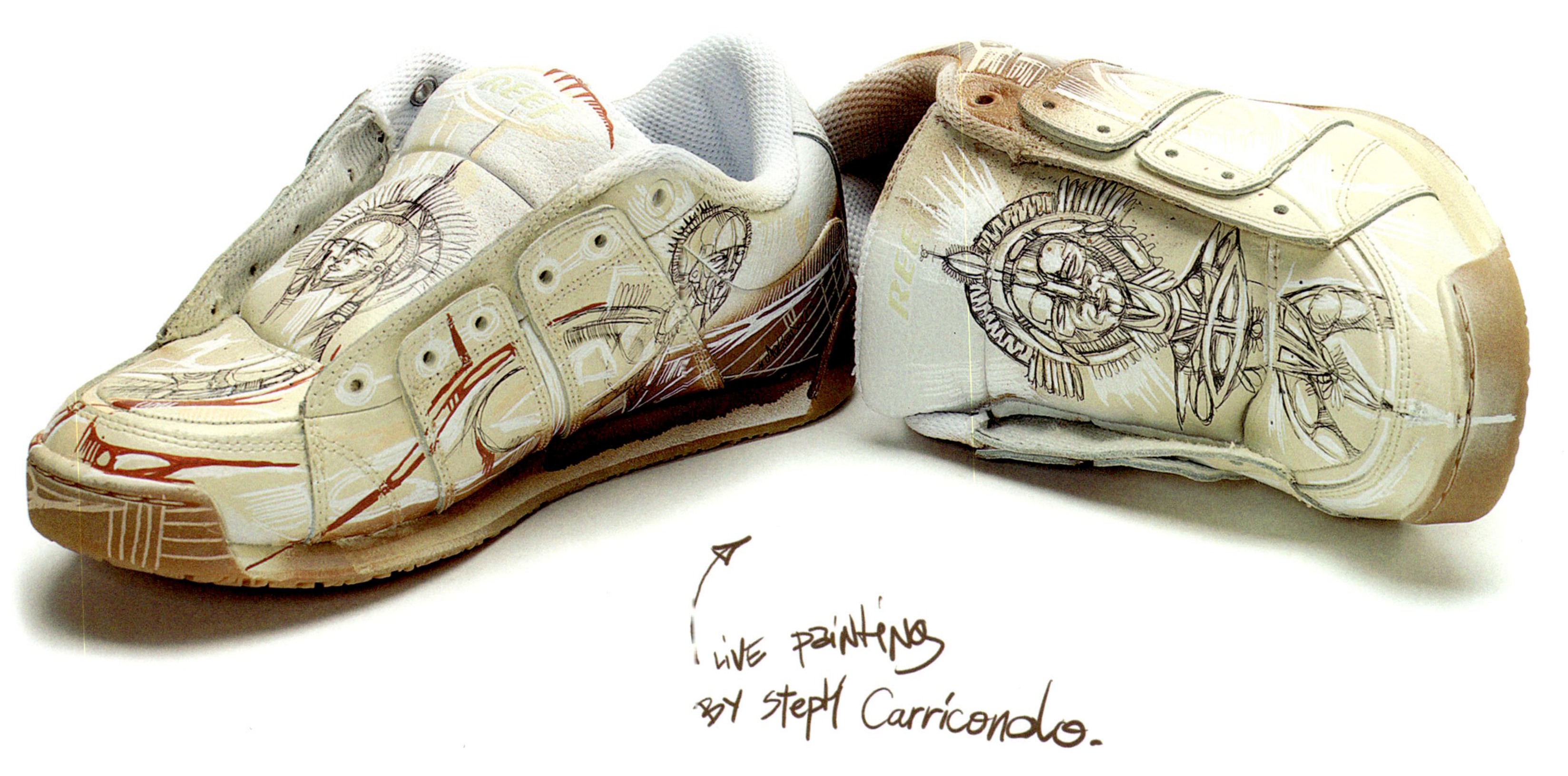
Live Painting
by Steph Carricondo.

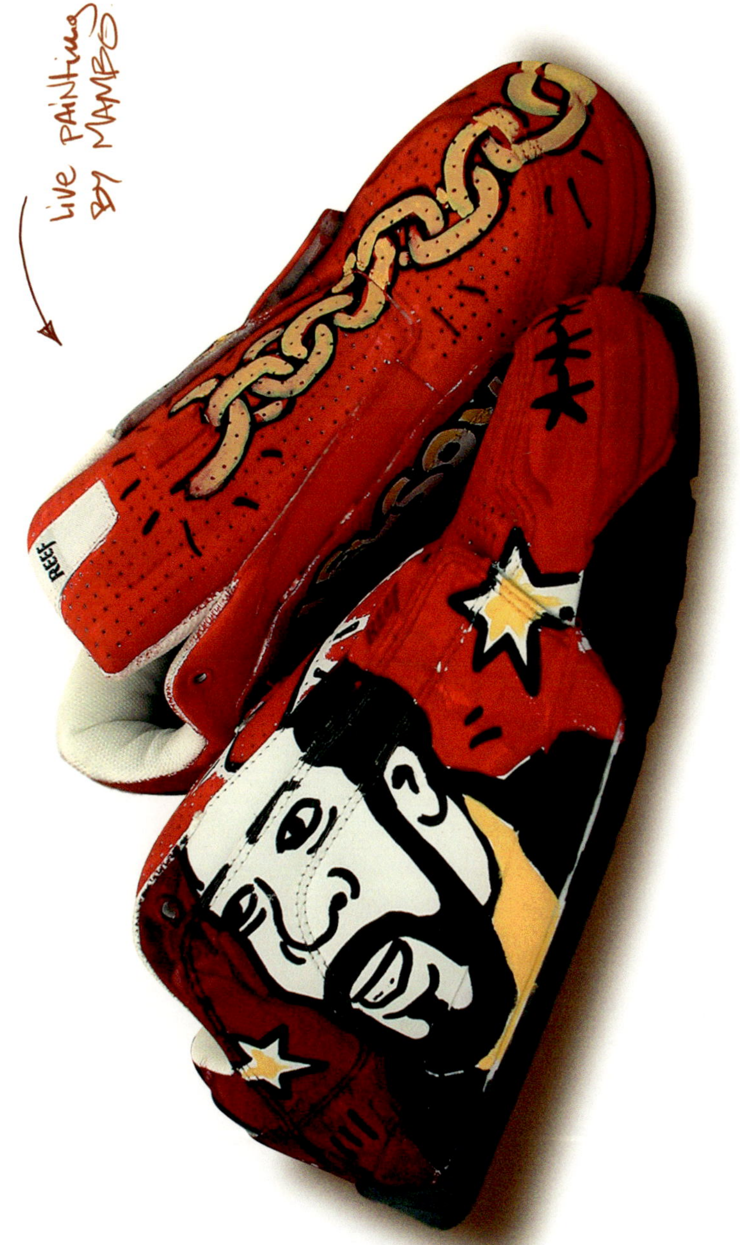
live pAinting
by MAMBO

ANGLET
July 2004 –

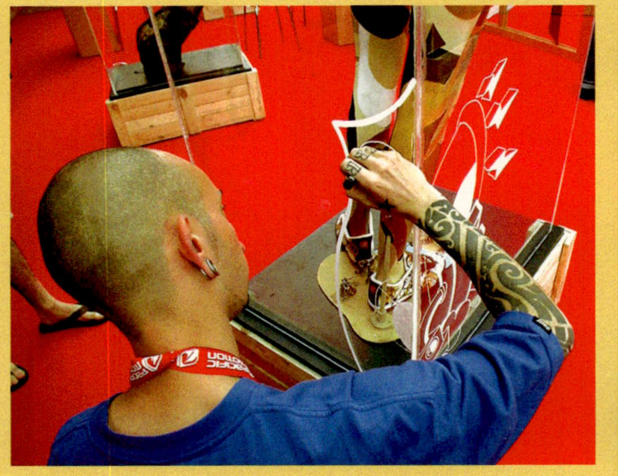

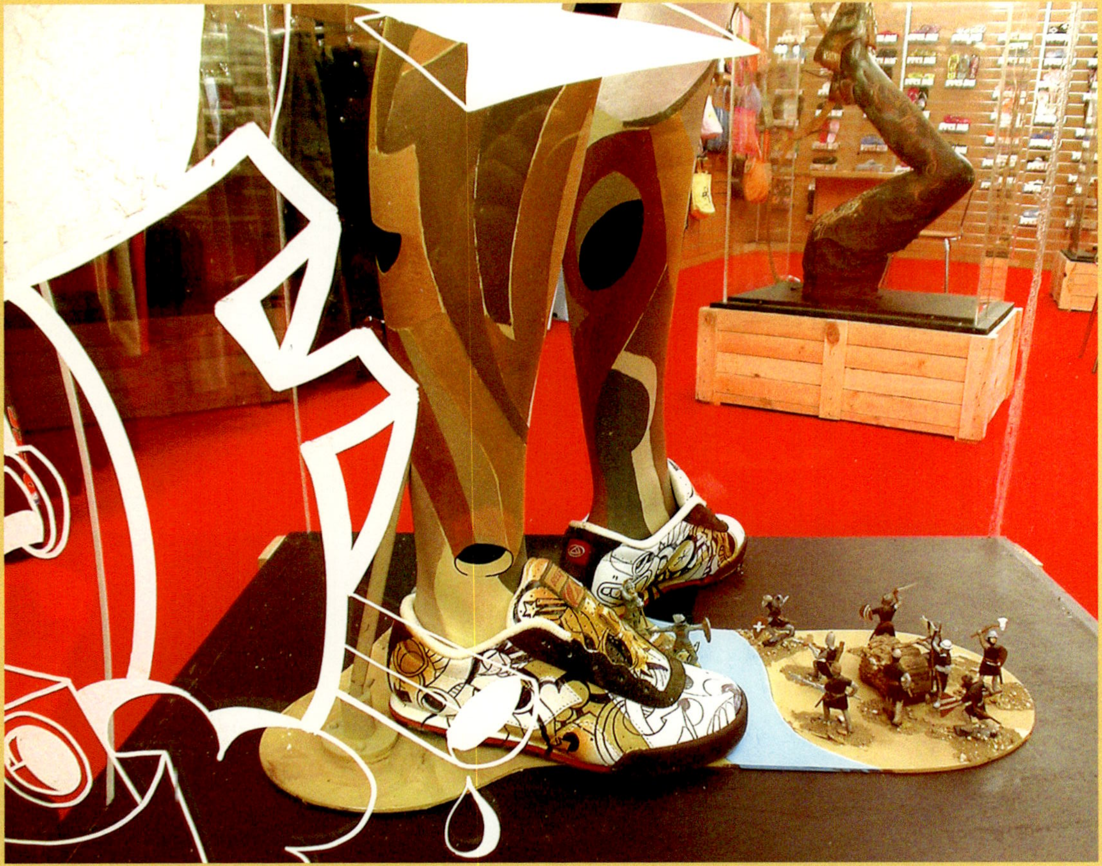

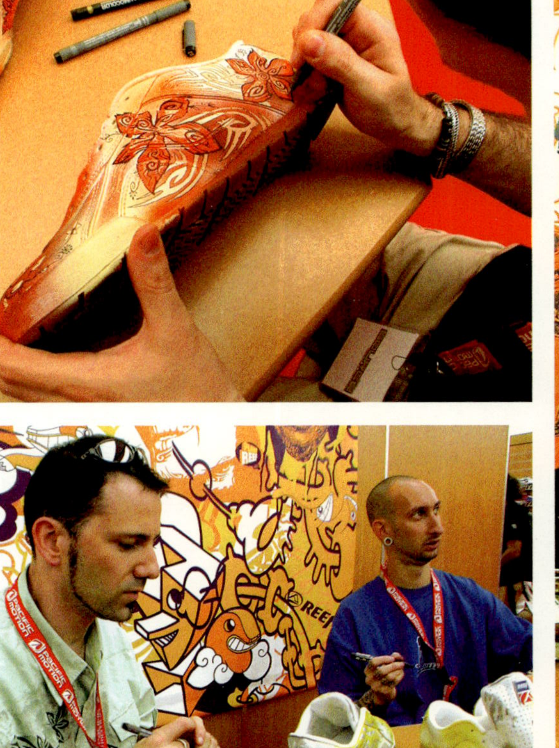
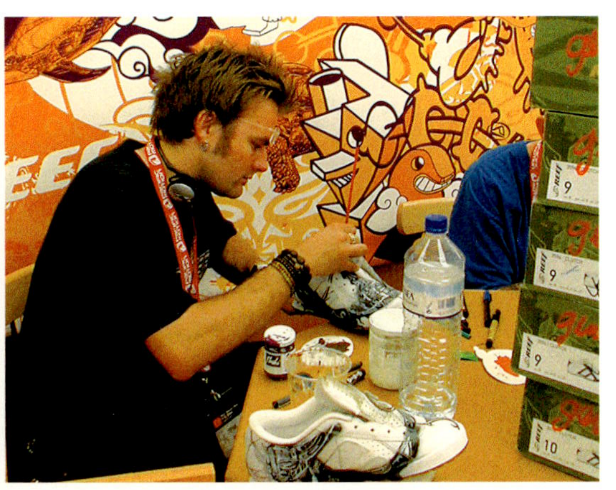
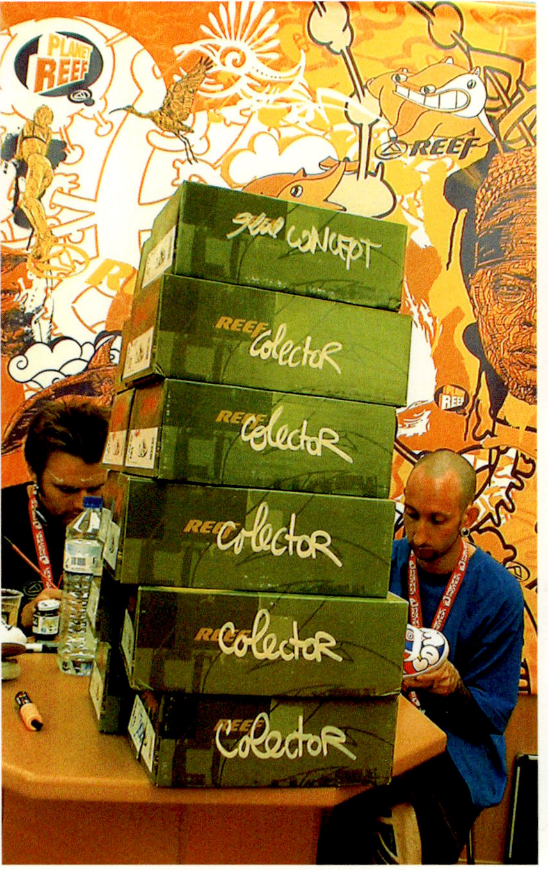
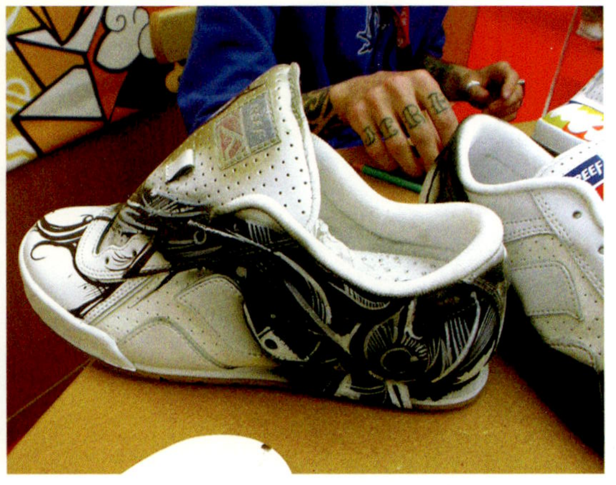
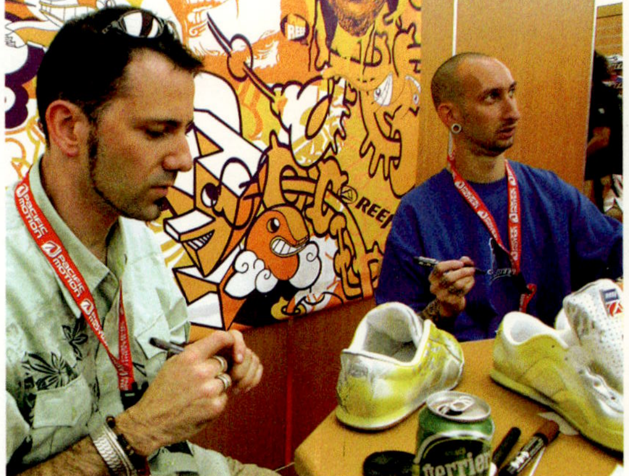

Steph Carricondo, Ned and Jerk 45 customize Reef collector shoes

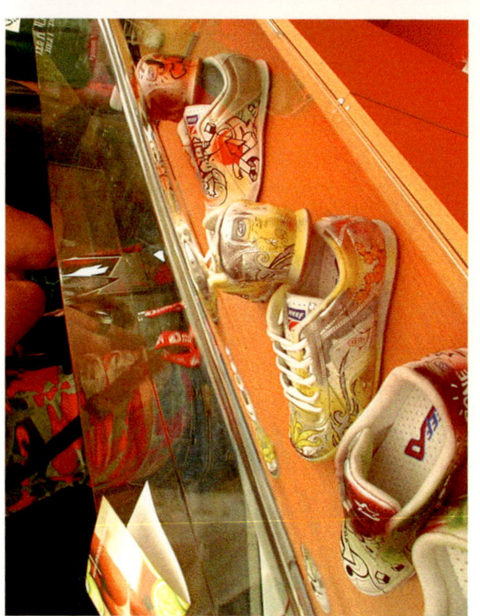
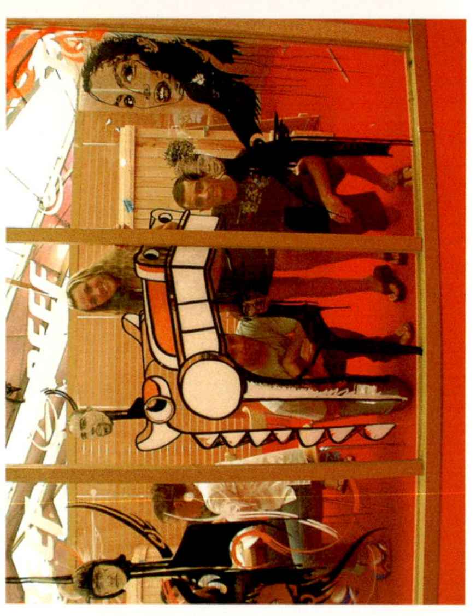

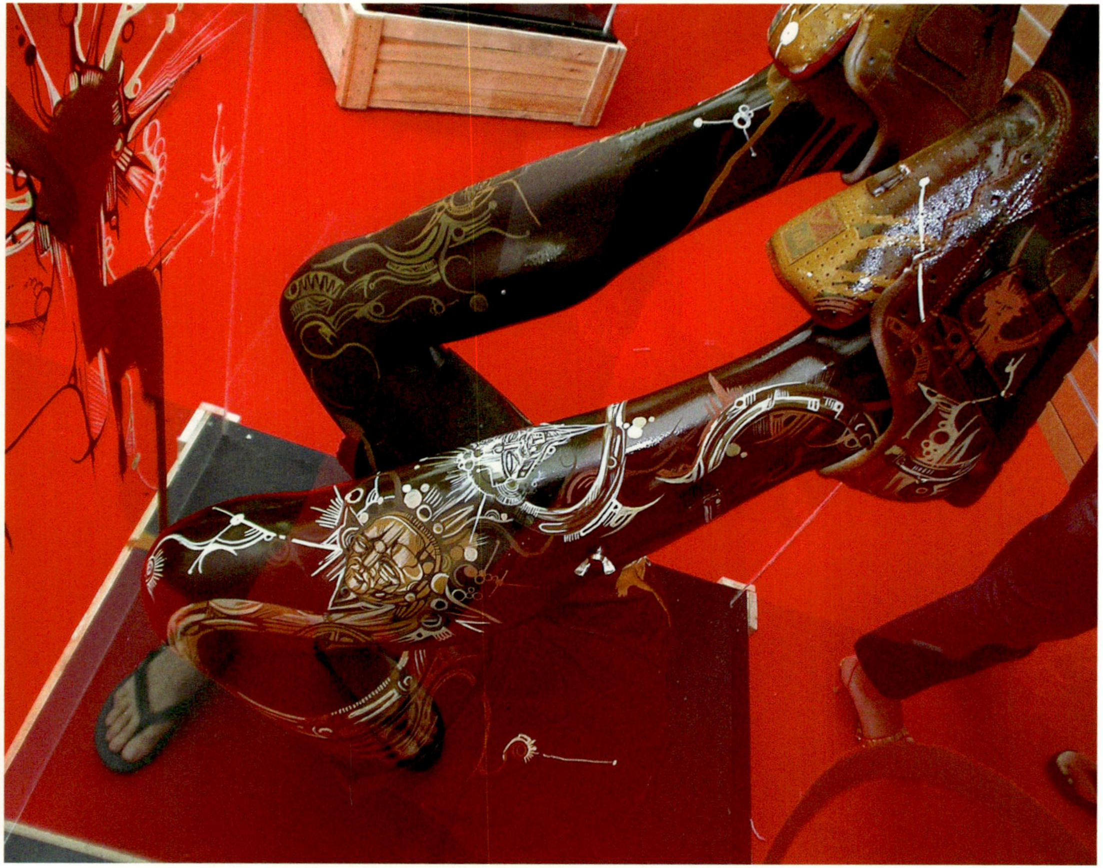

Painted shoes and mannequin display by Steph Carricondo

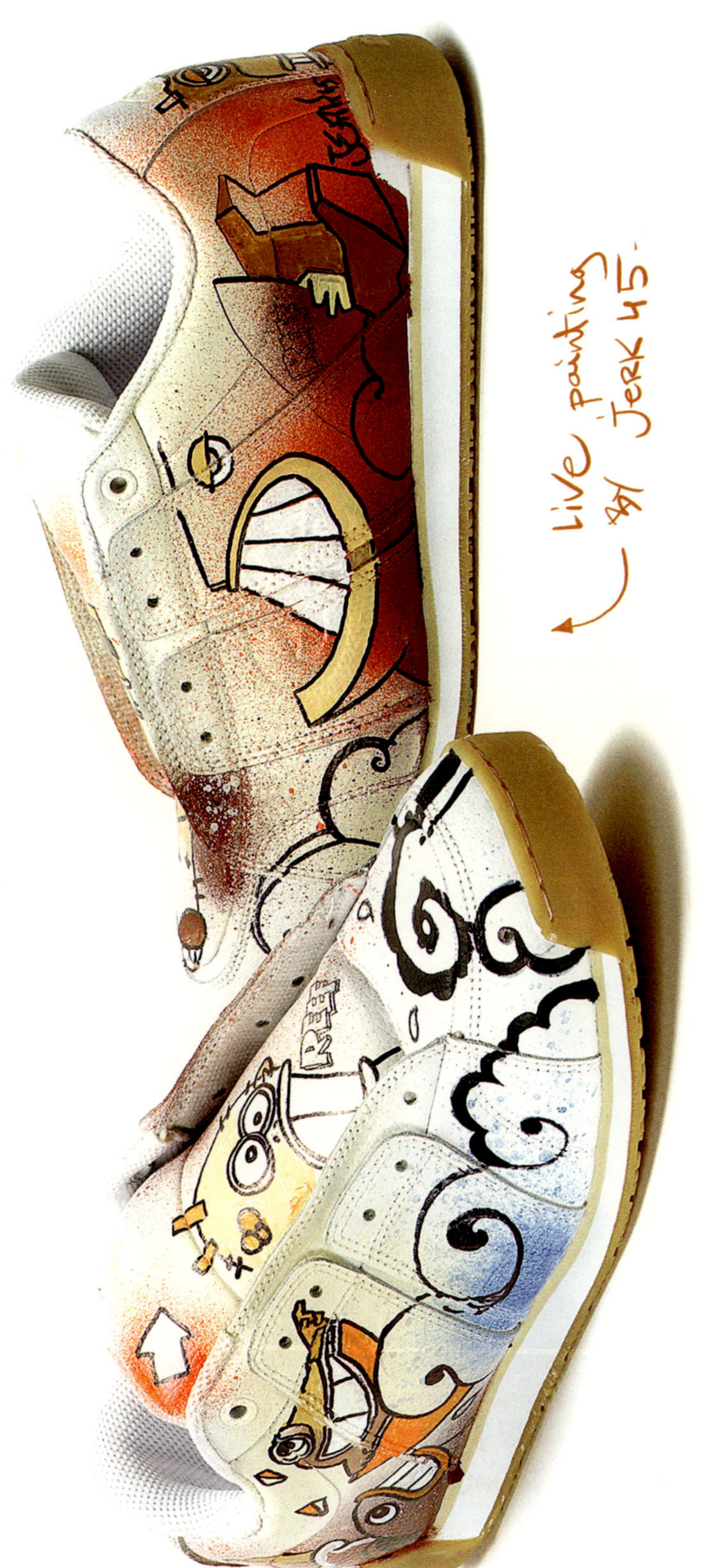

live painting
by Jerk 45 -

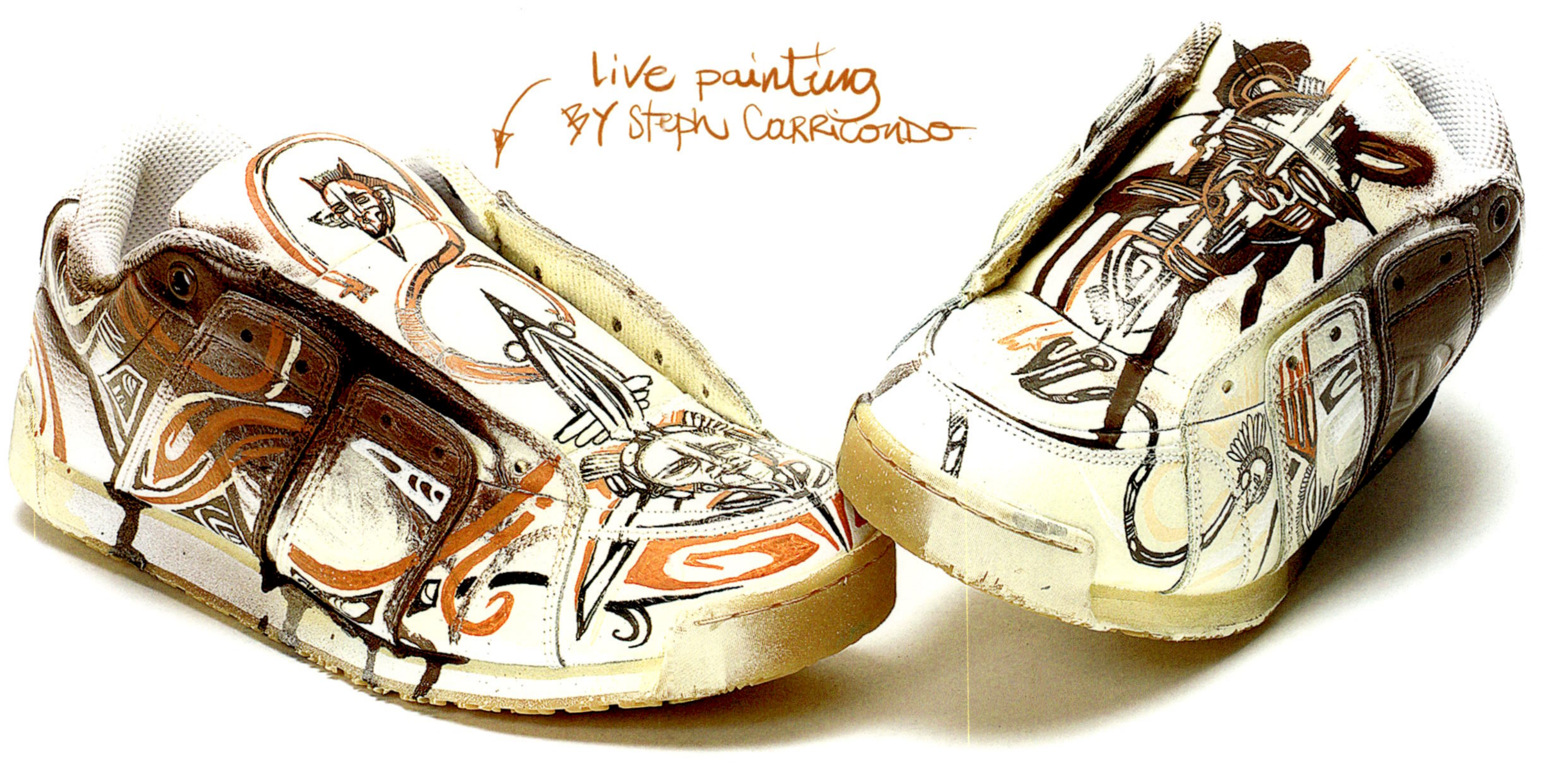
live painting
BY Steph Carricondo

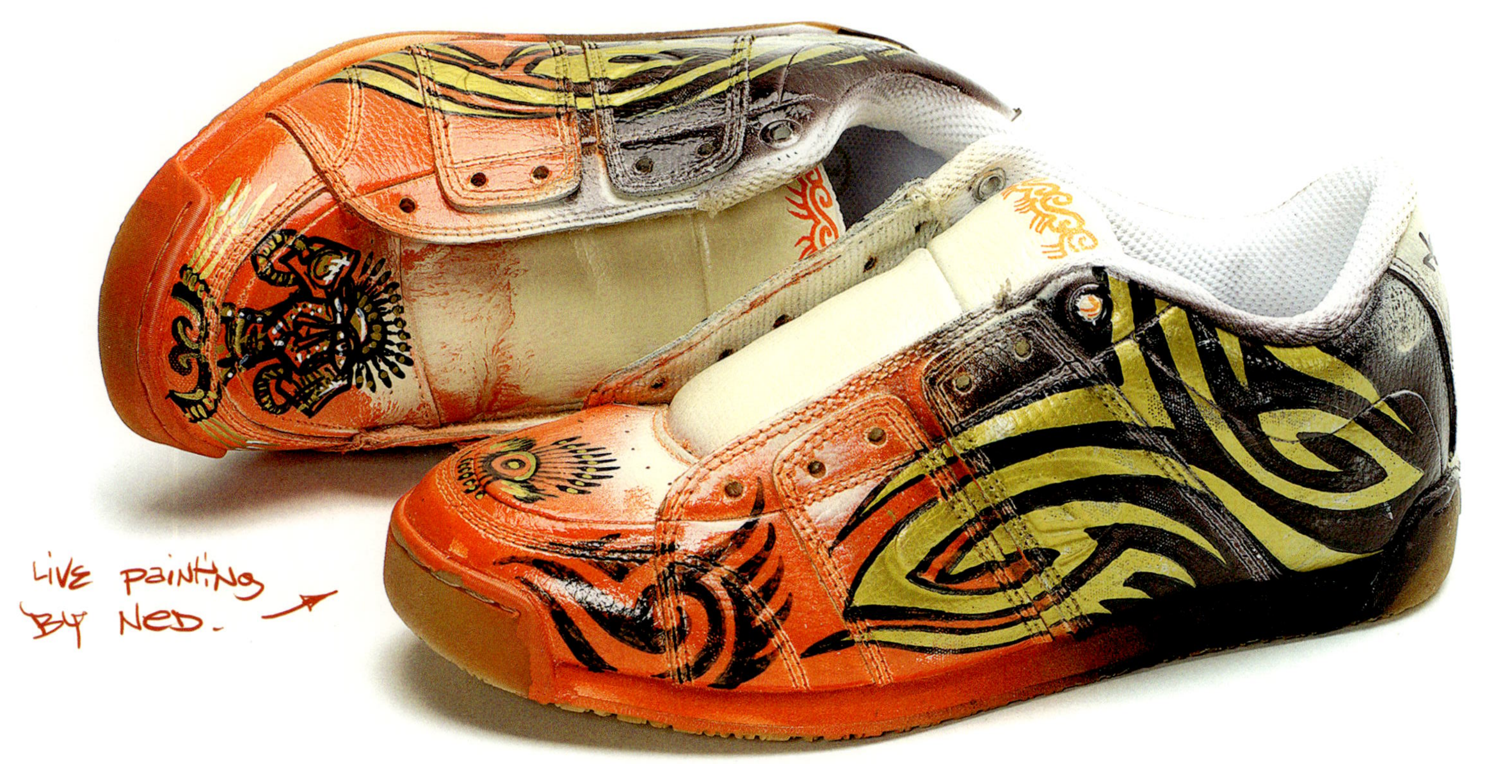

Live painting
by Ned.

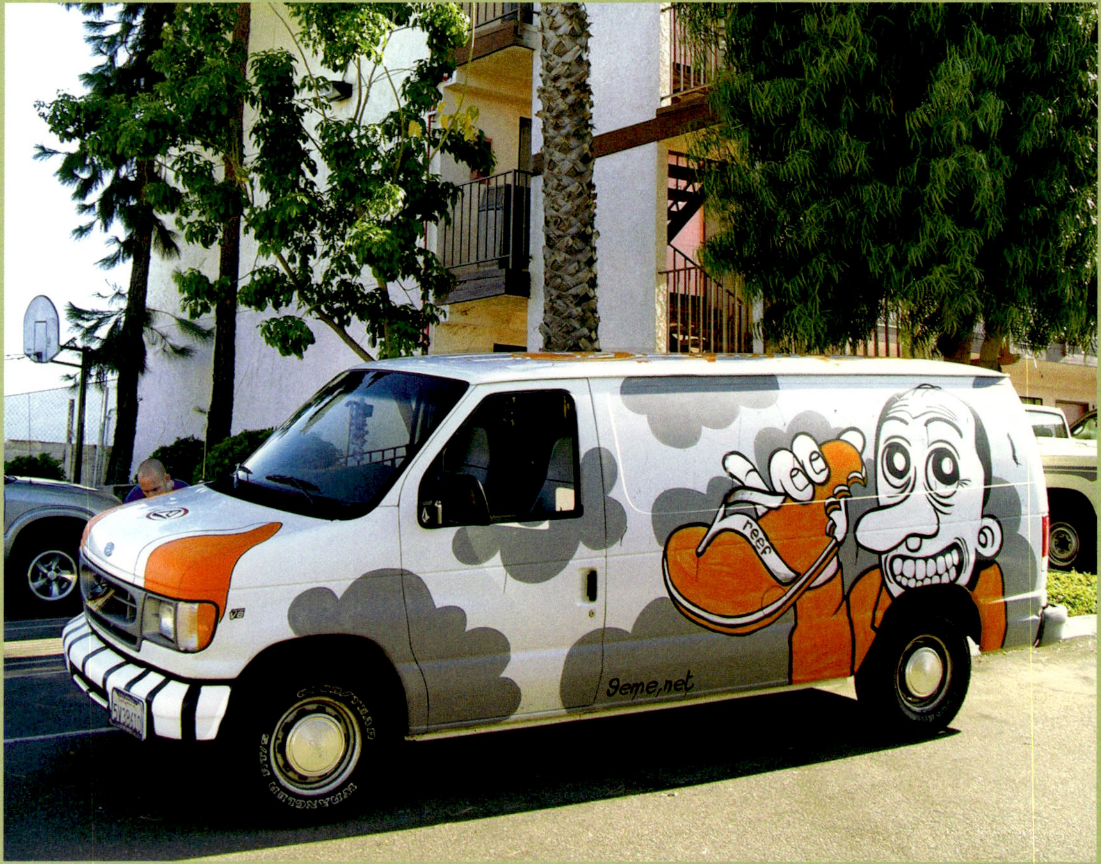

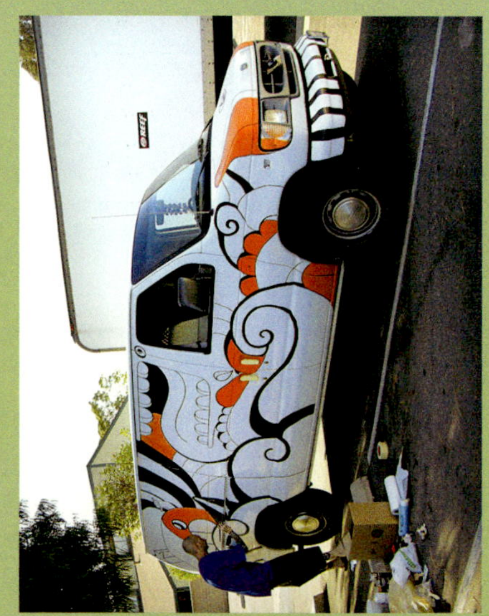

HUNTINGTON BEACH
July - 2004 -

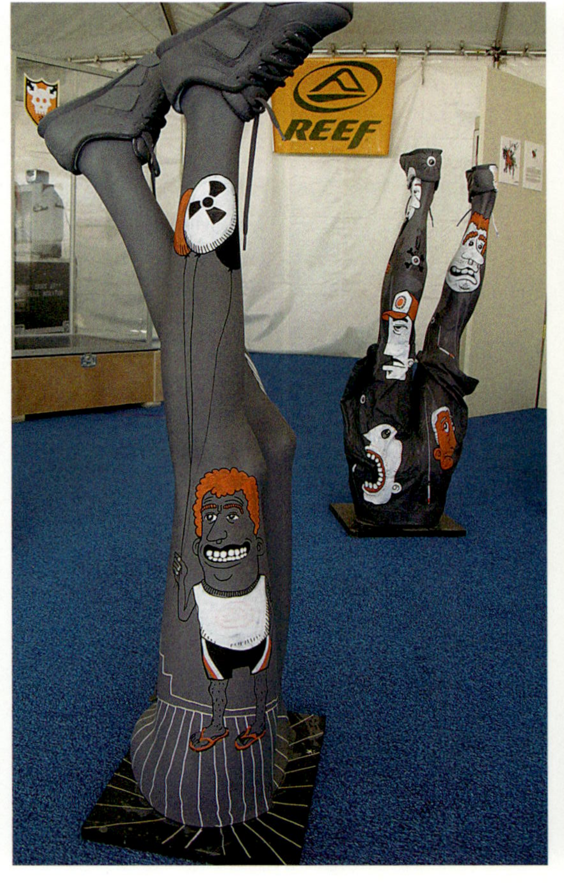

REEF
GATE N°27 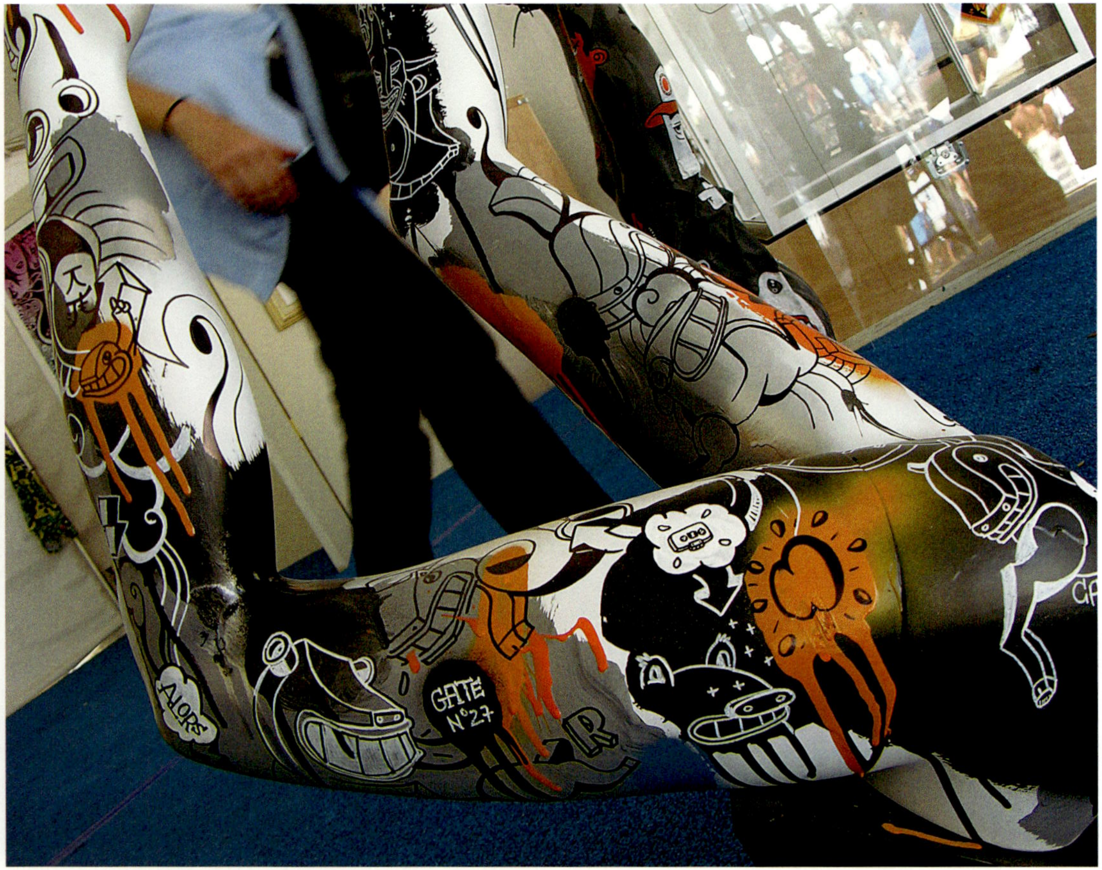
ALORS

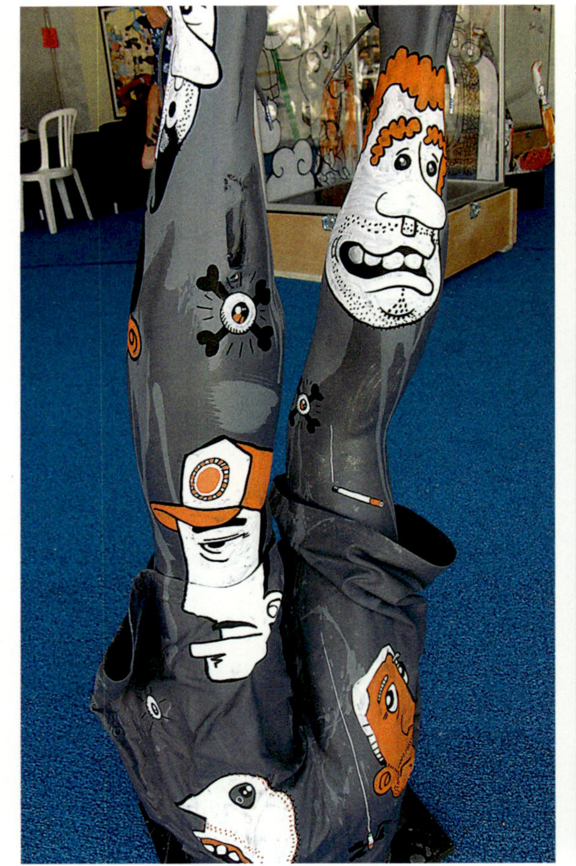

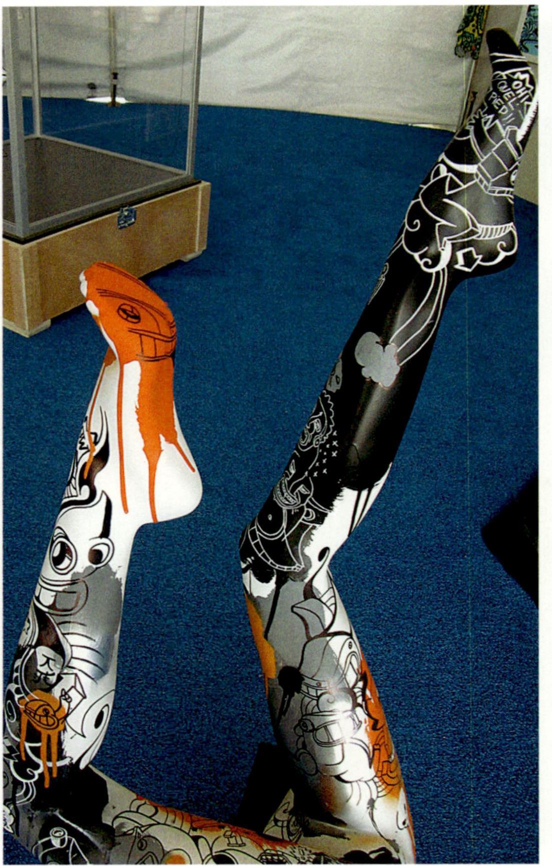

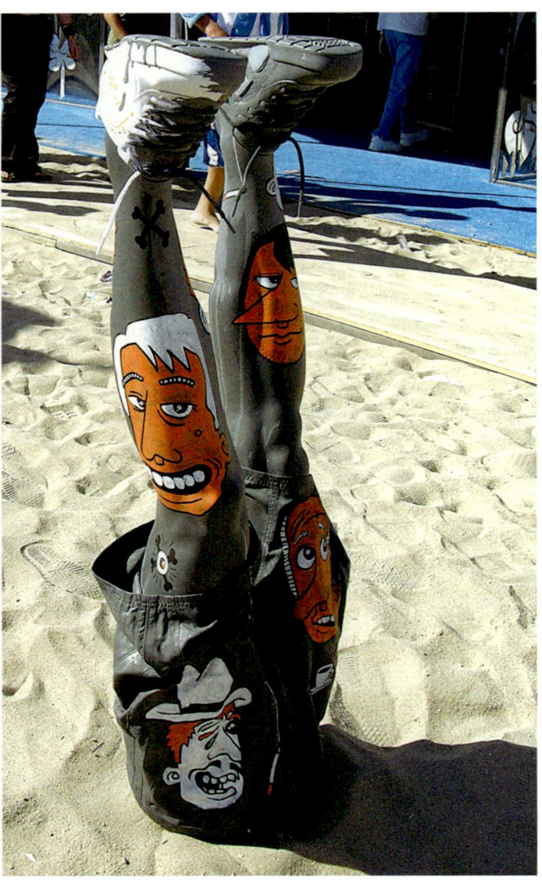

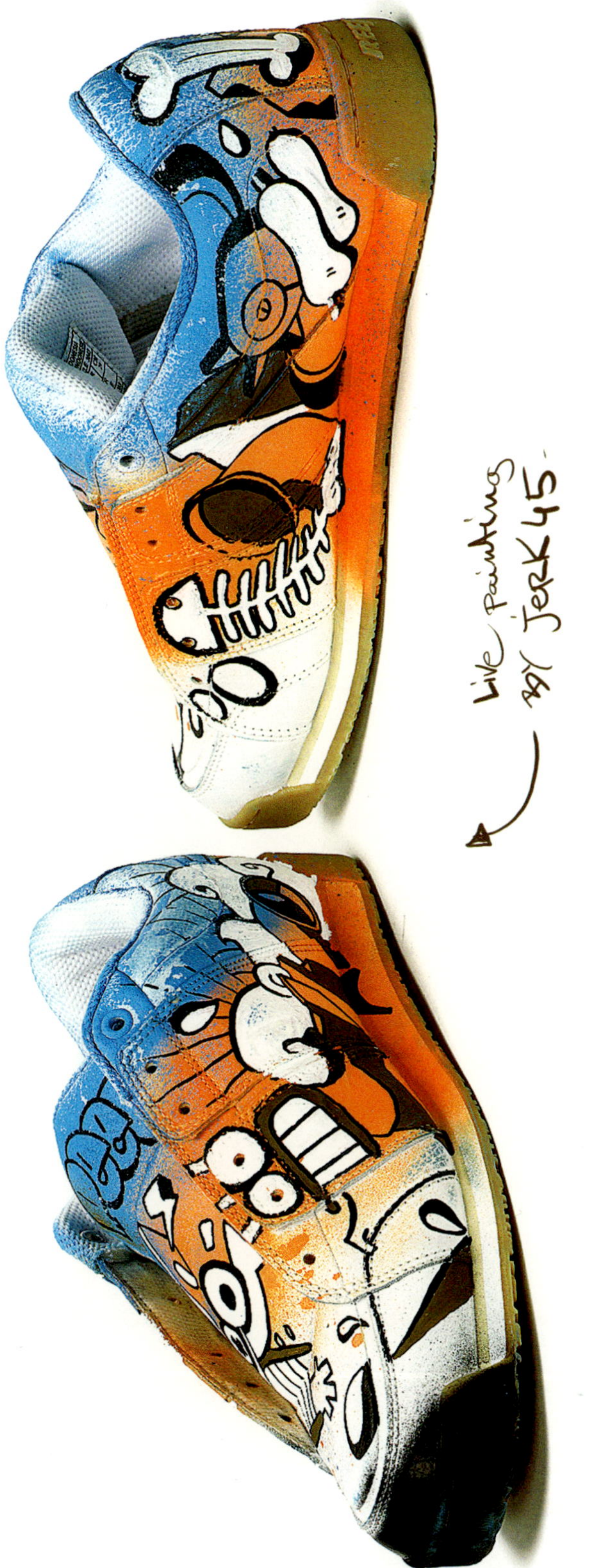

Live Painting
by JERK 45

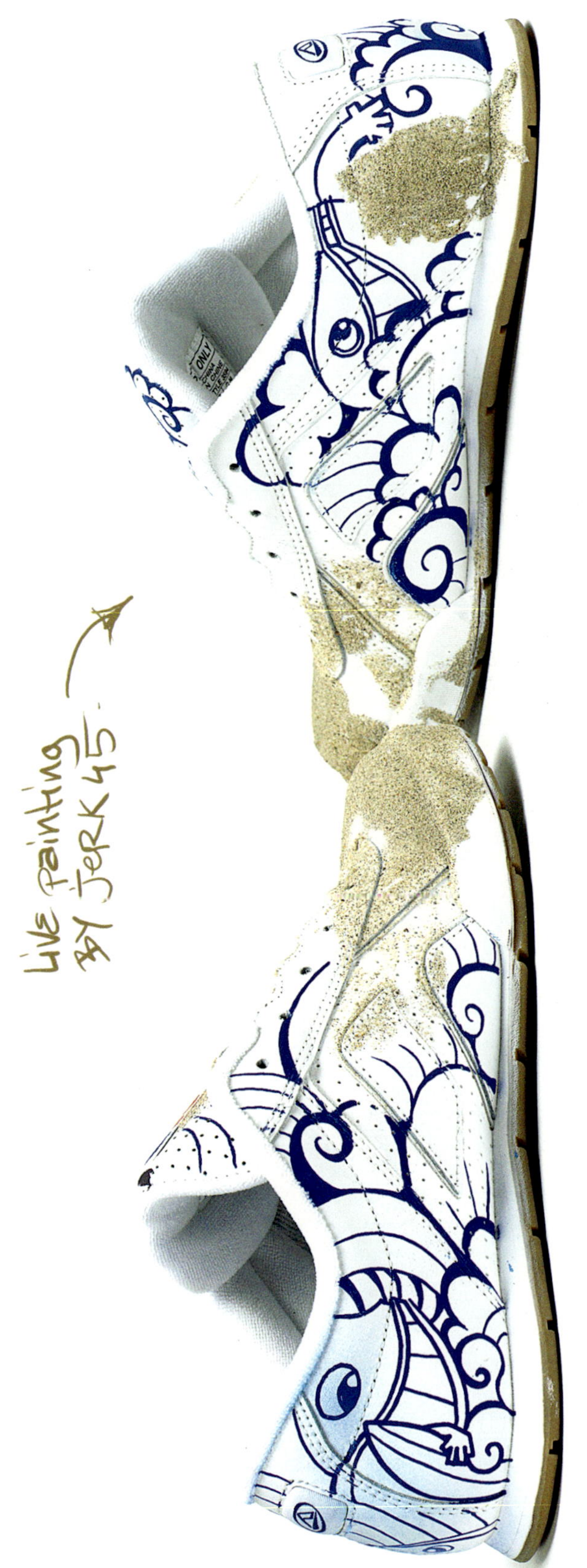
Live Painting
By Jerk 45

→ Live Painting
BY Mambo

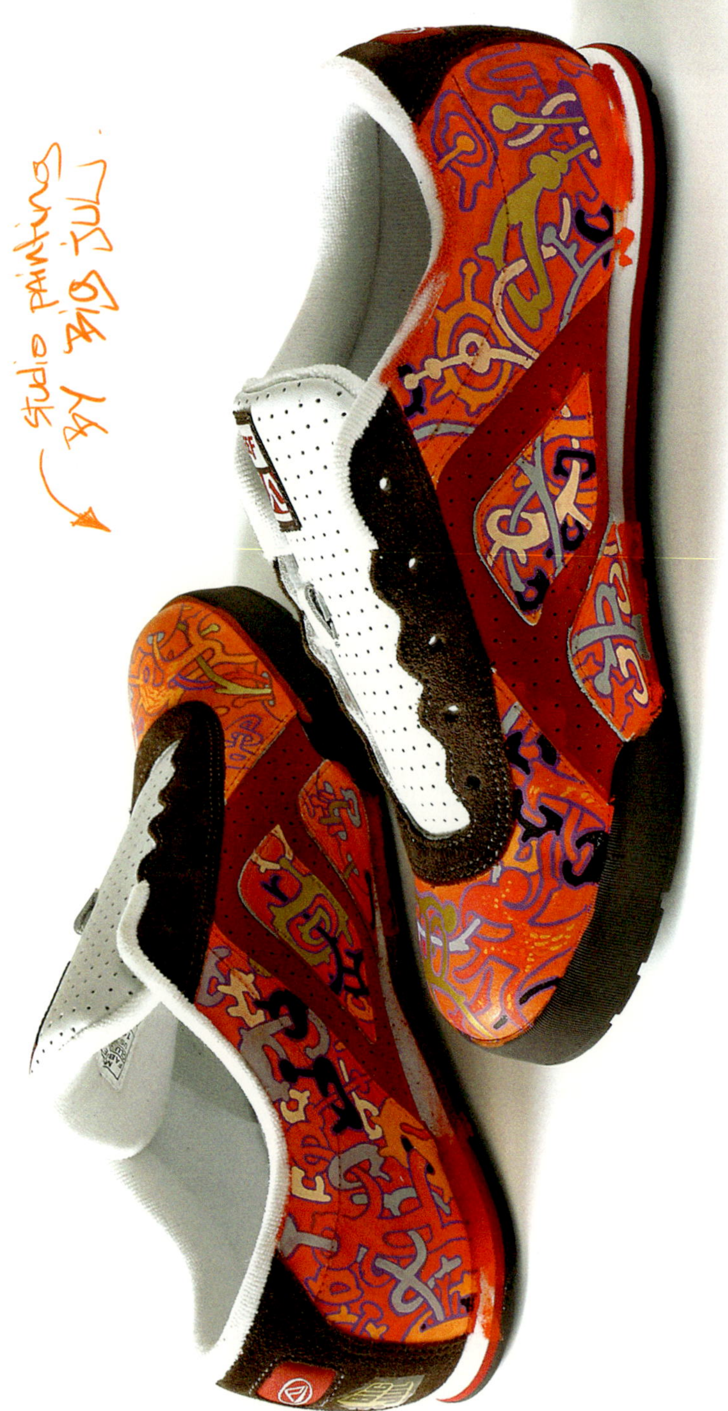
studio painting
BY BIG JUL

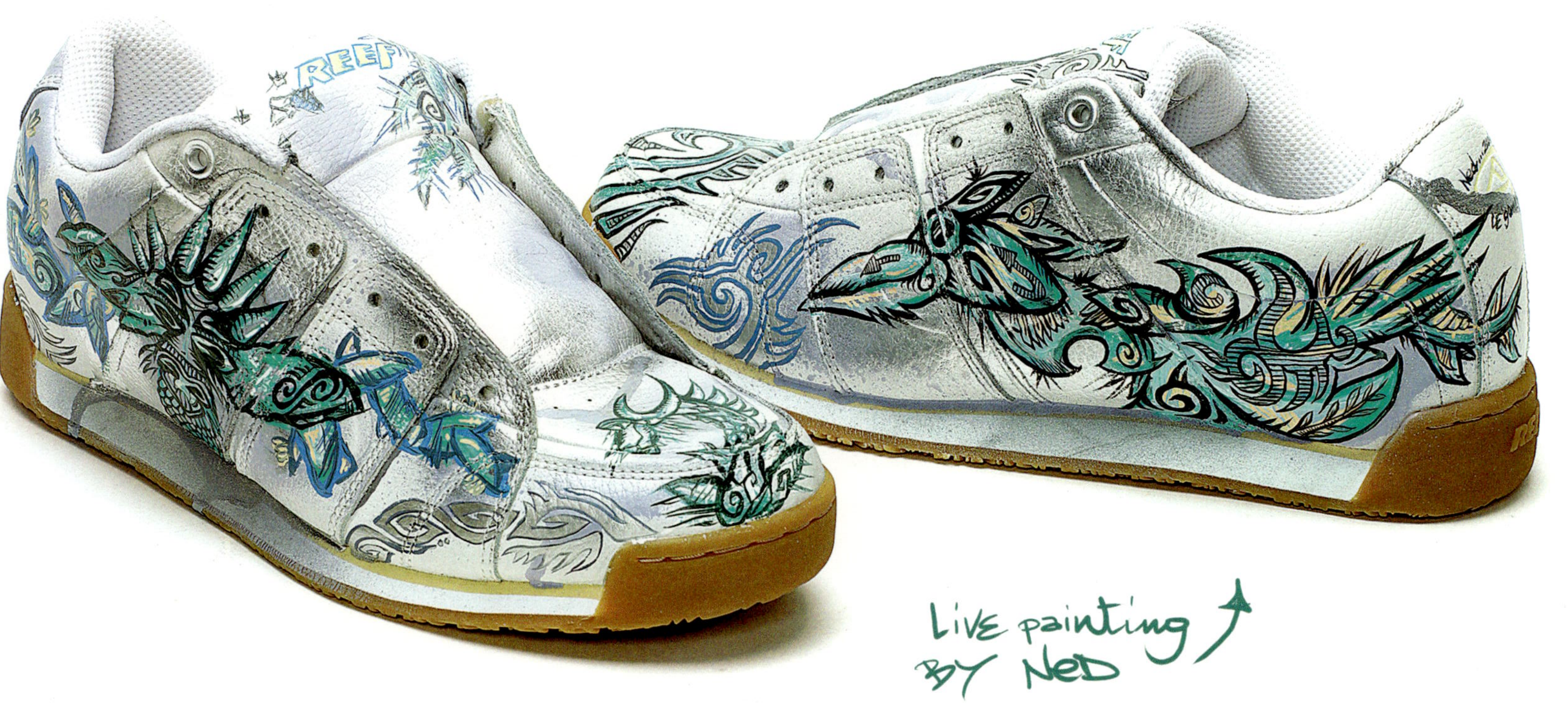
LIVE painting
BY NeD

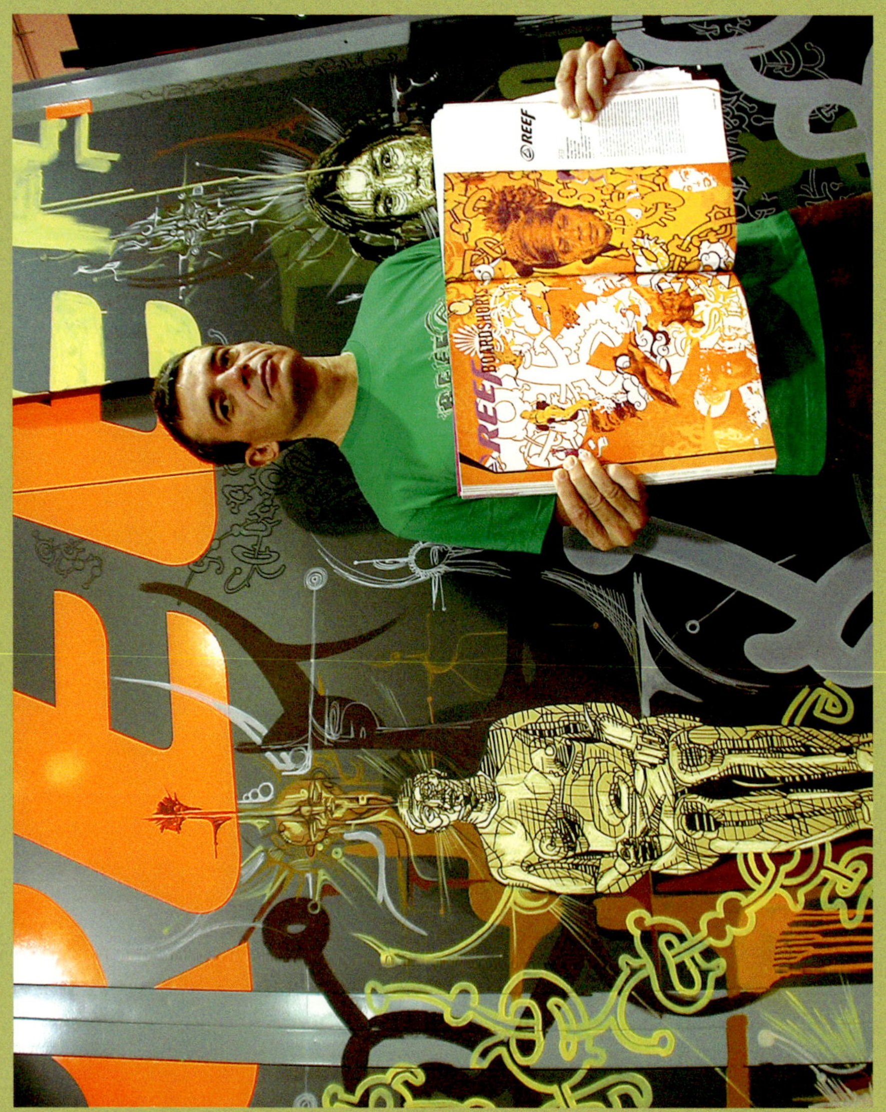

"SAN DiEGO

september 2004—

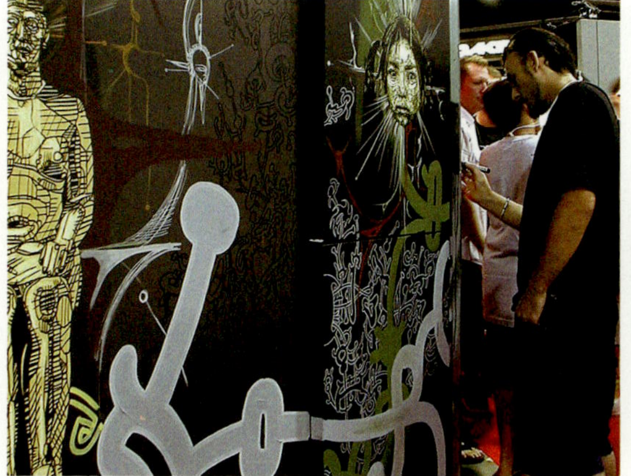
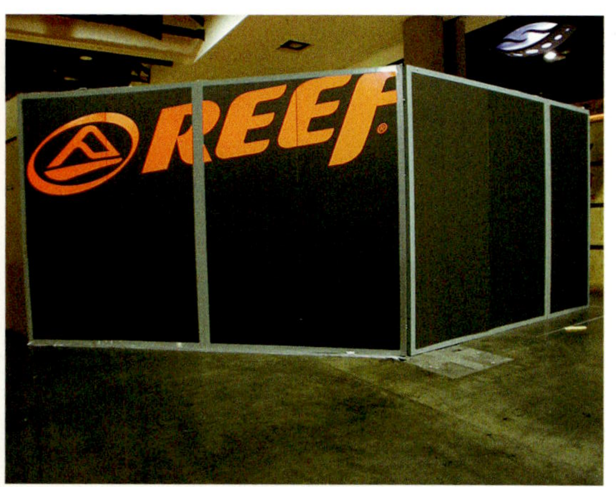
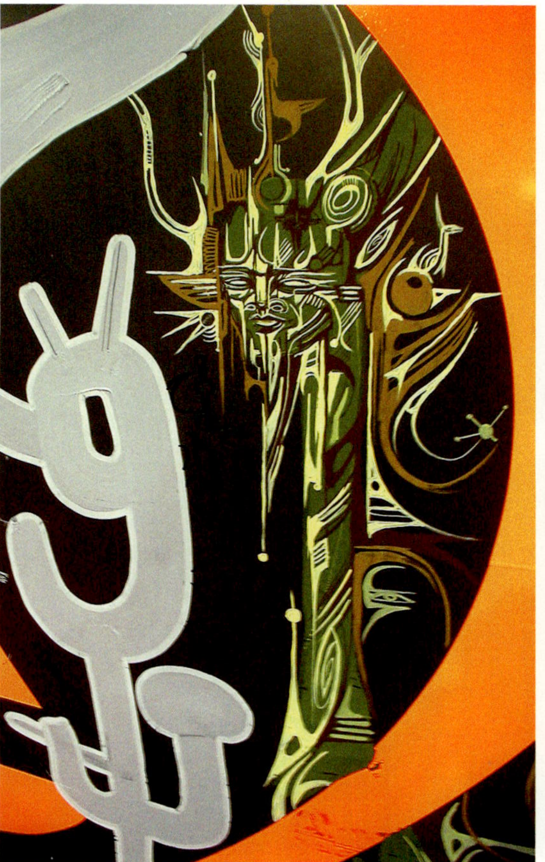
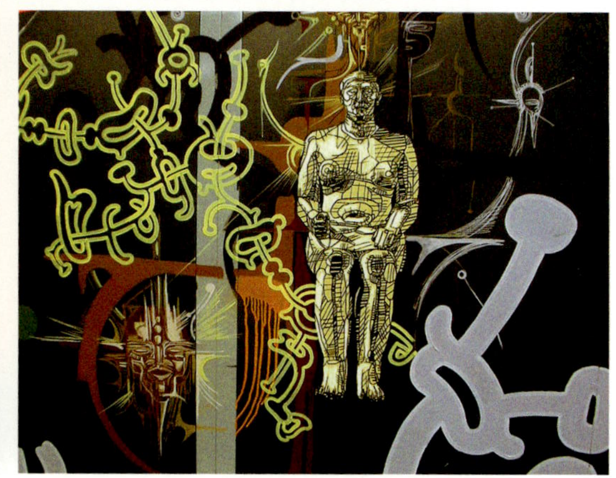
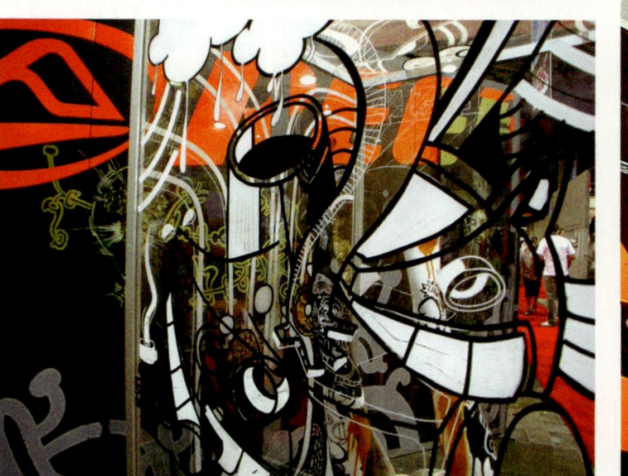

SAN DiEGO

Reef trade show booth panel painted by Big Jul and Steph Carricondo

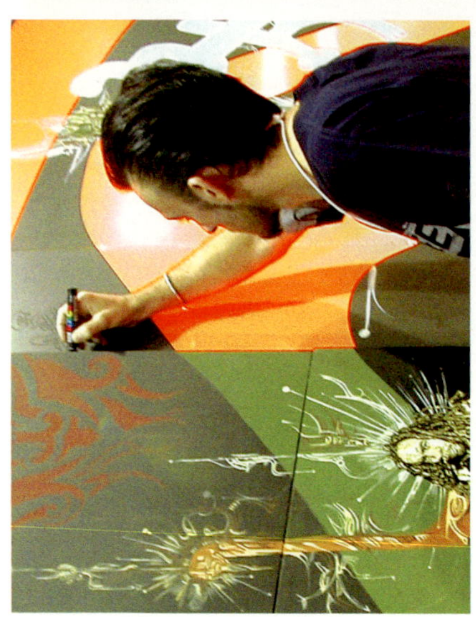

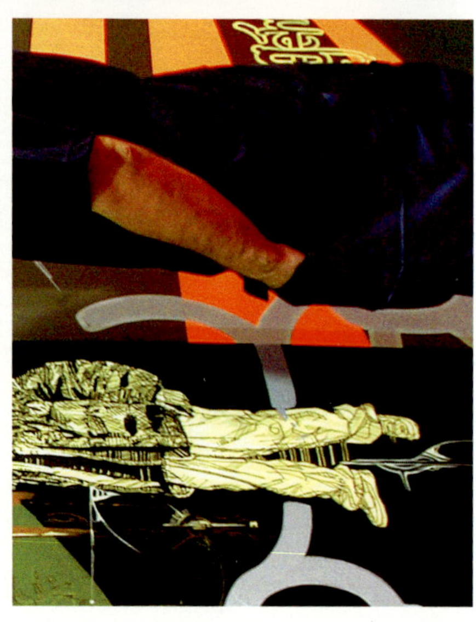

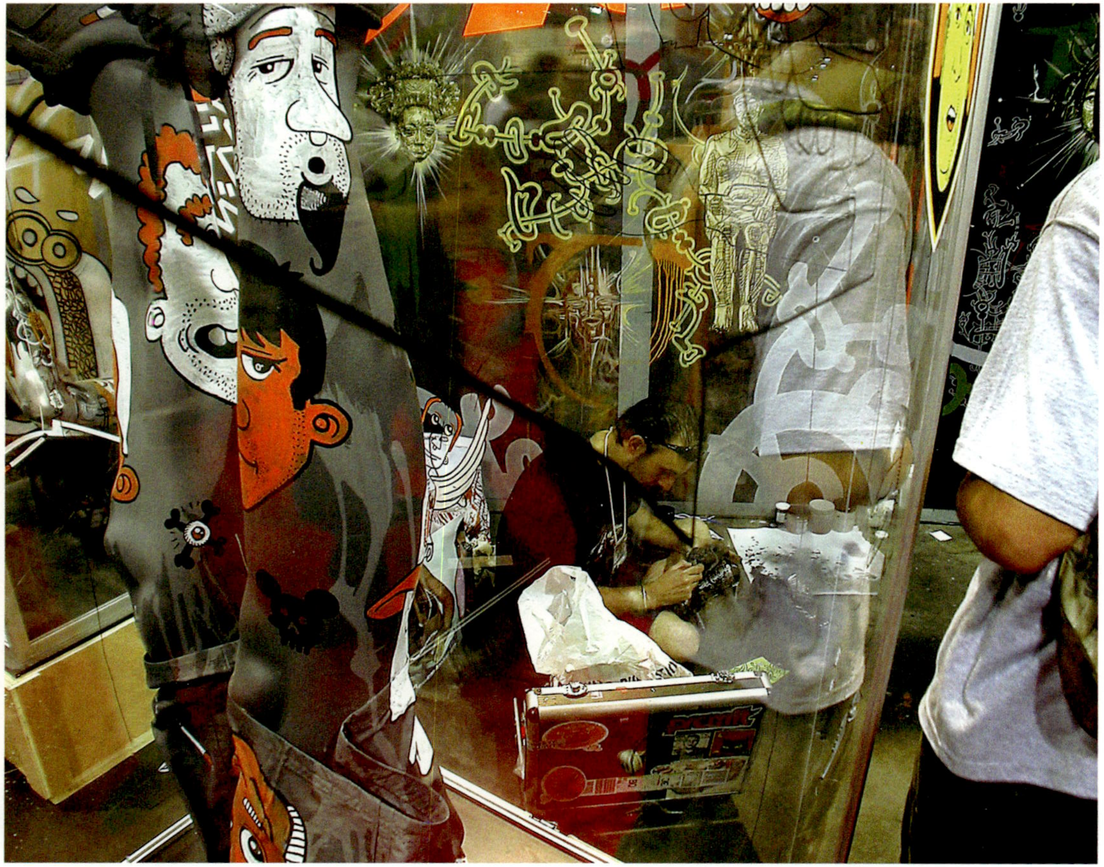

SAN DiEGO

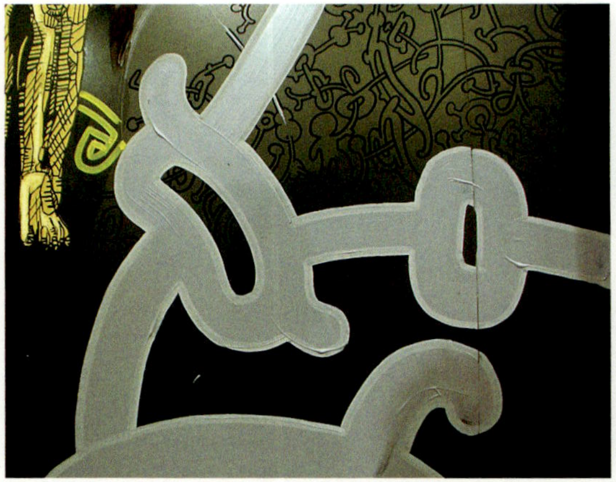

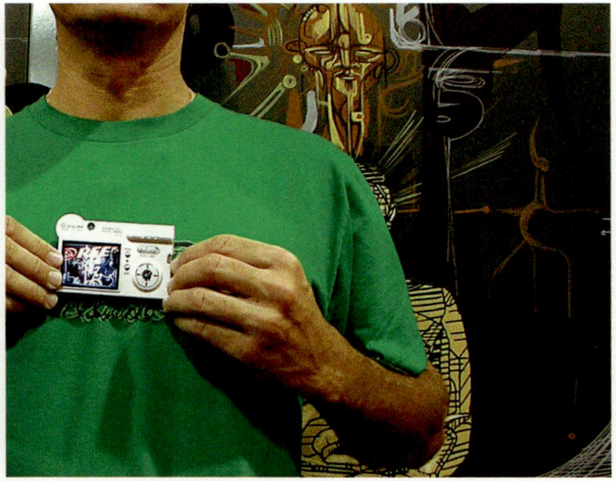

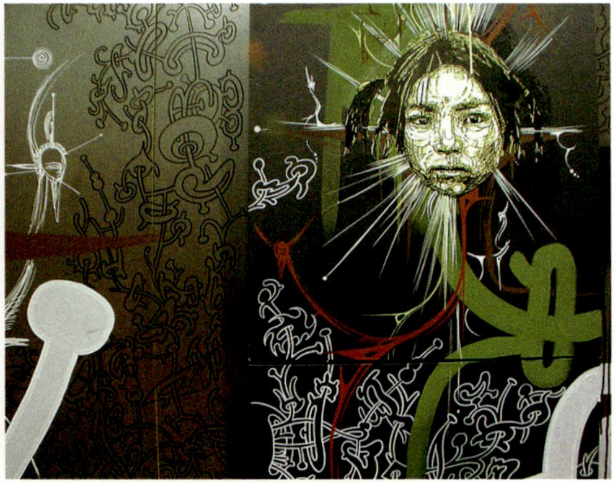

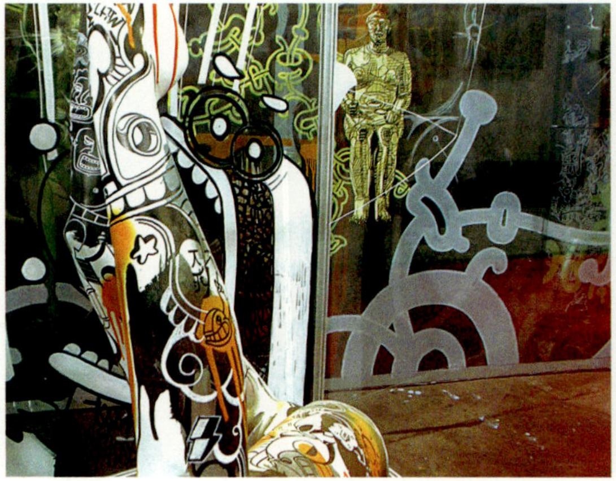

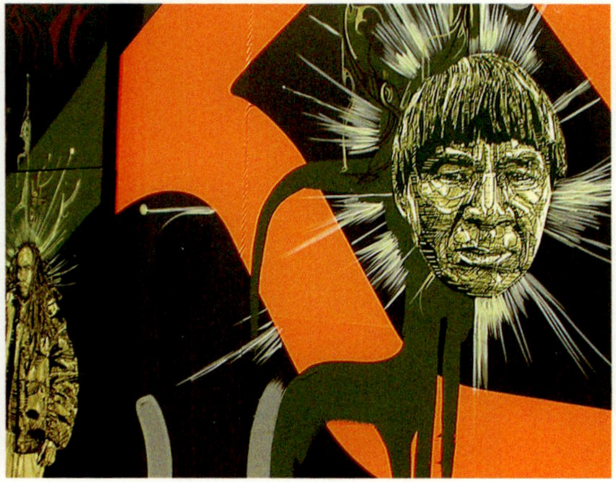

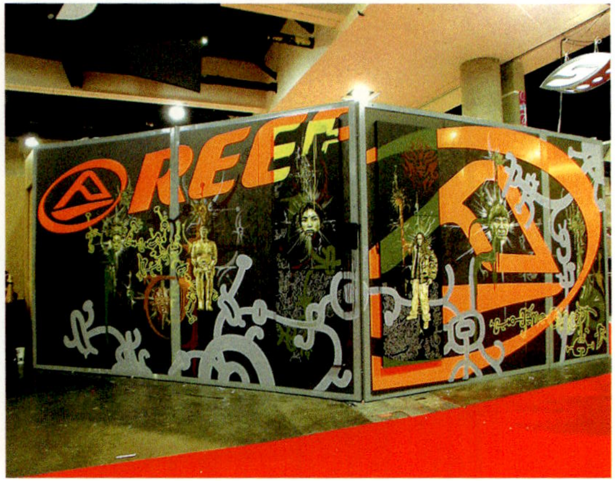

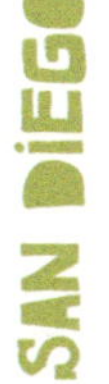

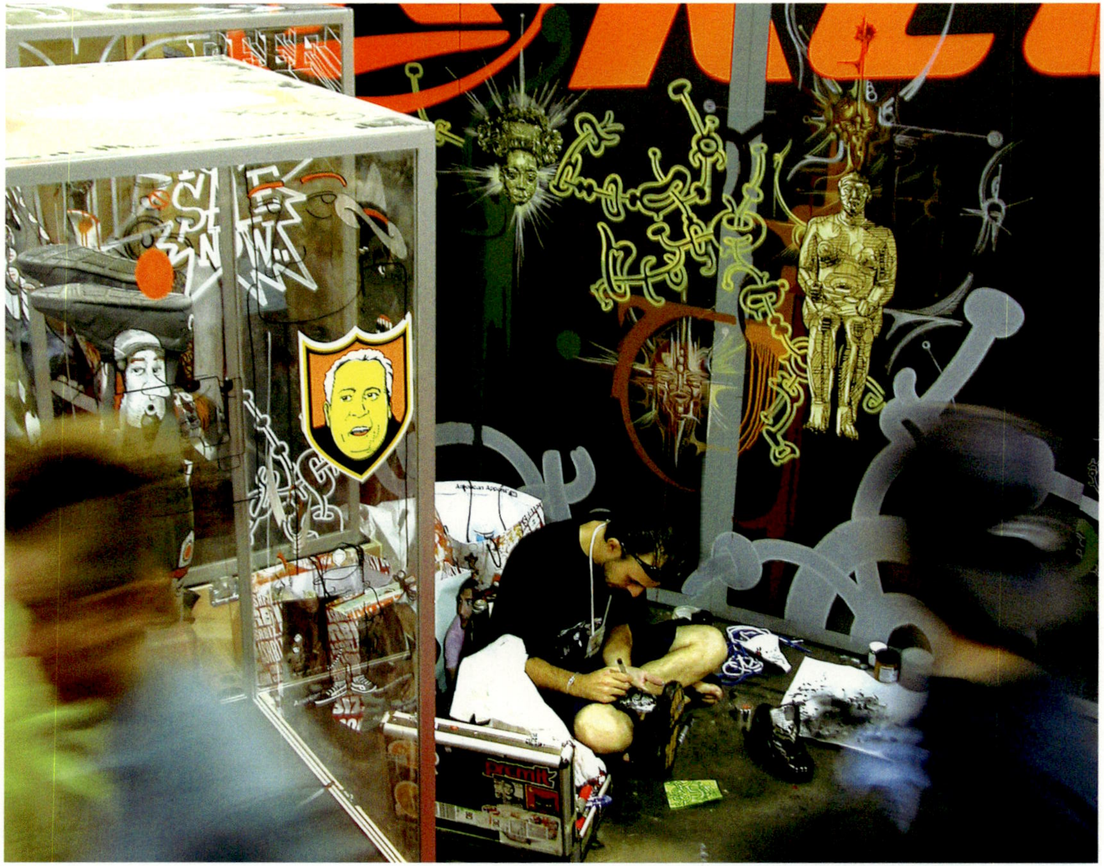

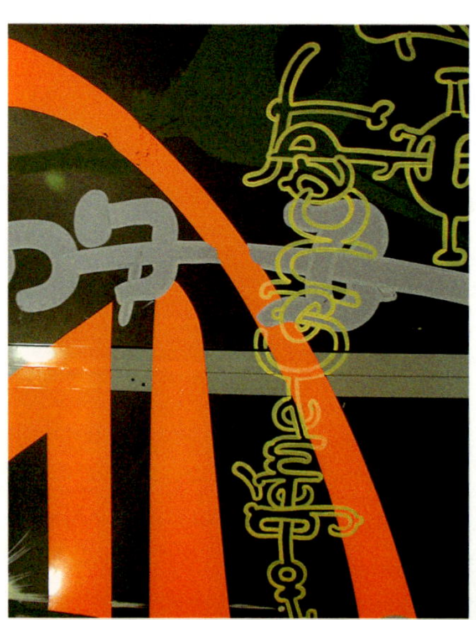

live painting by Big Jul

SAN DiEGO

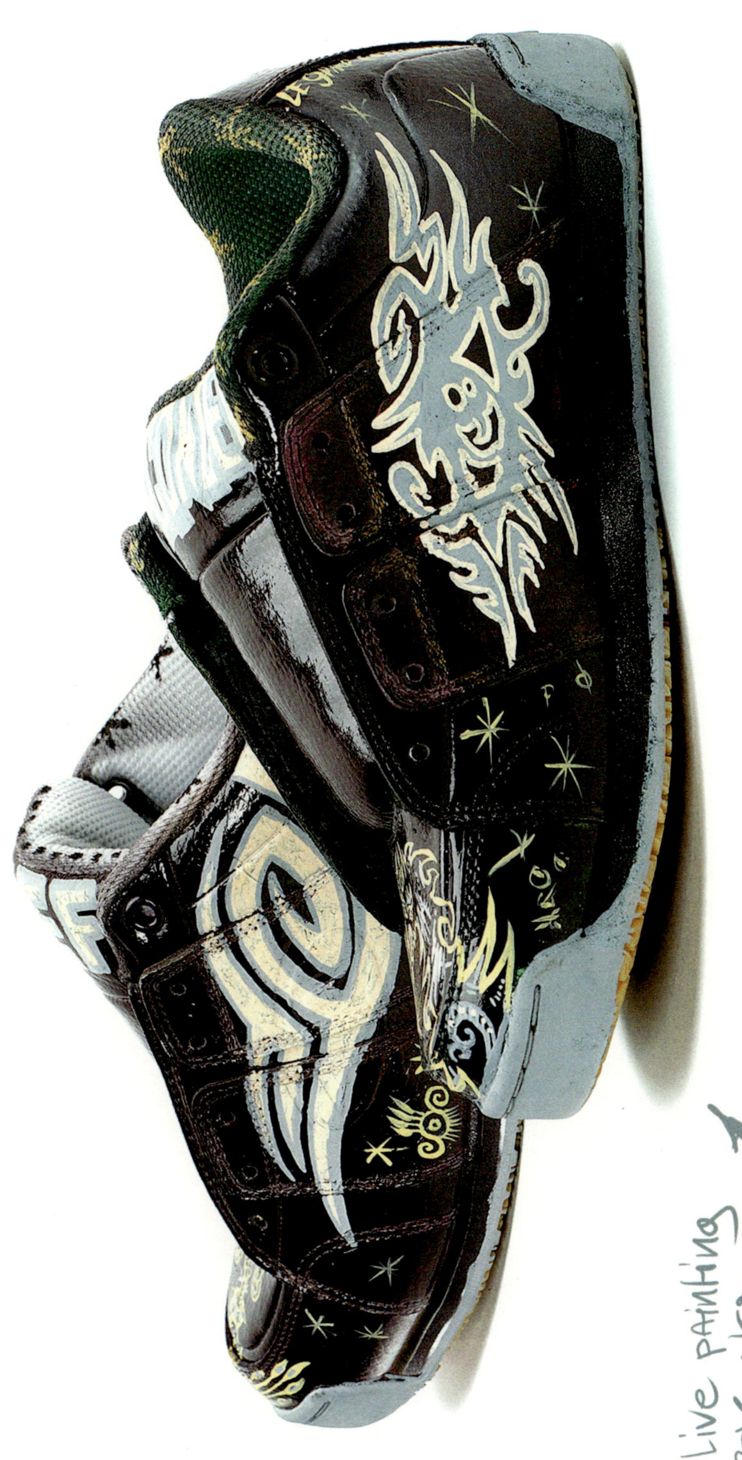
live painting
BY NED

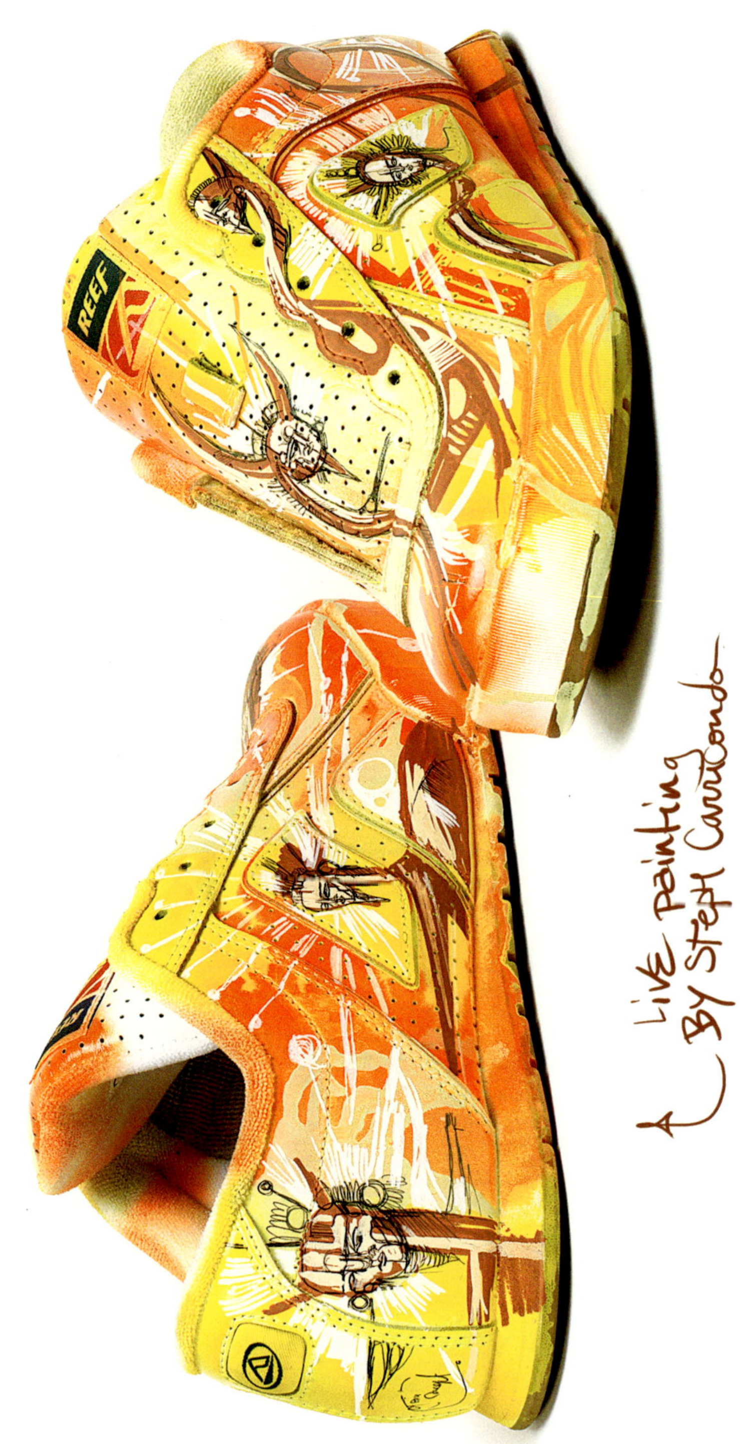

REEF
Live painting
By Steph Carimondo

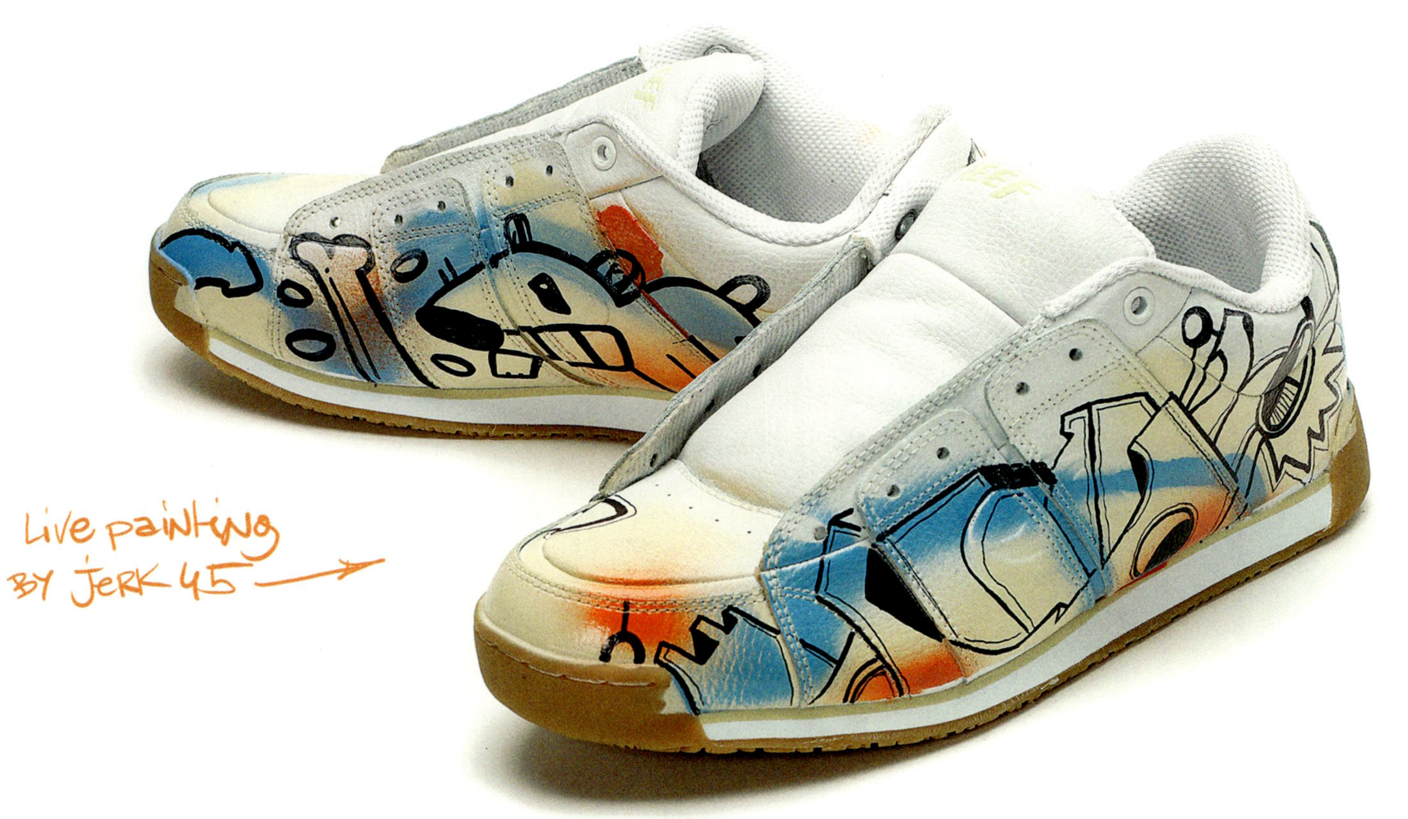
live painting
BY JeRK 45

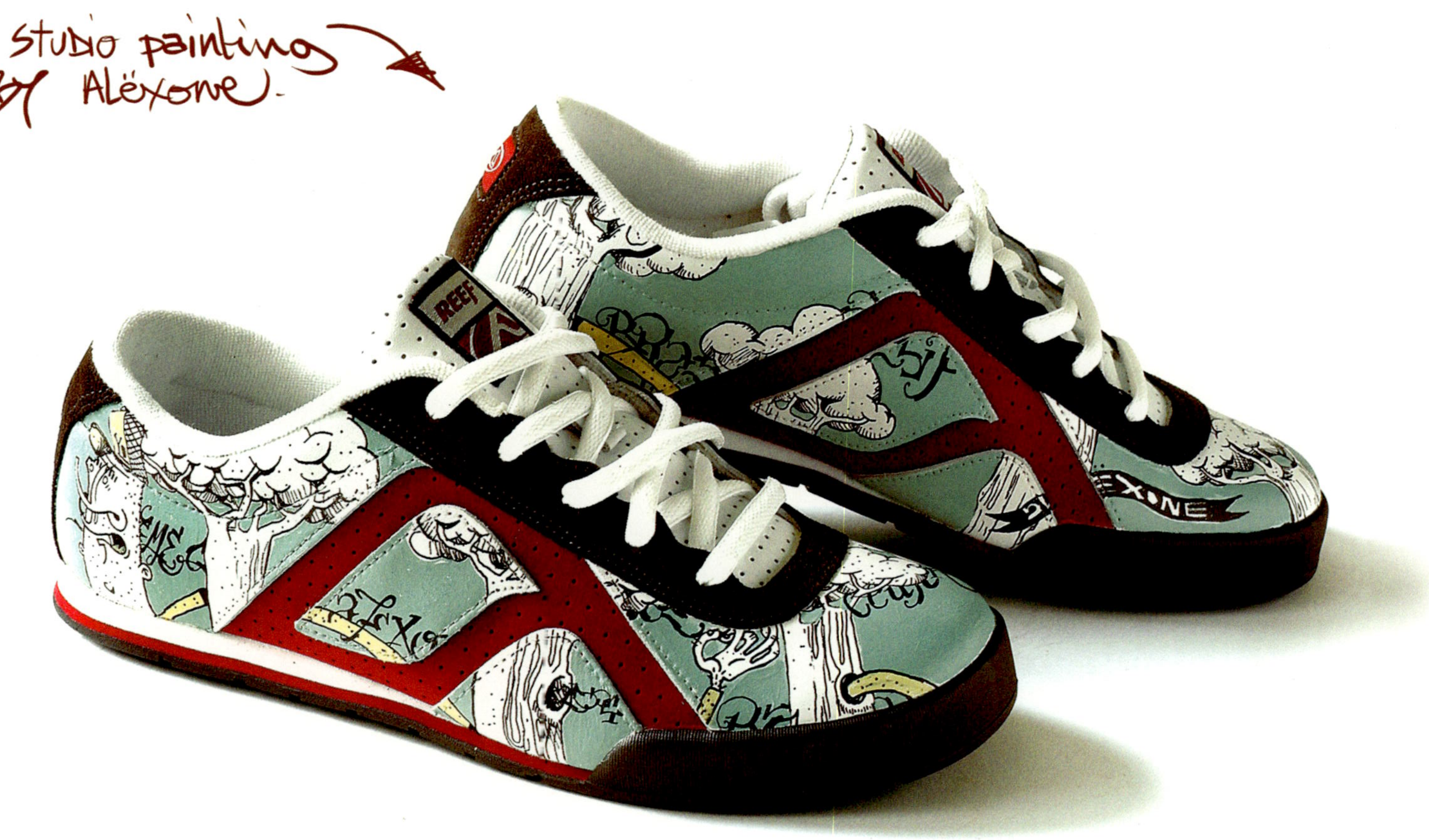

studio painting
BY Aléxone.
REEF

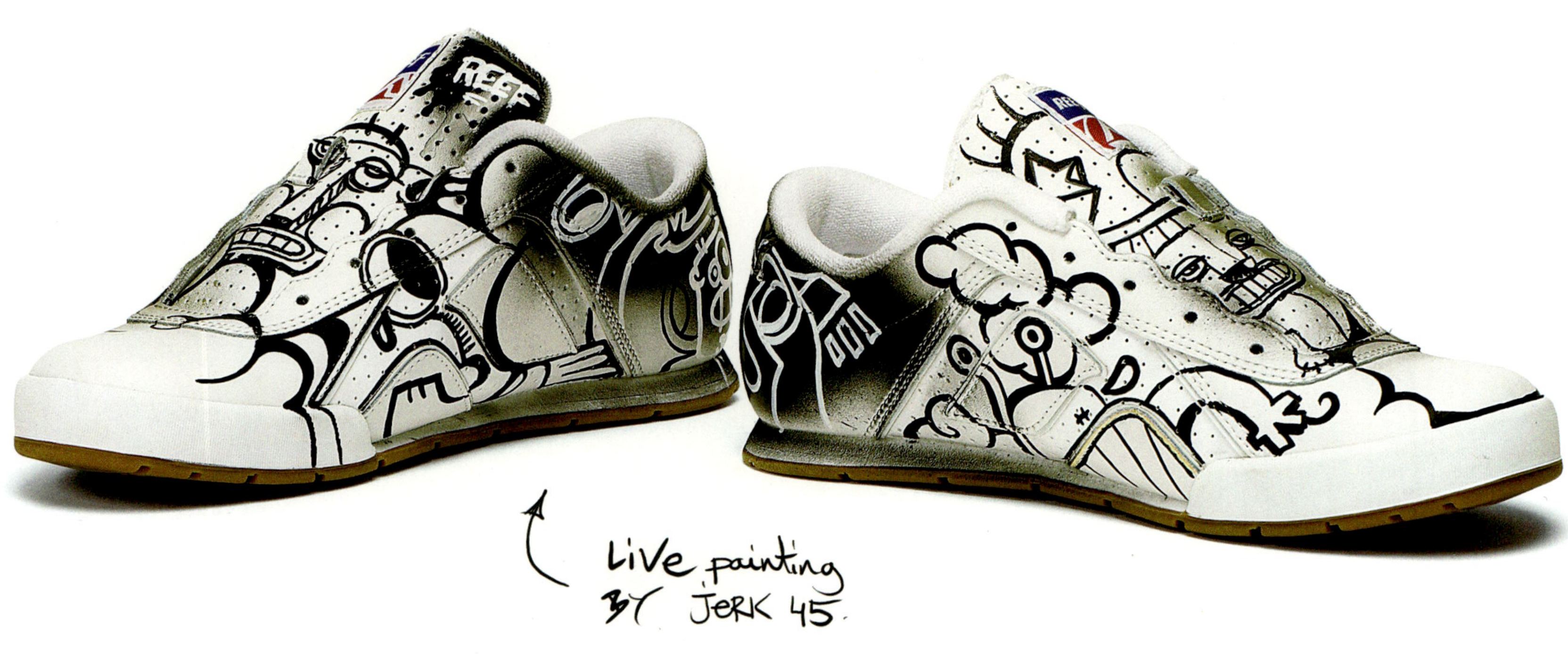

Live painting
by JERK 45.

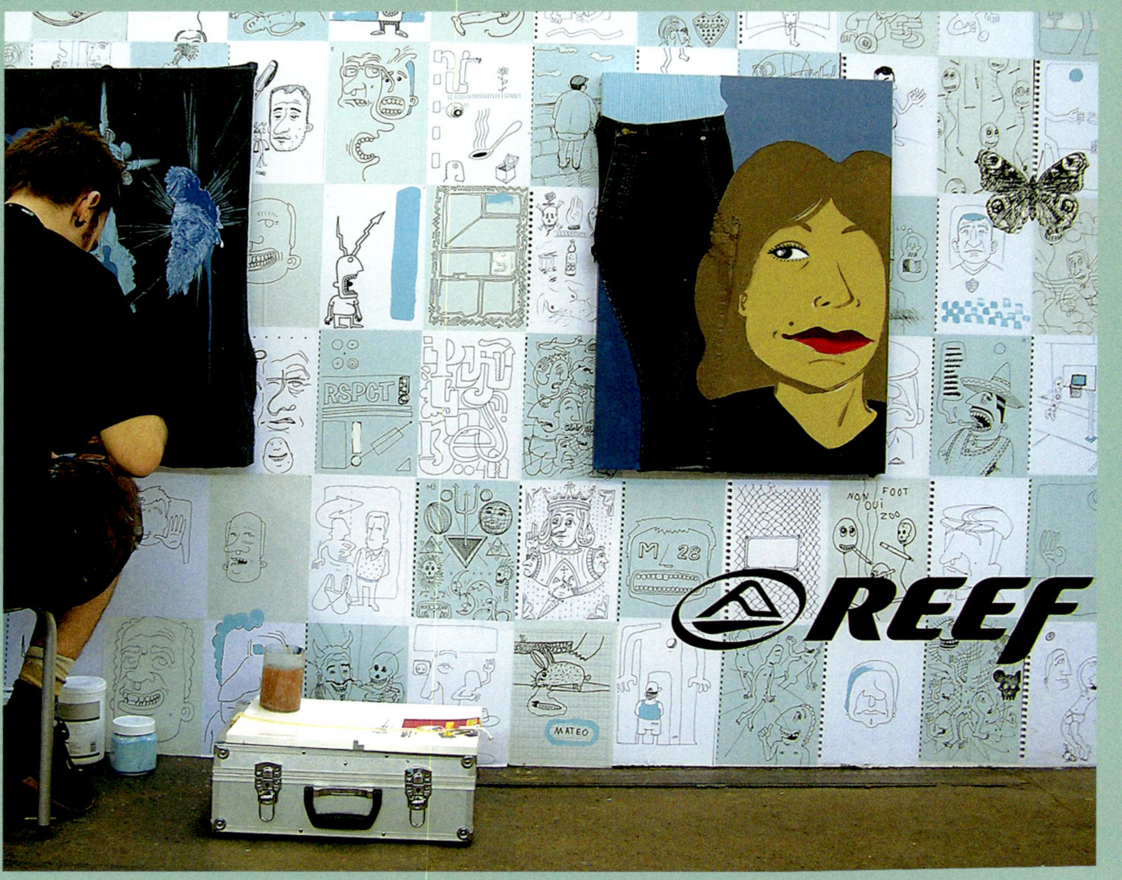
REEF
'BERLiN
January 2005-

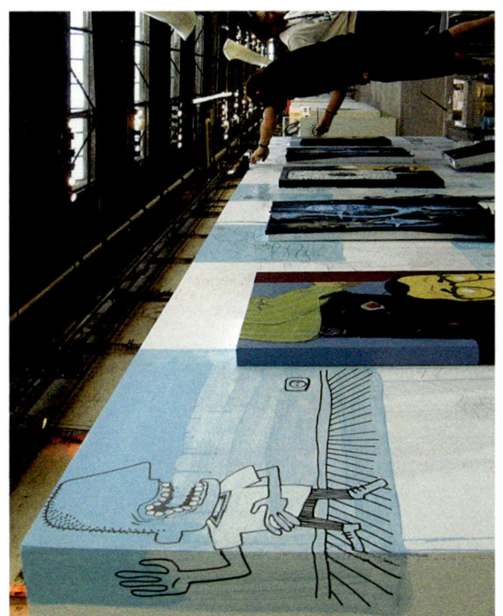
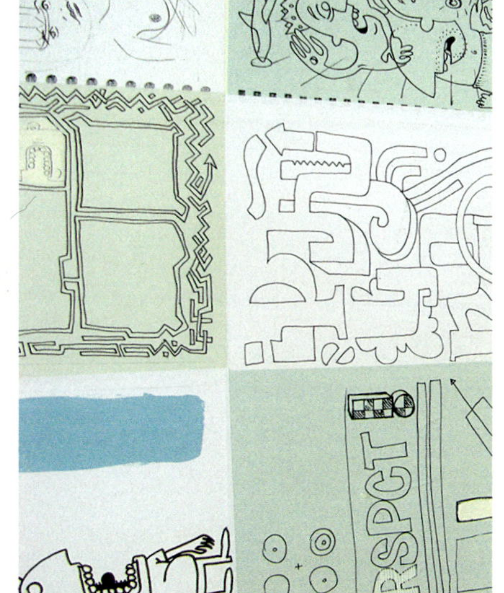

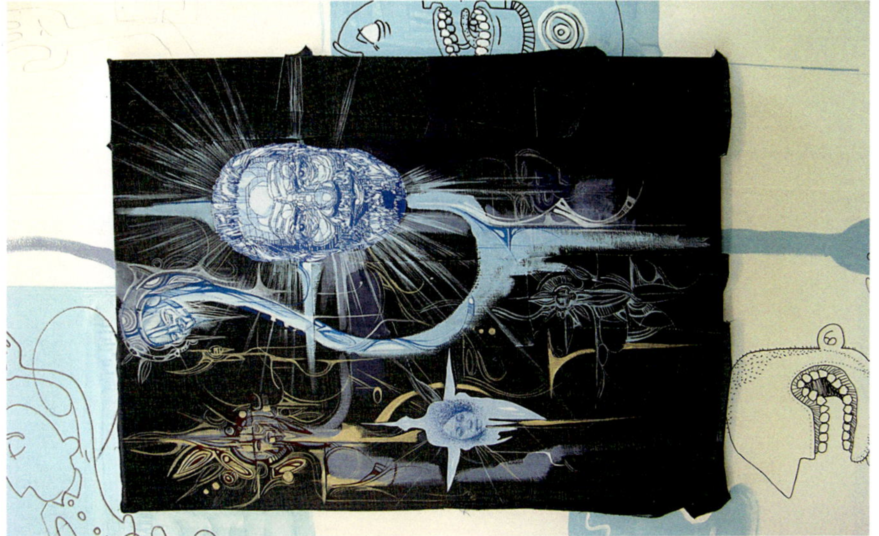
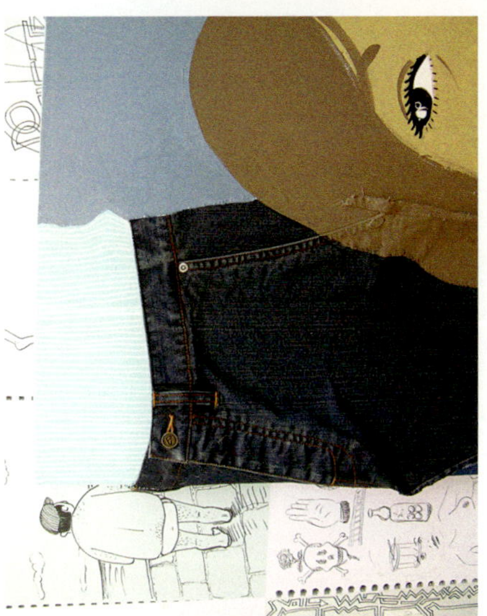
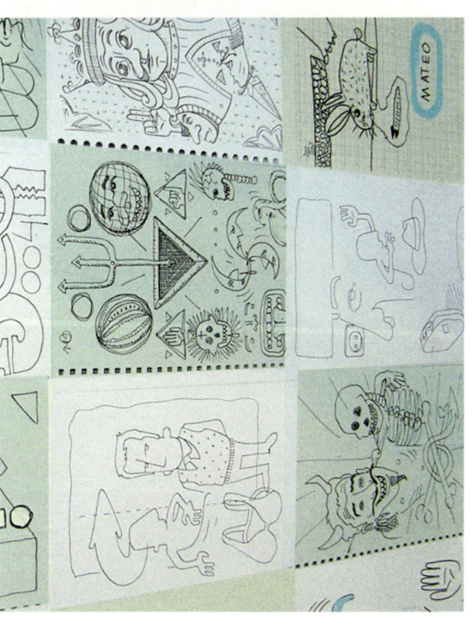

BERLiN

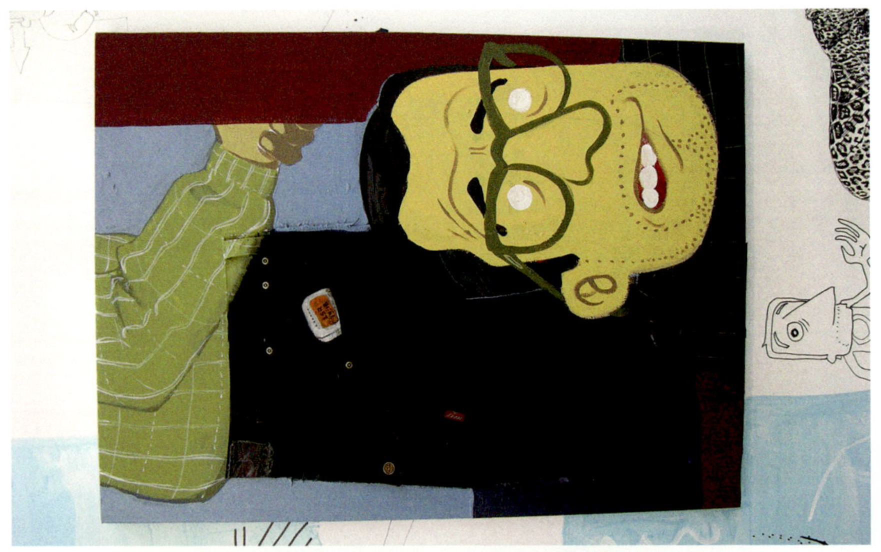

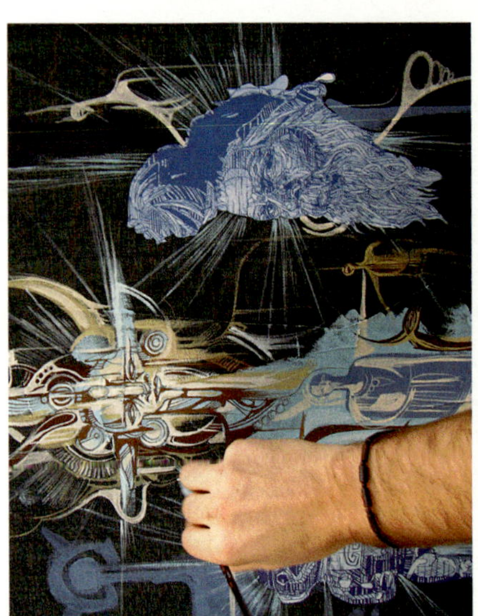

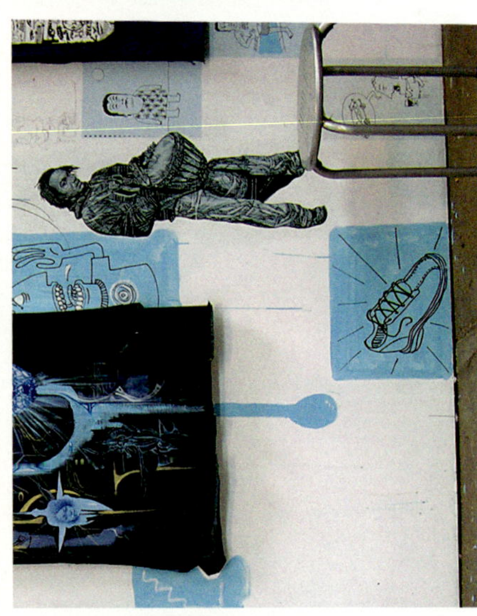

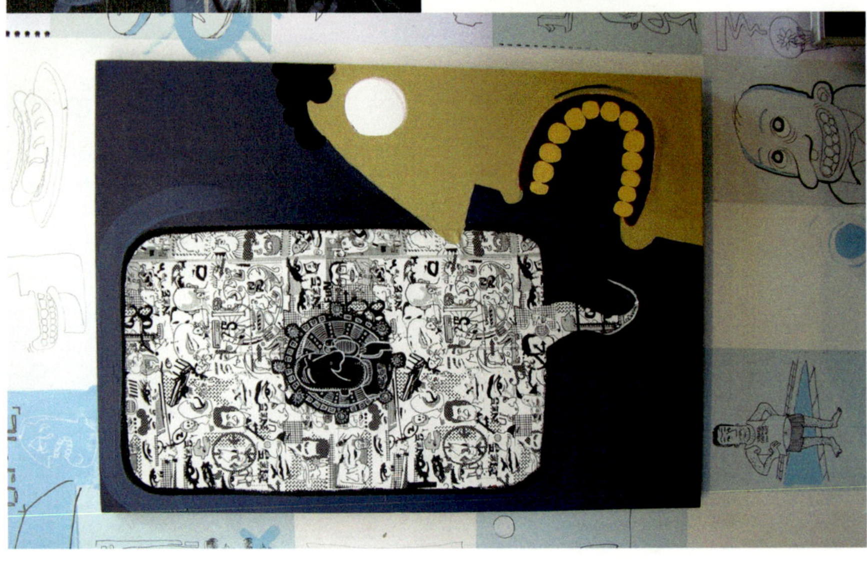

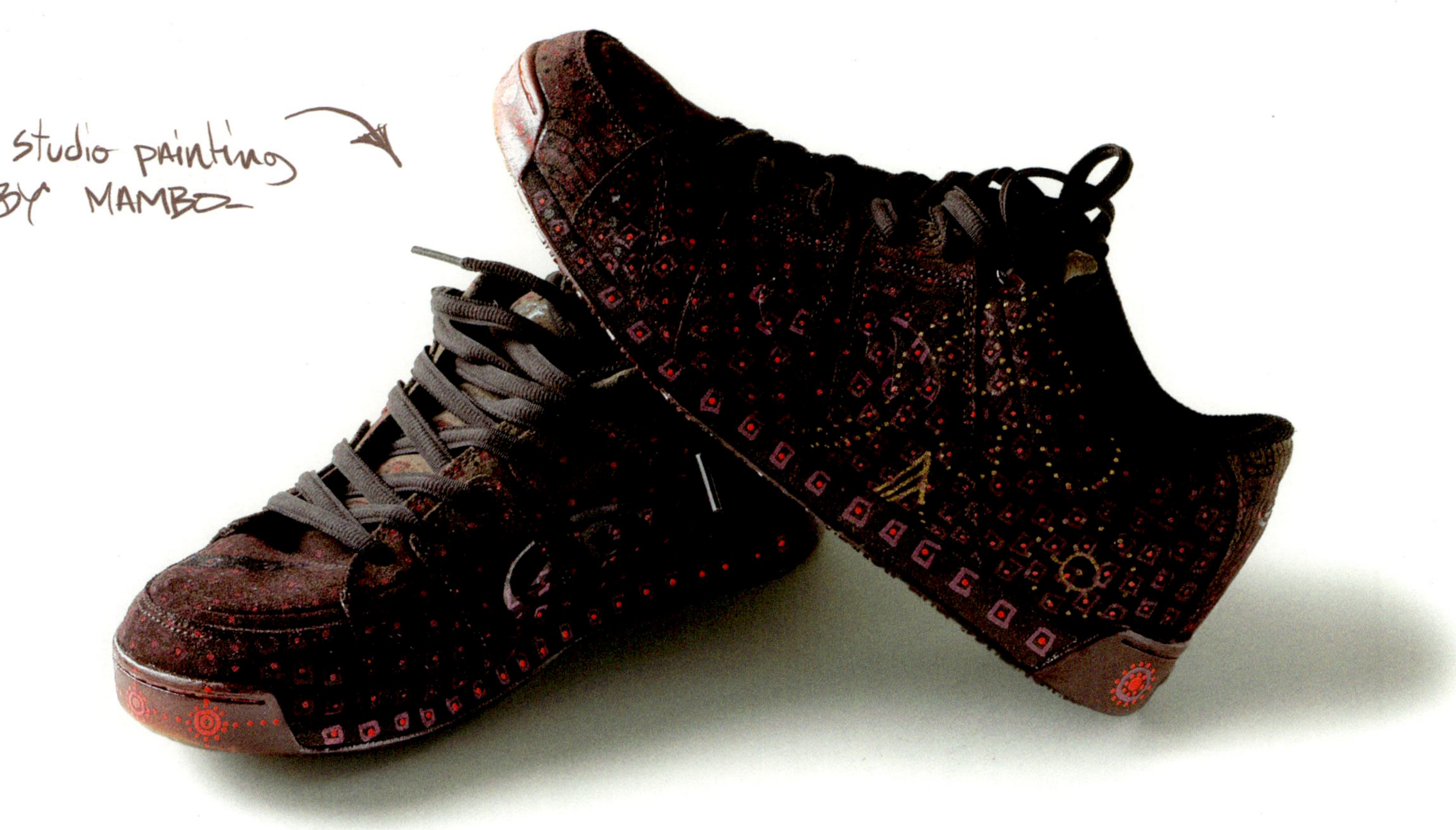
studio painting
By MAMBO

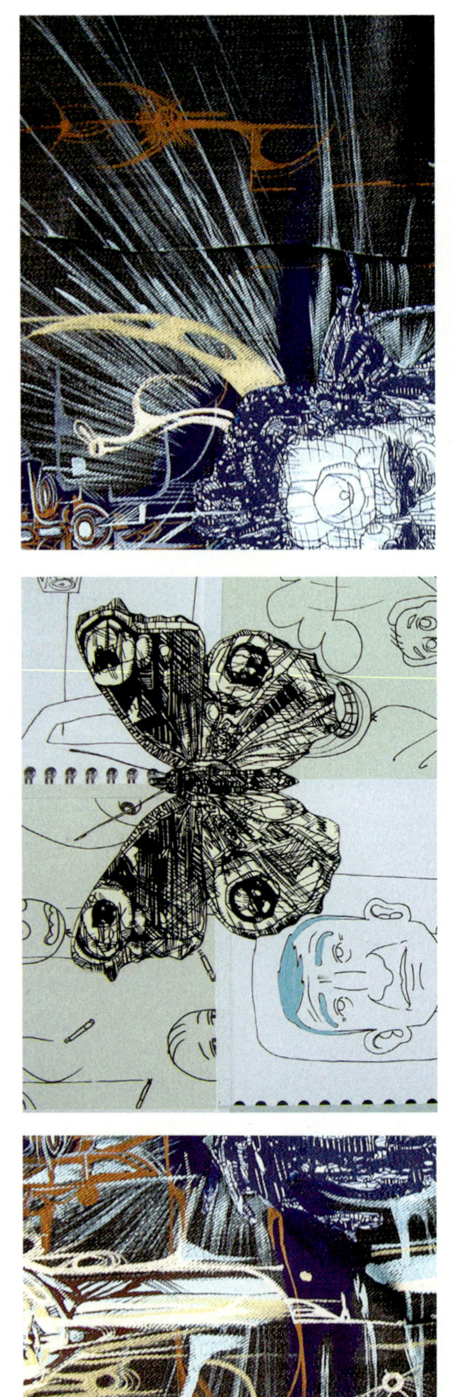
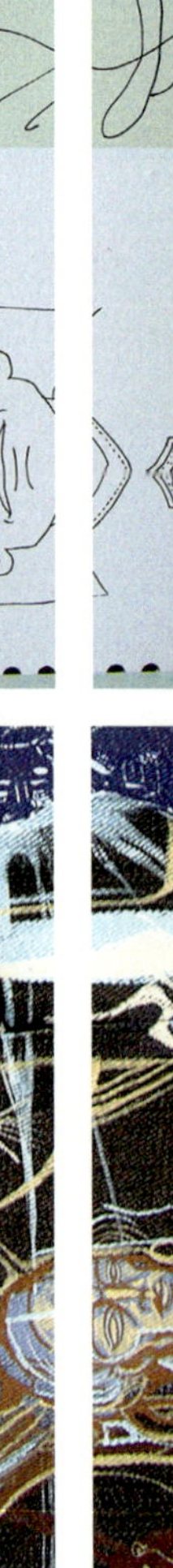
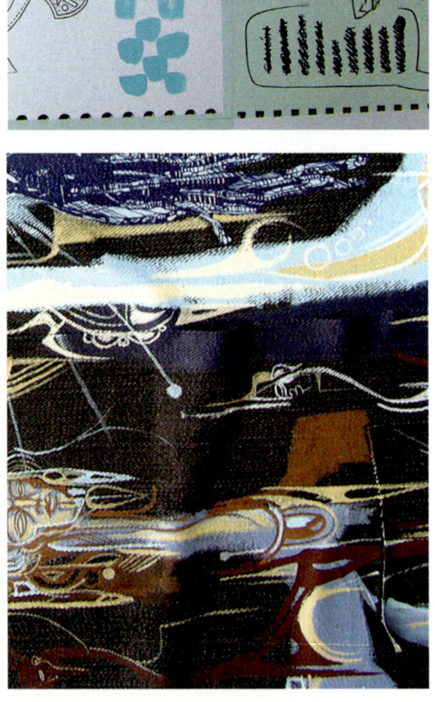
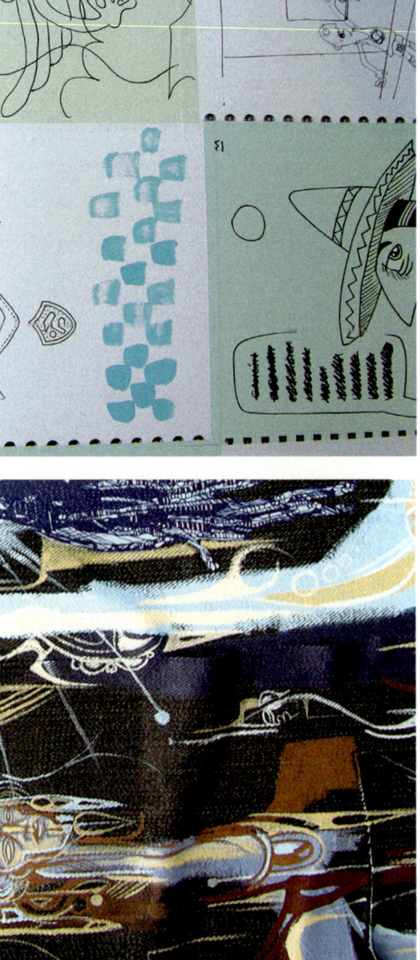

Mambo and Steph Carricondo

BERLiN

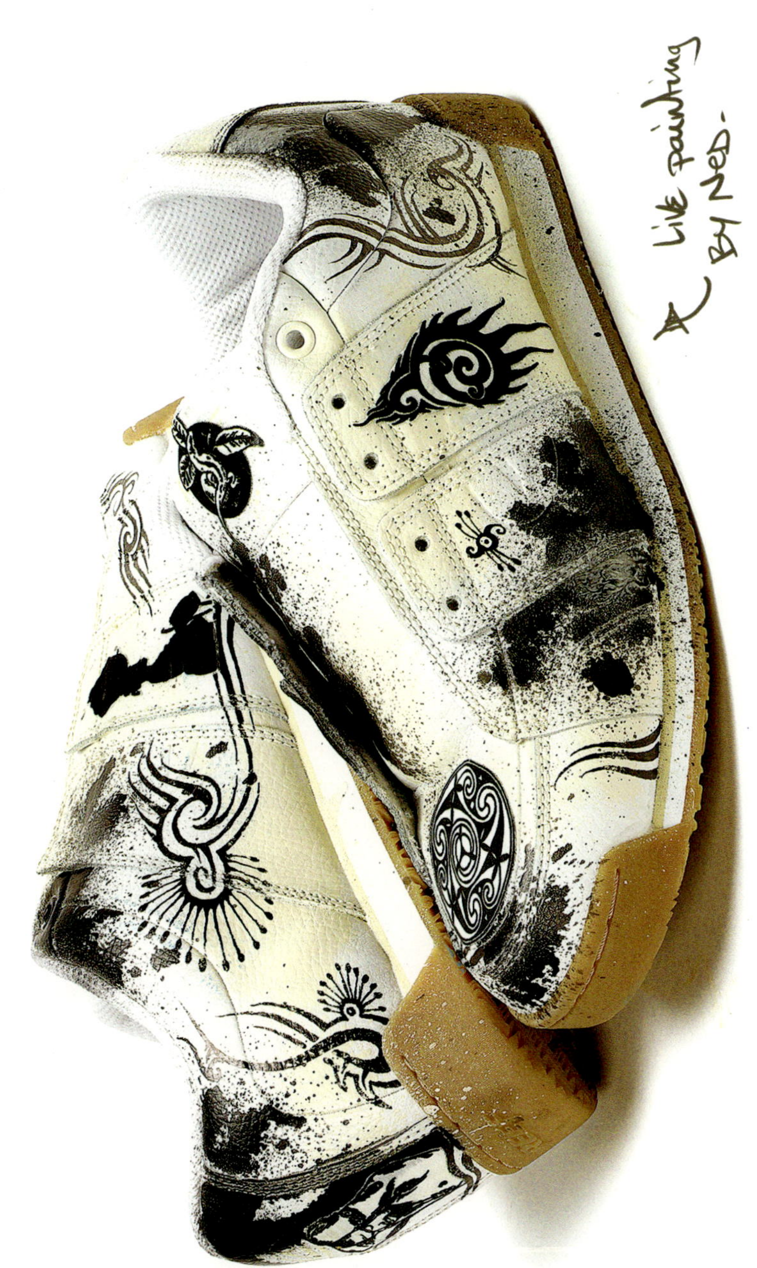

like painting
By Ned.-

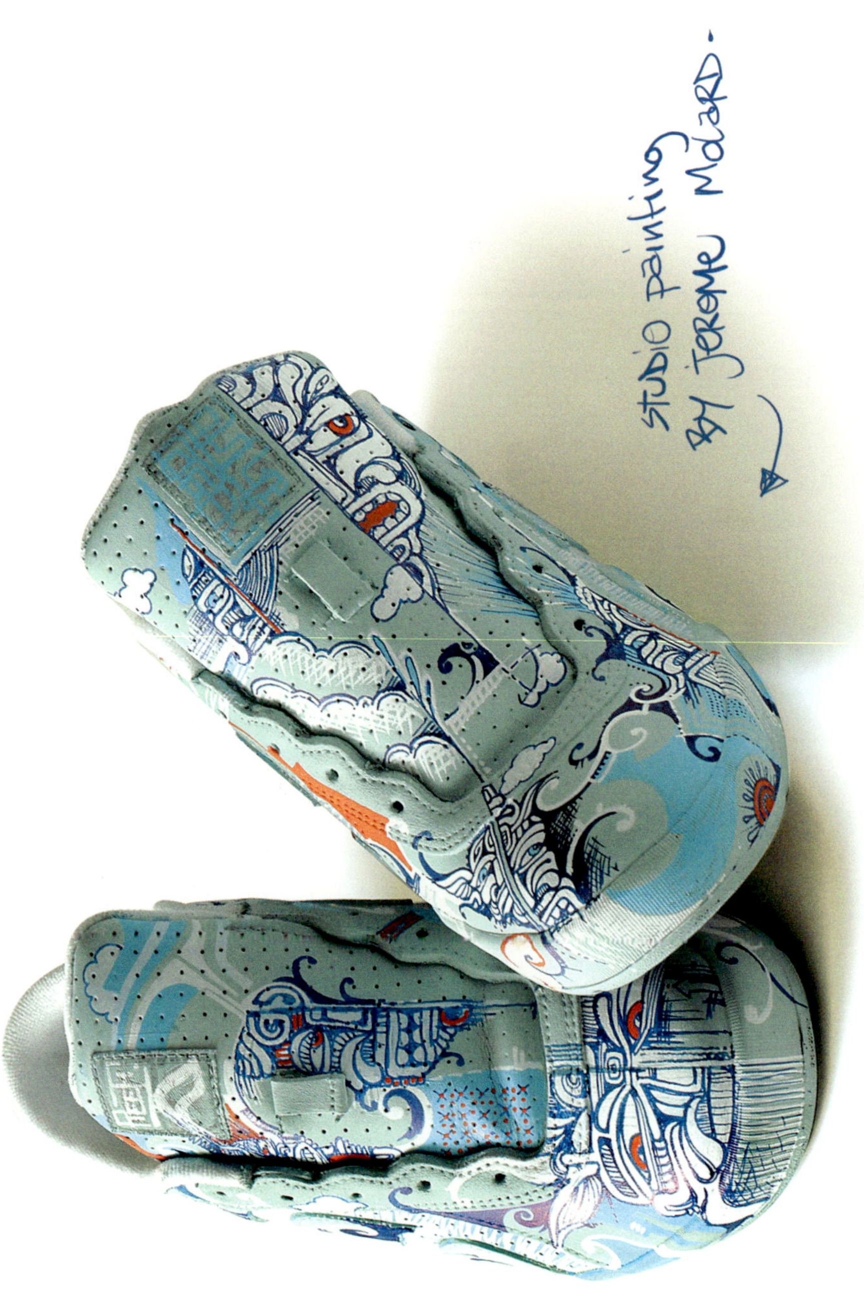
studio painting
By Jerome Mdard.

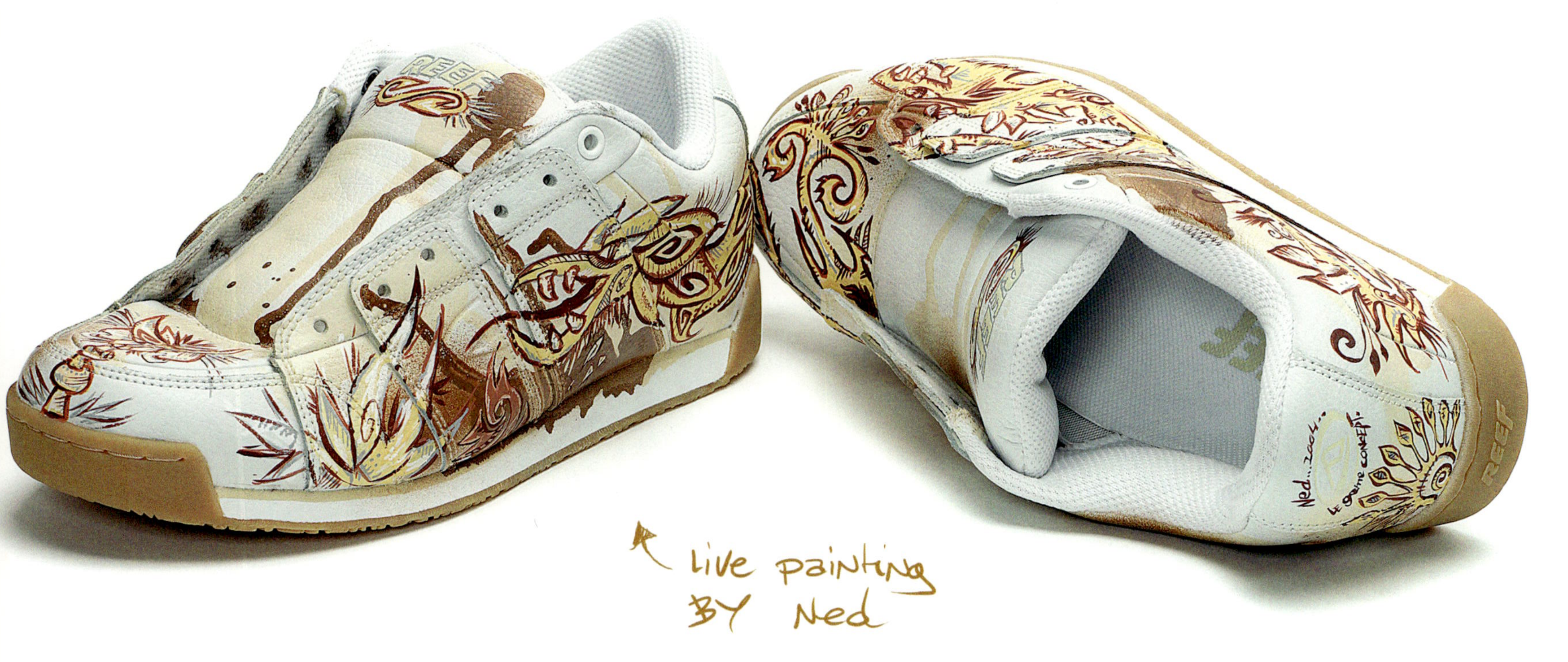

A live painting
BY Ned

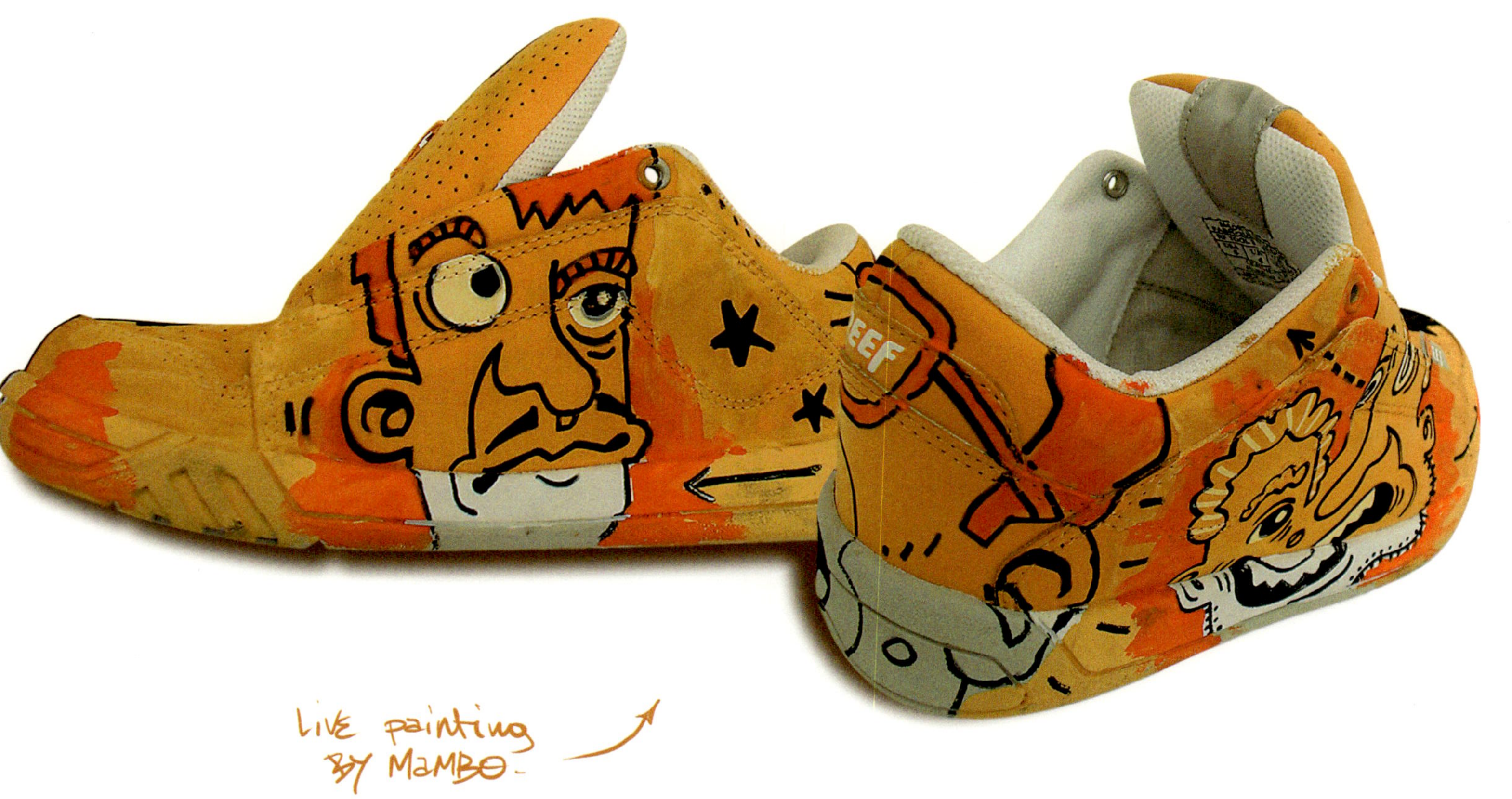

Live painting
by MAMBO →

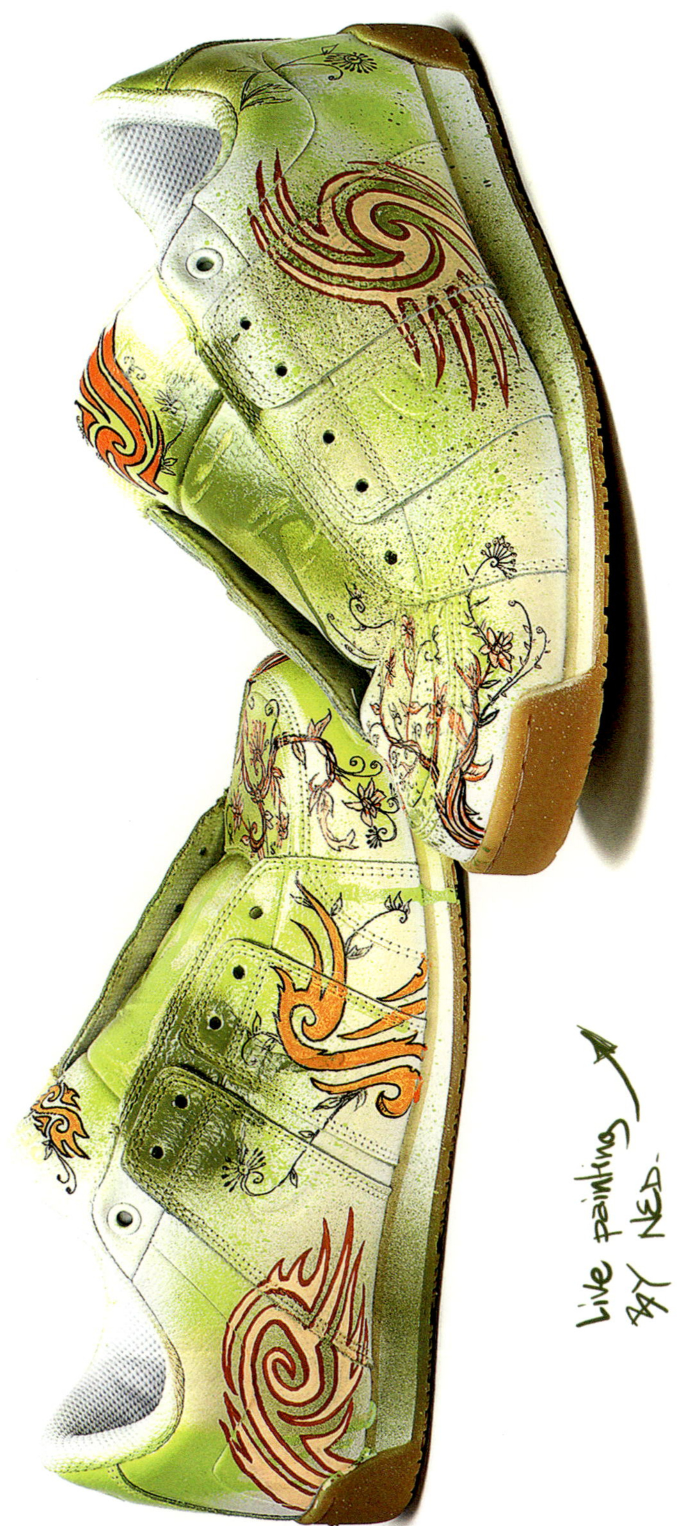

Live painting
by Ned.

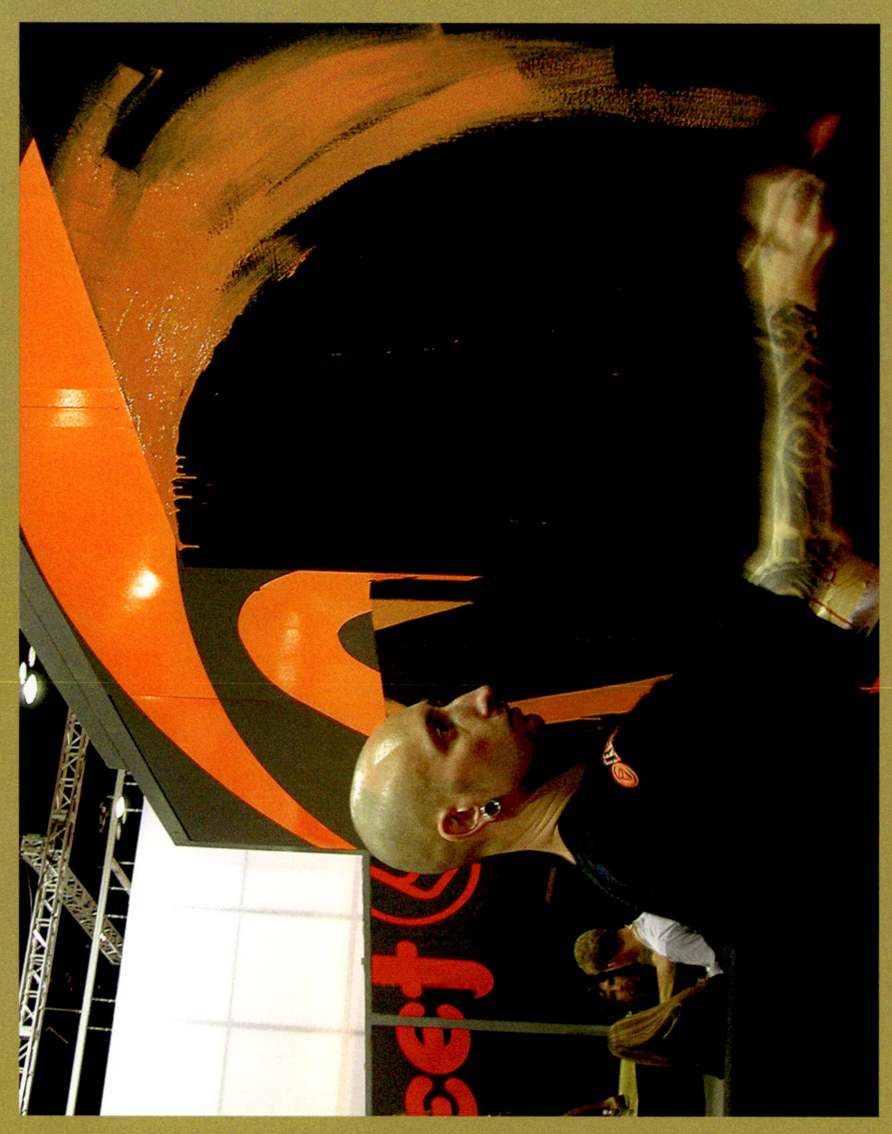

'SAN DIEGO January 2005.

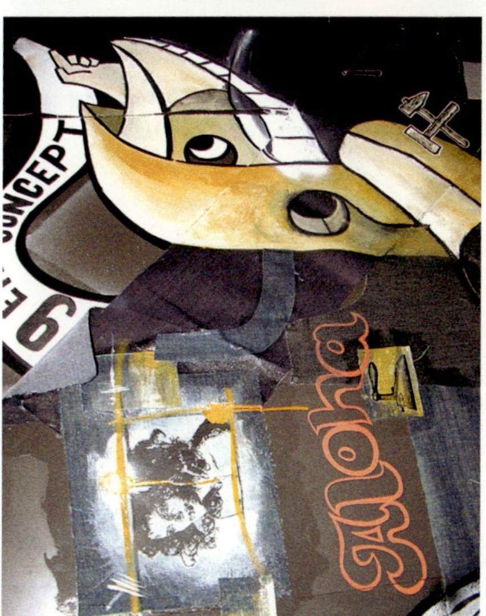
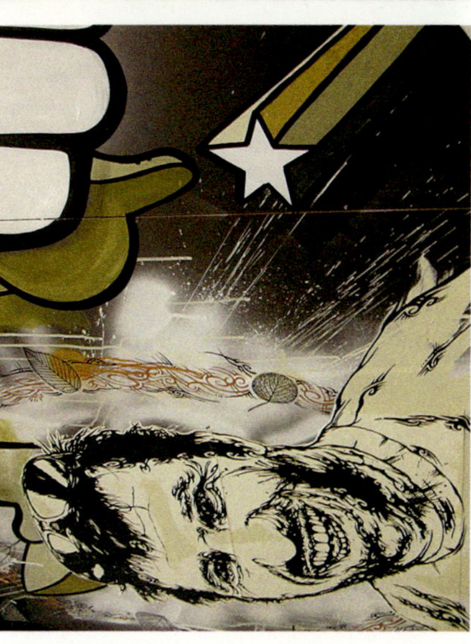

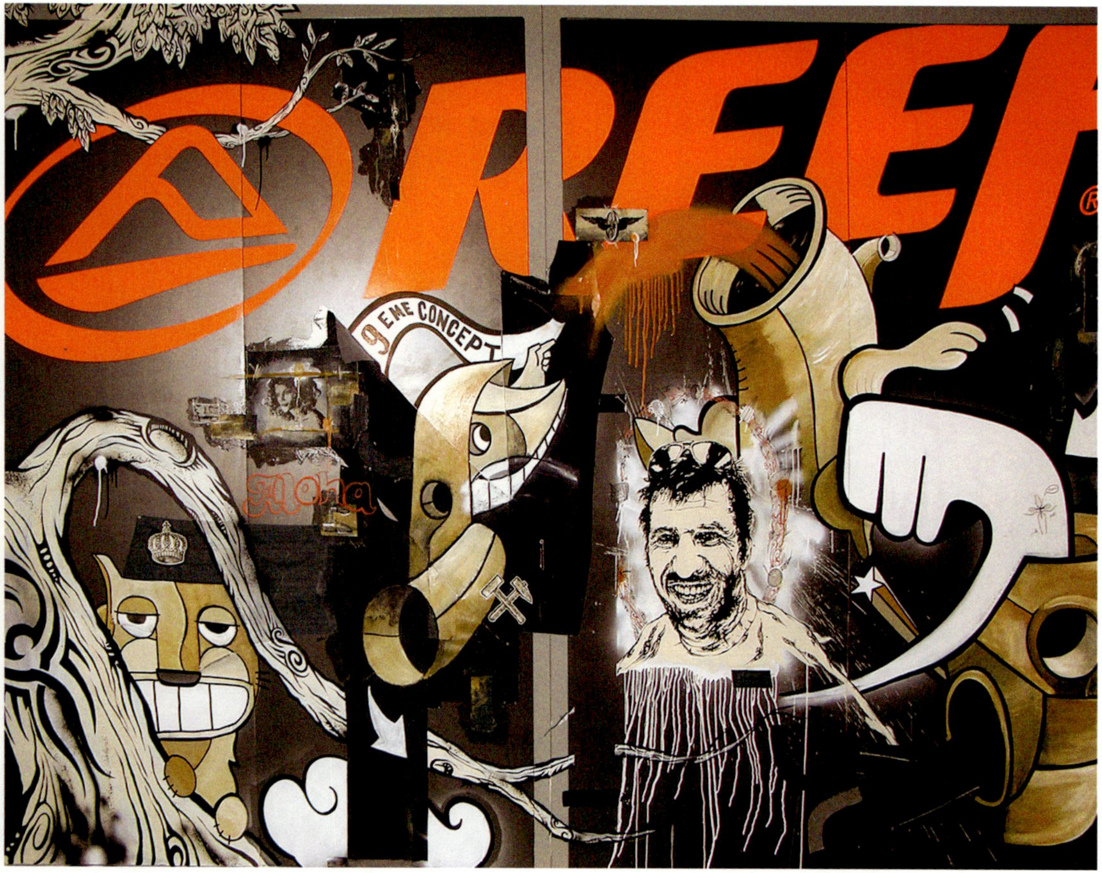

Live painting by Ned and Jerk 45

SAN DiEGO

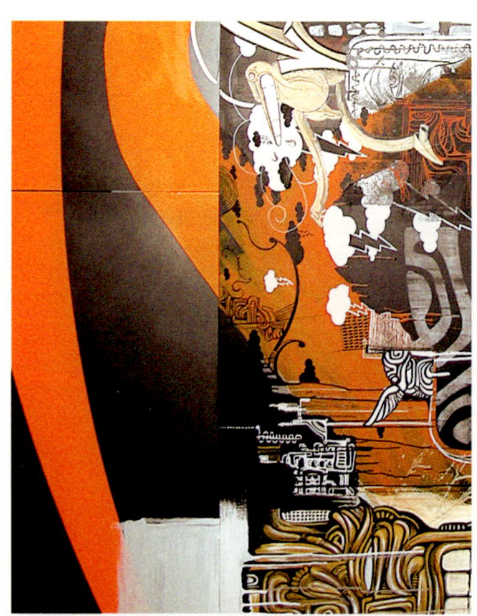
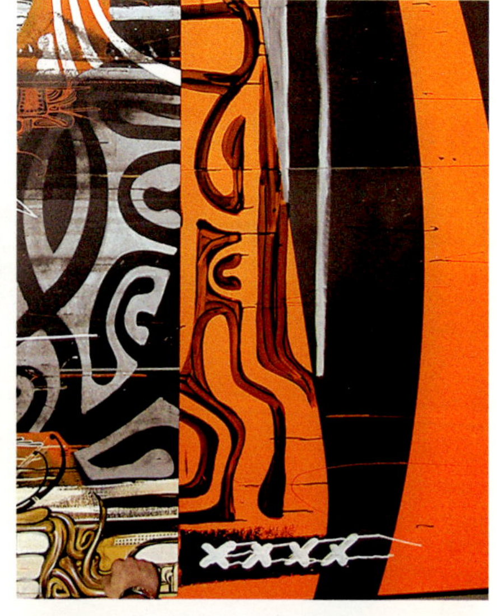
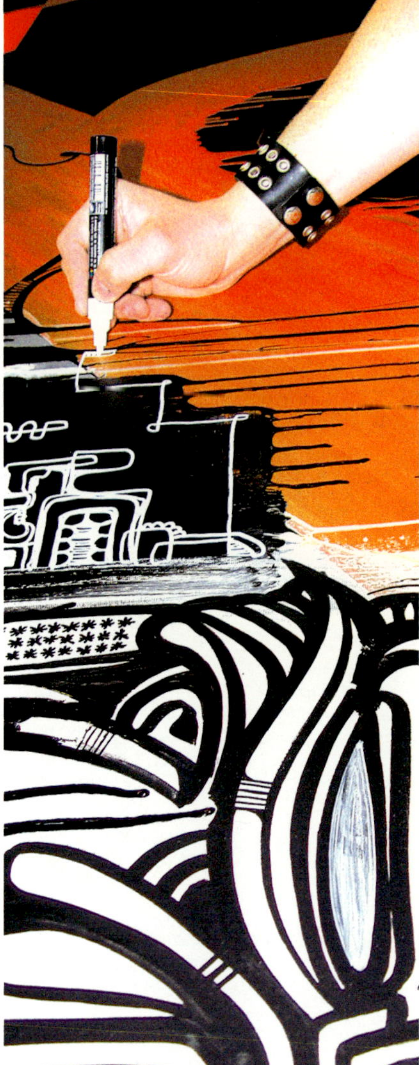
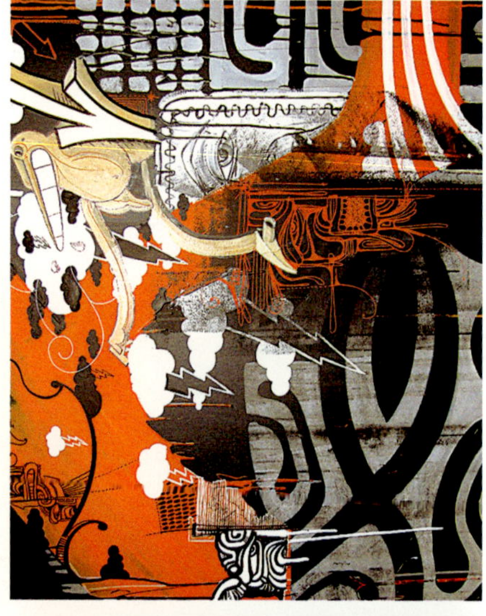
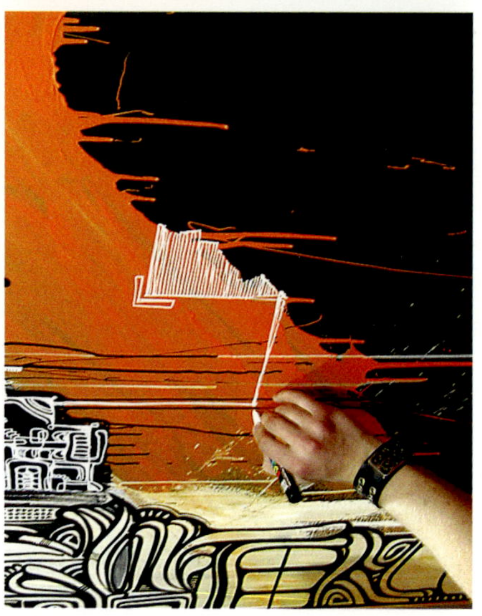

Live painting by Jérome Molard and Jerk45

SAN DiEGO

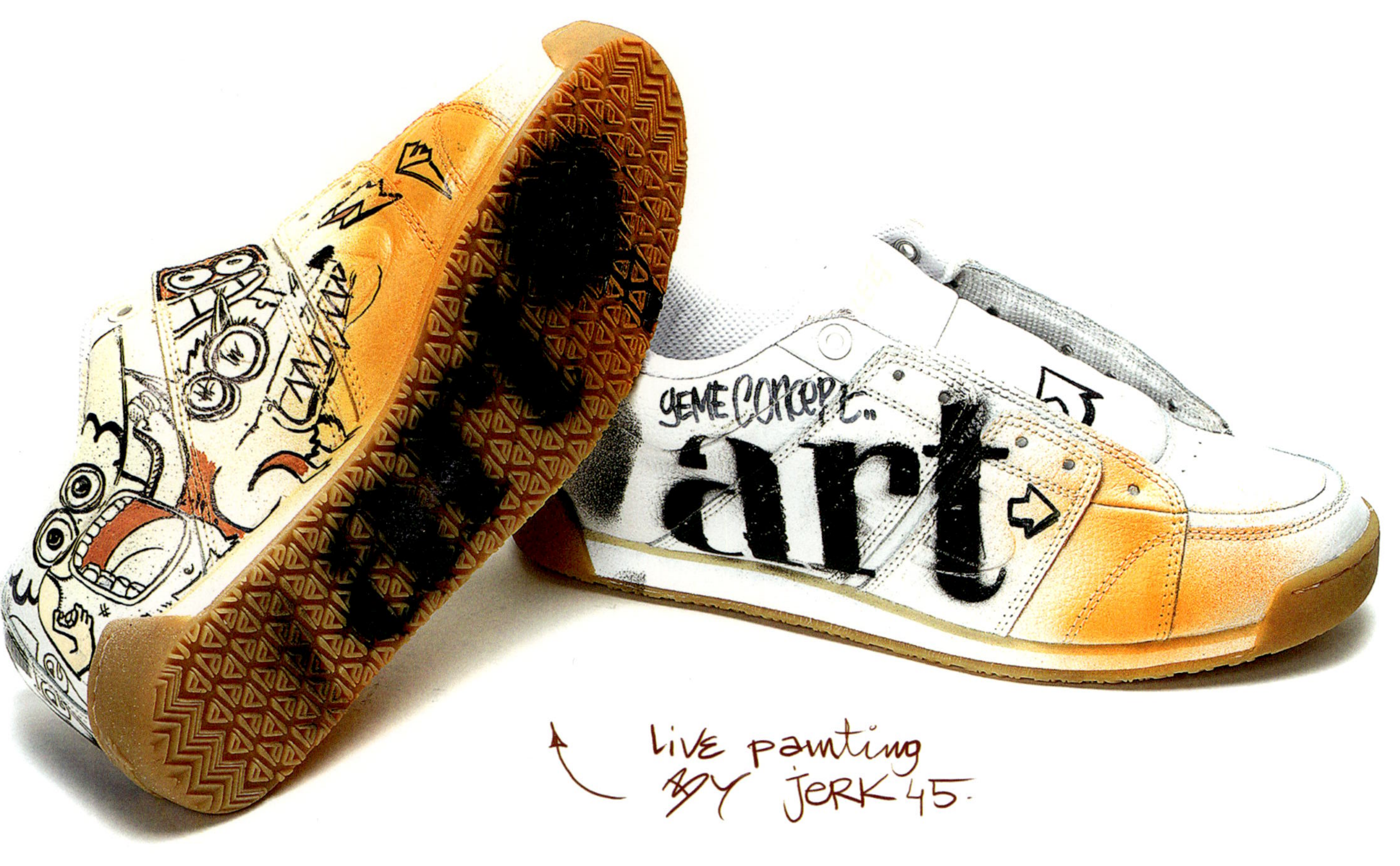

gene concept..
art
live painting
by JERK 45.

live painting
By Steph Carricondo

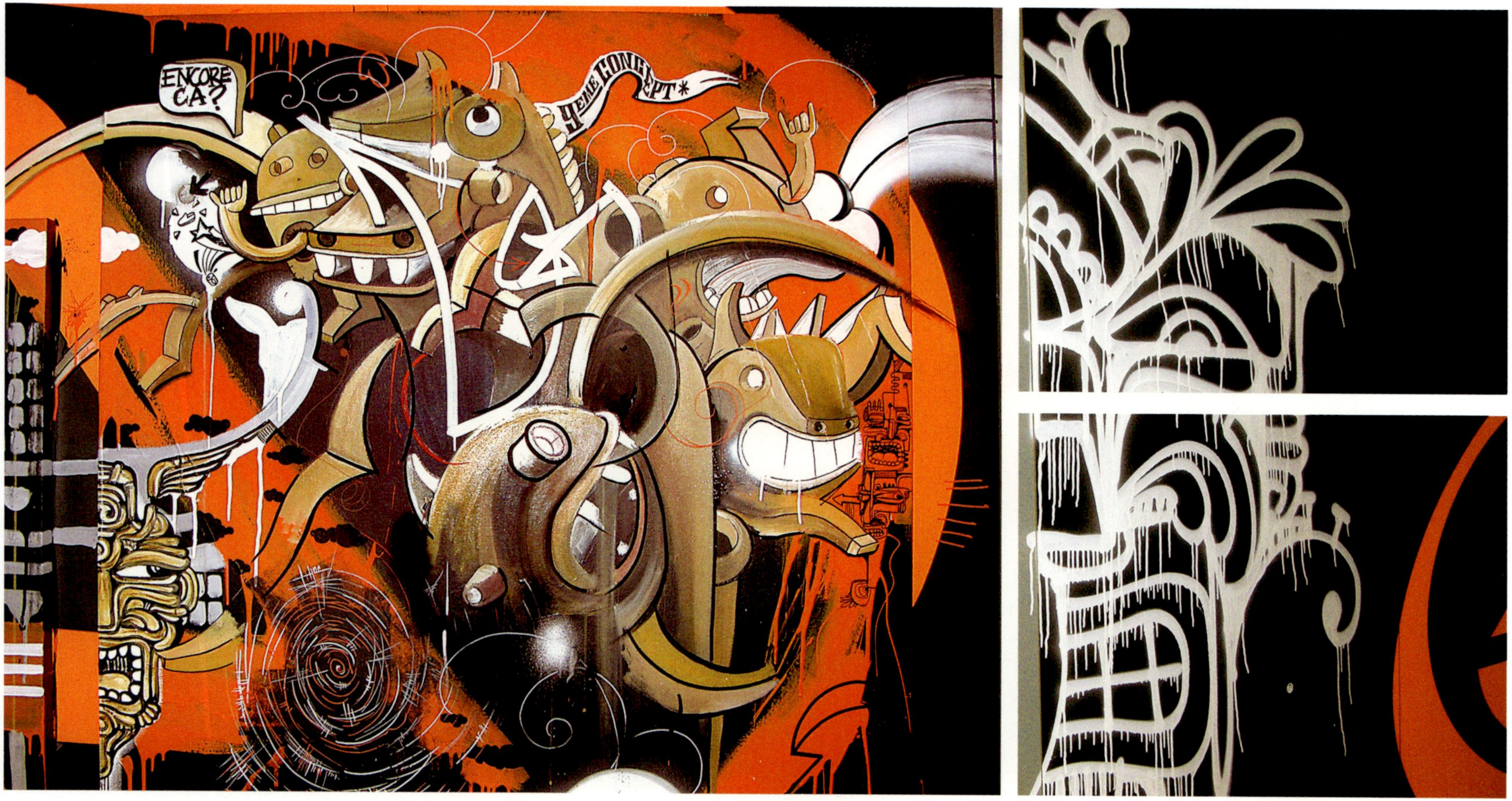

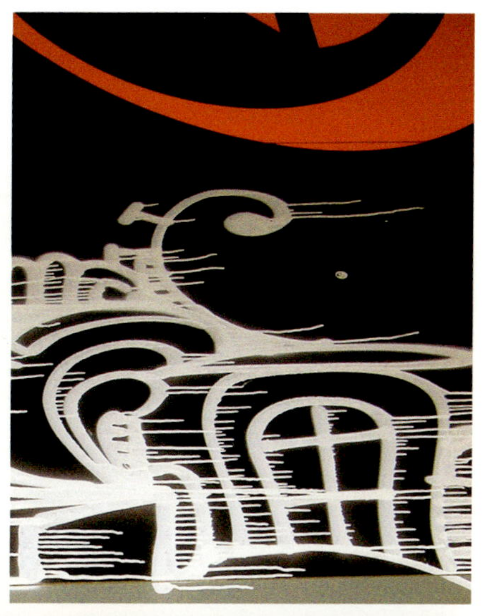

107

SAN DiEGo

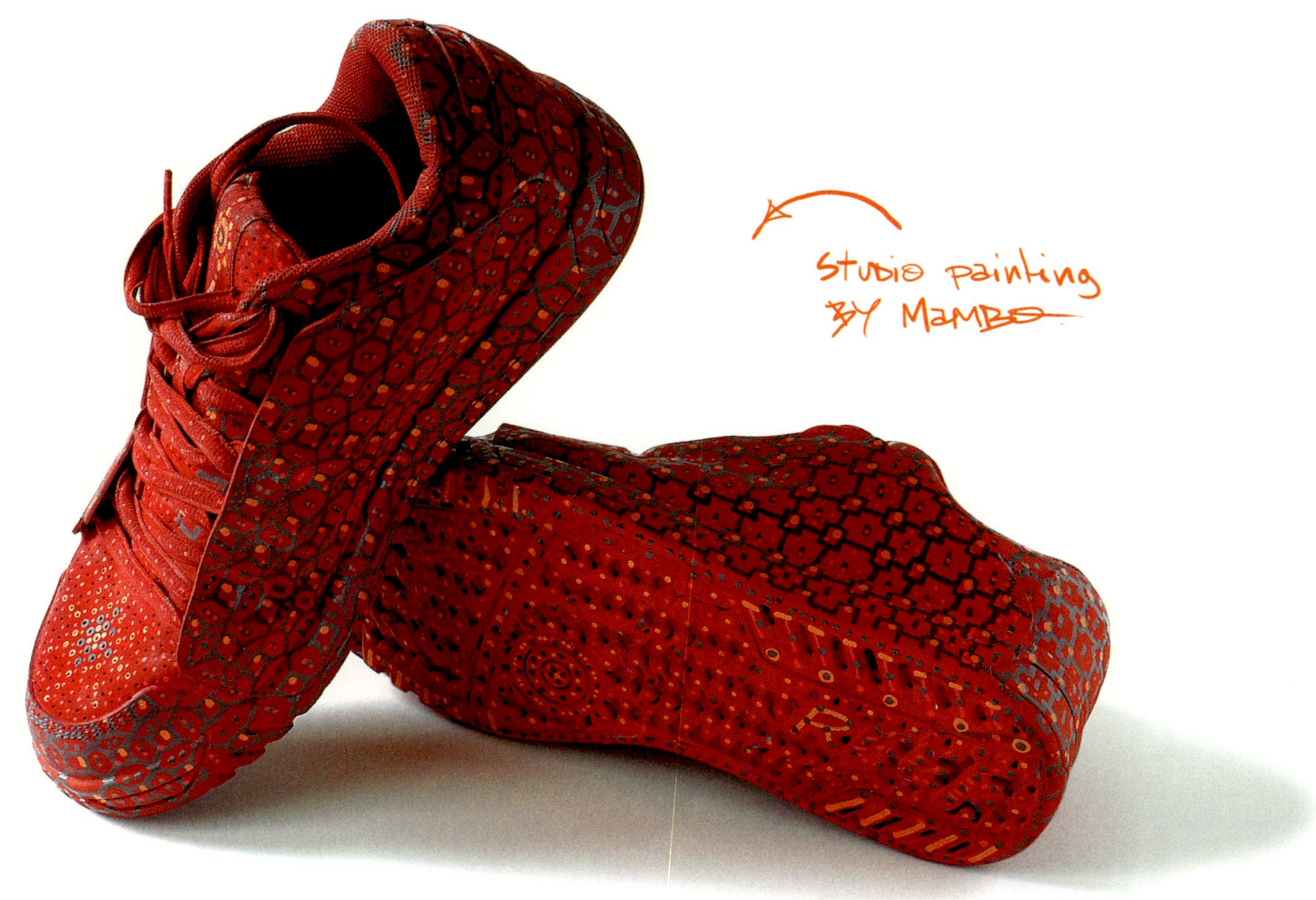

Studio painting
by Mambo

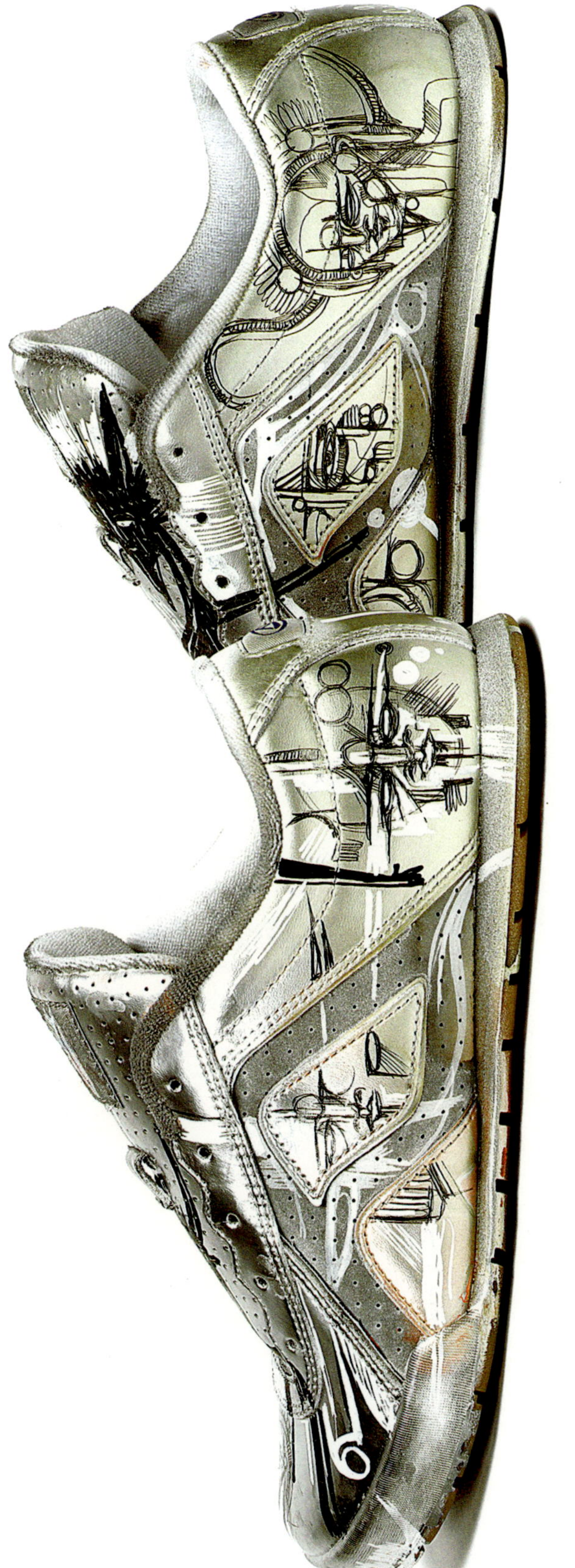

LIVE PAINTING
BY SETH CARICONDO.

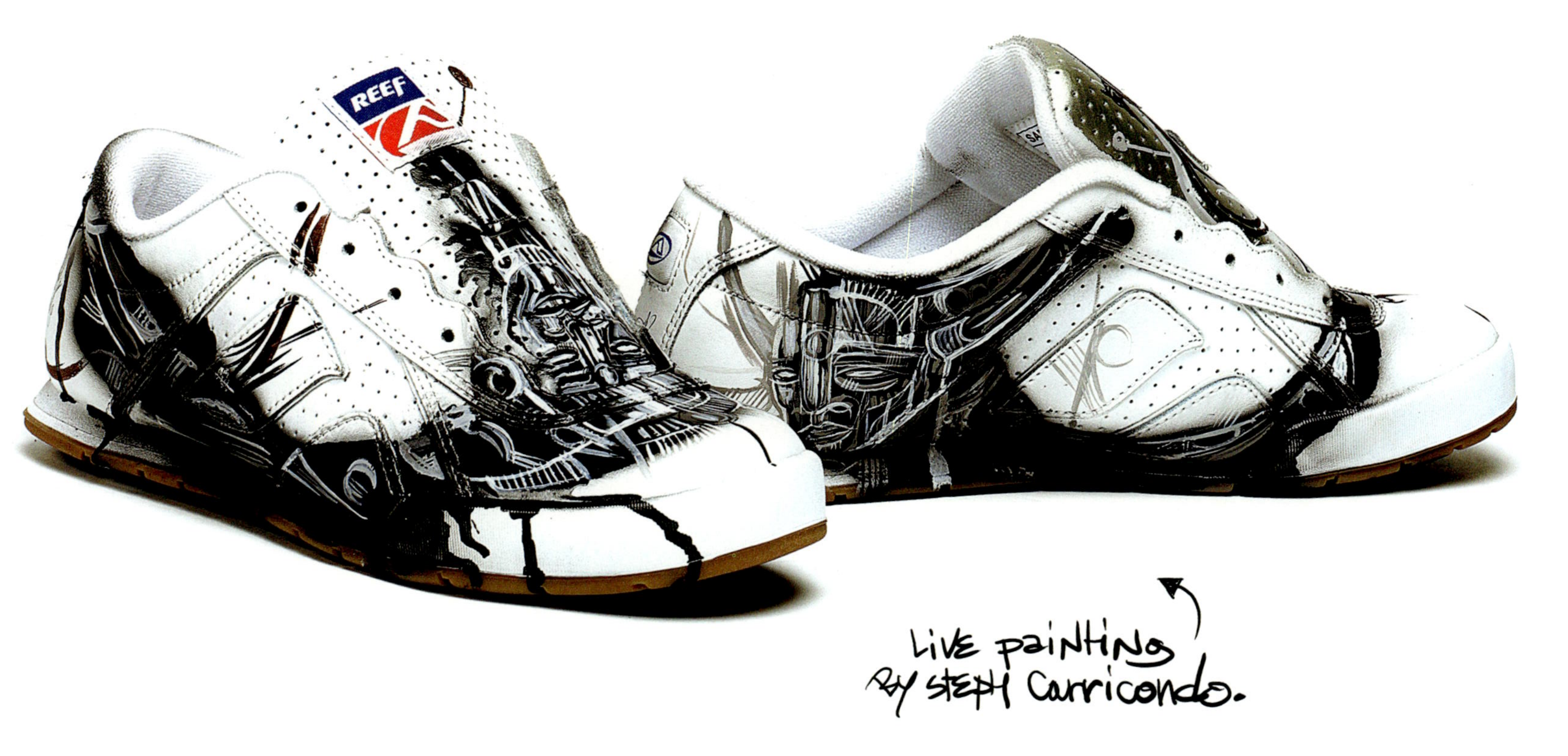

REEF
live painting
by steph carricondo.

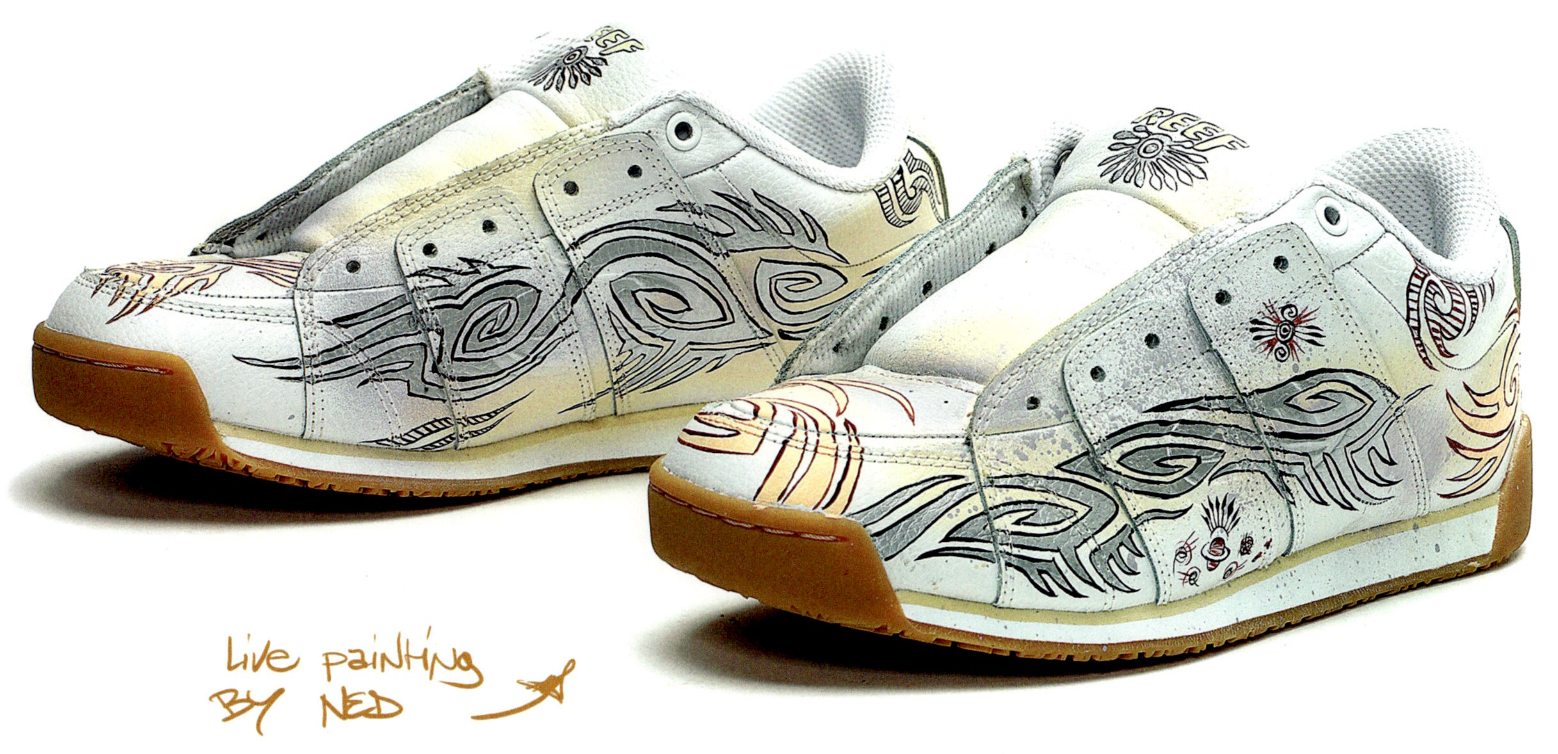
Live painting
BY NED

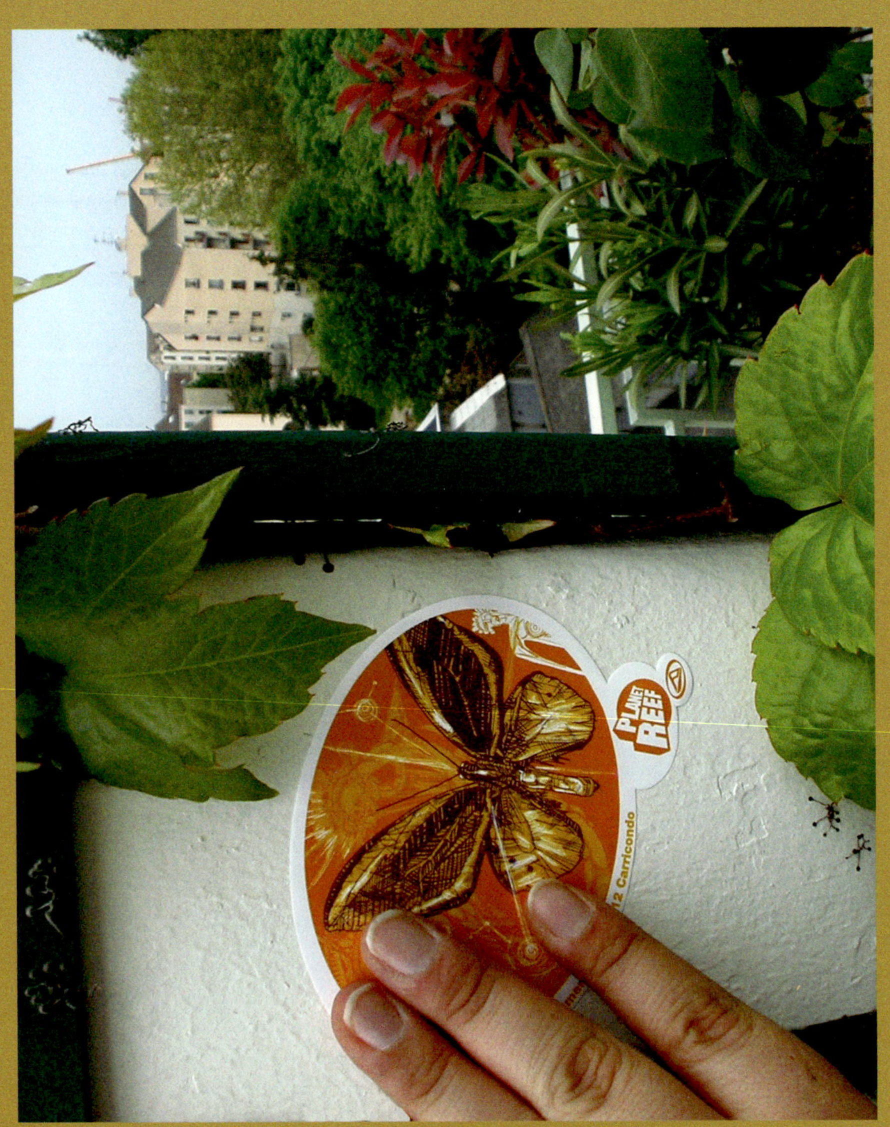

STICKERS Worldwide

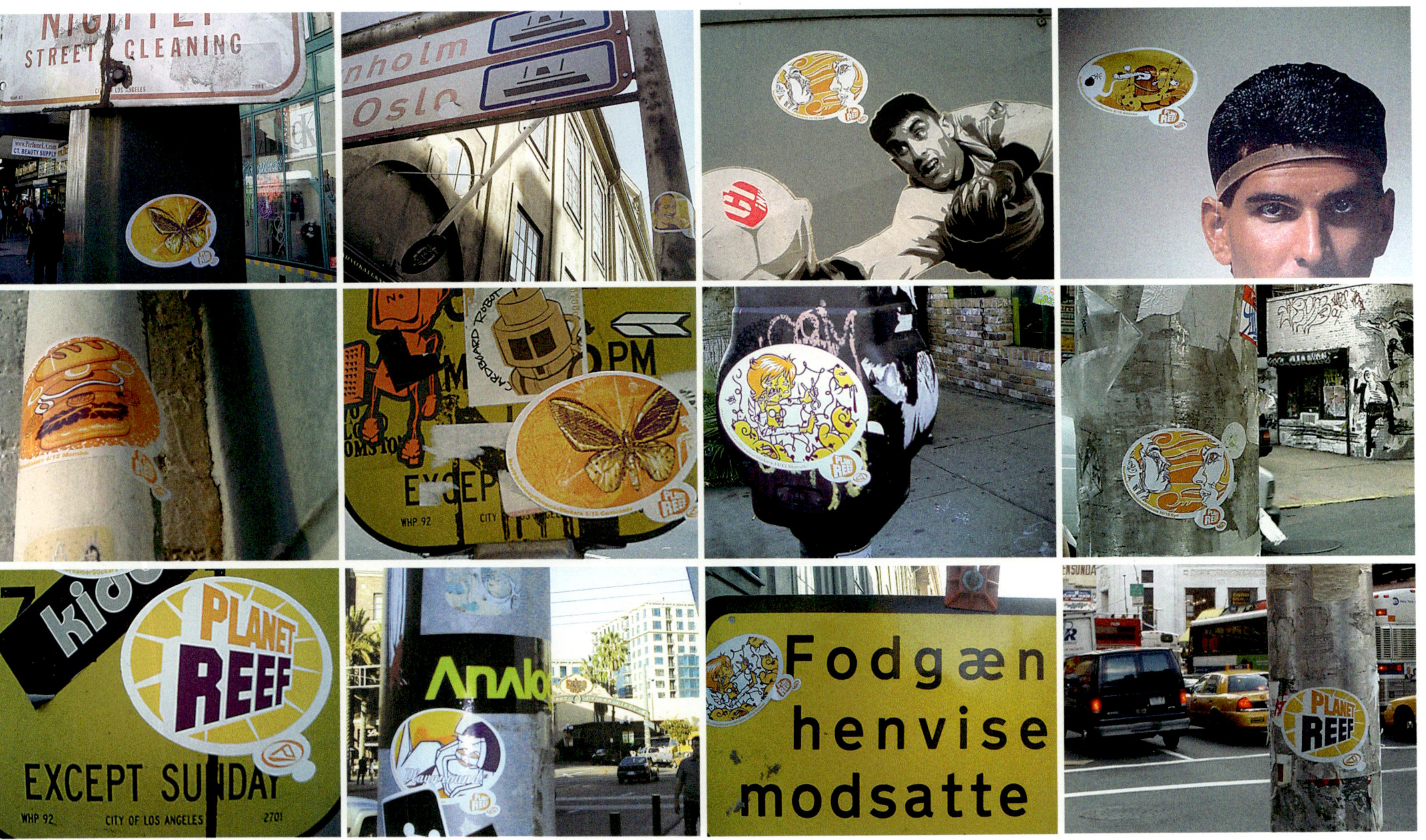

Seen in Los Angeles, Coppenhagen, Las Vegas, Del Mar, New York, Berlin, Paris...

Reef9thConceptDreamerStickers 2/12 Ned
PLANET REEF
Reef9thConcept4DreamerStickers 5/12 Alëxone
PLANET REEF
Reef9thConceptDreamerStickers 12/12 Romain
PLANET REEF
Playground*
Reef9thConceptDreamerStickers 3/12 Jerk 45
PLANET REEF
Reef9thConceptDreamerStickers 11/12 Veenom
PLANET REEF
Reef9thConceptDreamerStickers 7/12 Clément
PLANET REEF

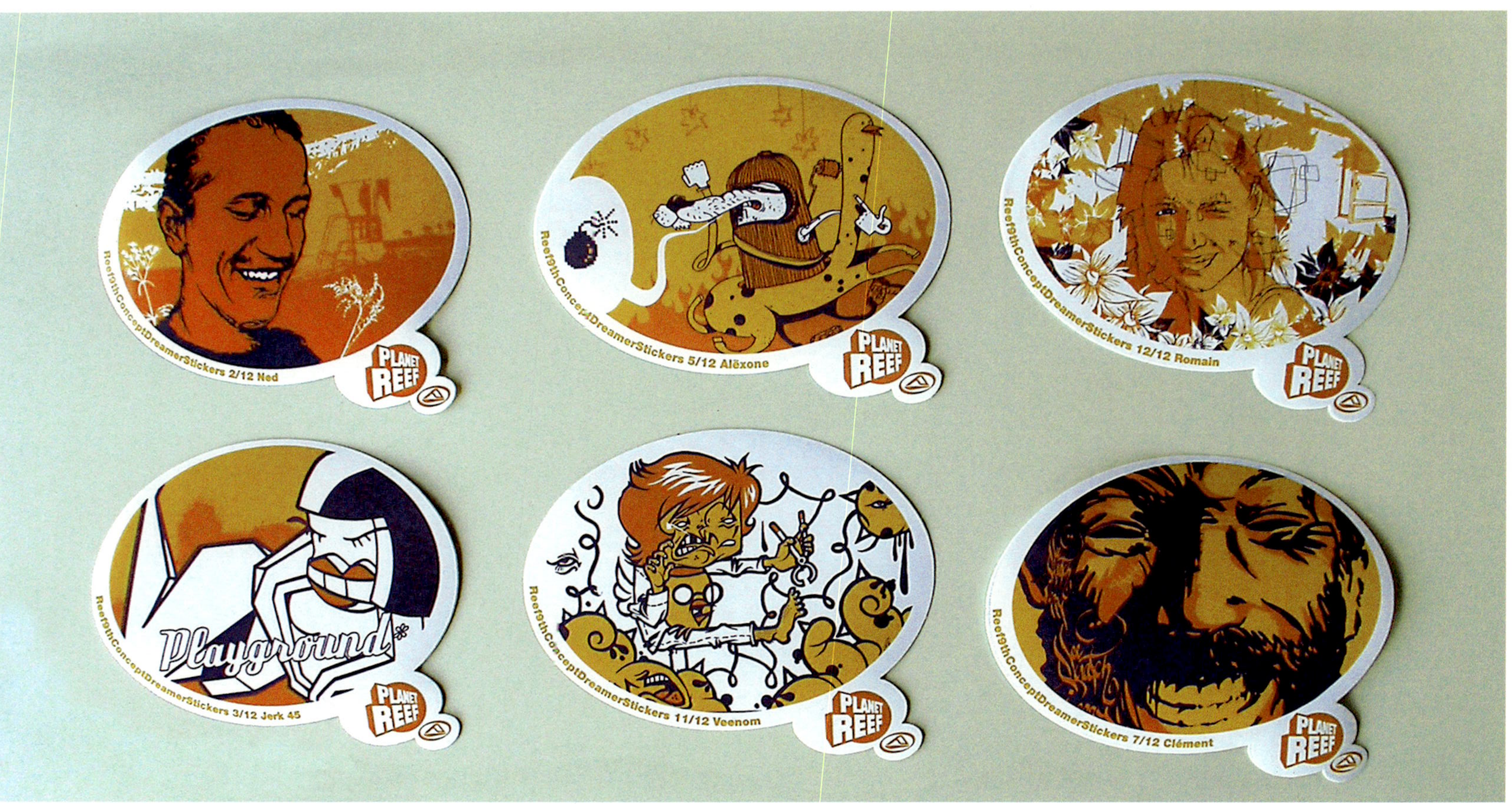

STICKERS

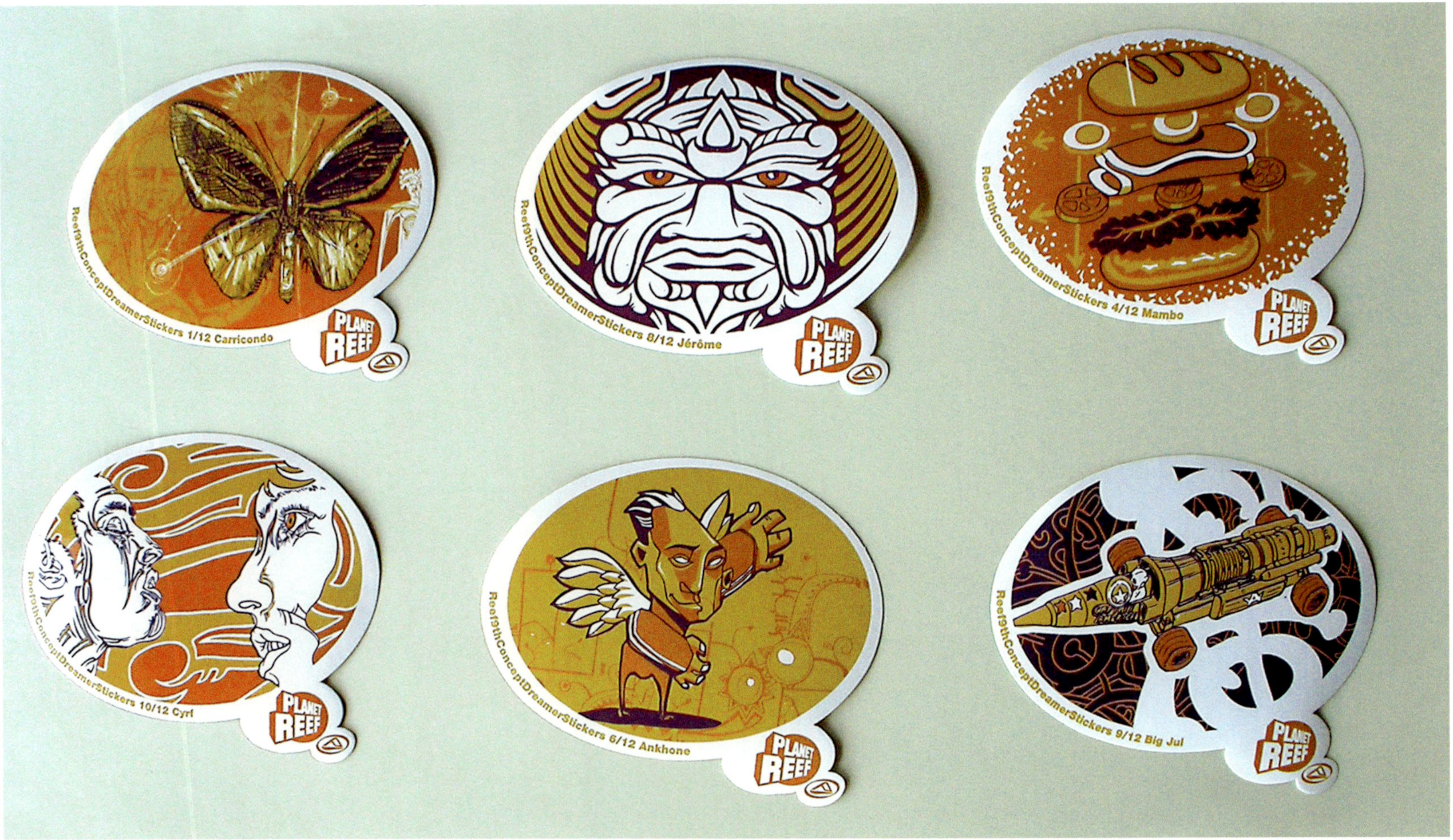

Reef9thConceptDreamerStickers 4/12 Mambo
Reef9thConceptDreamerStickers 9/12 Big Jul
Reef9thConceptDreamerStickers 8/12 Jérôme
Reef9thConceptDreamerStickers 6/12 Ankhone
Reef9thConceptDreamerStickers 1/12 Carricondo
Reef9thConceptDreamerStickers 10/12 Cyrl
PLANET REEF

STICKERS

Seen in Los Angeles, Bredene, Coppenhagen, Hollywood, Munchen, Berlin, Newport Beach, San Diego, Tokyo...

自民 PLANET REEF
石原慎太郎
東京都議会議員
村上英子 弁士
横断禁止
郵便 POST
日本郵政公社 JAPAN POST
KIRIN キリンビール ラーメン 餃子
岐阜屋
GRILL
質

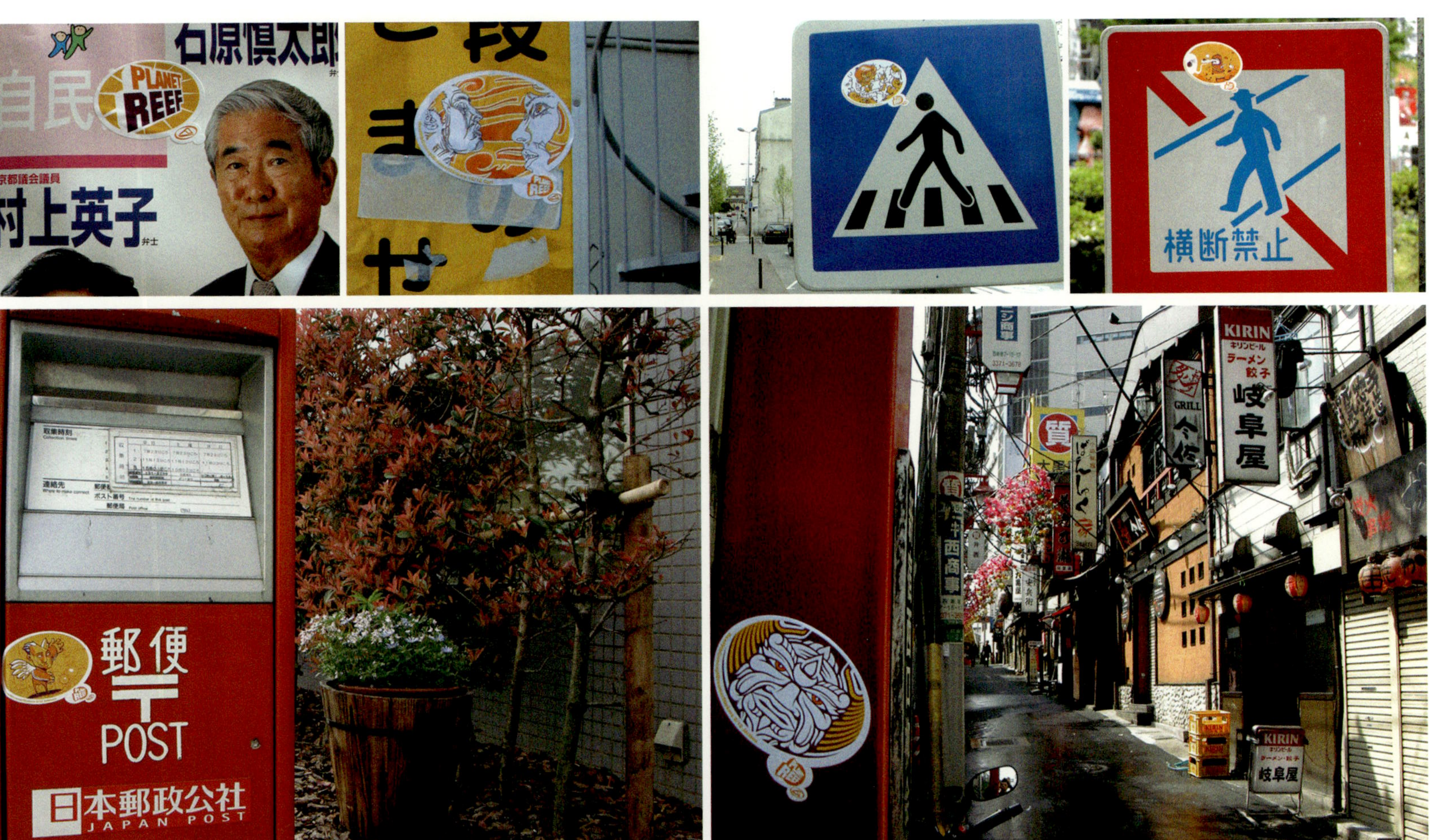

117

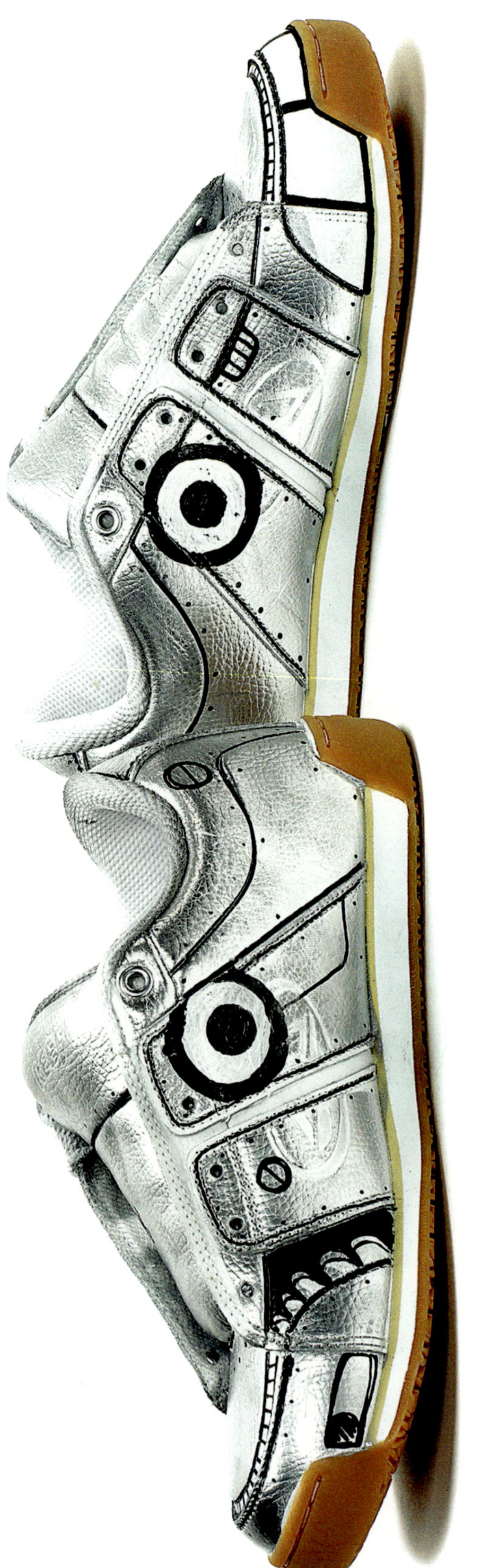
Live painting
by Jerk 45

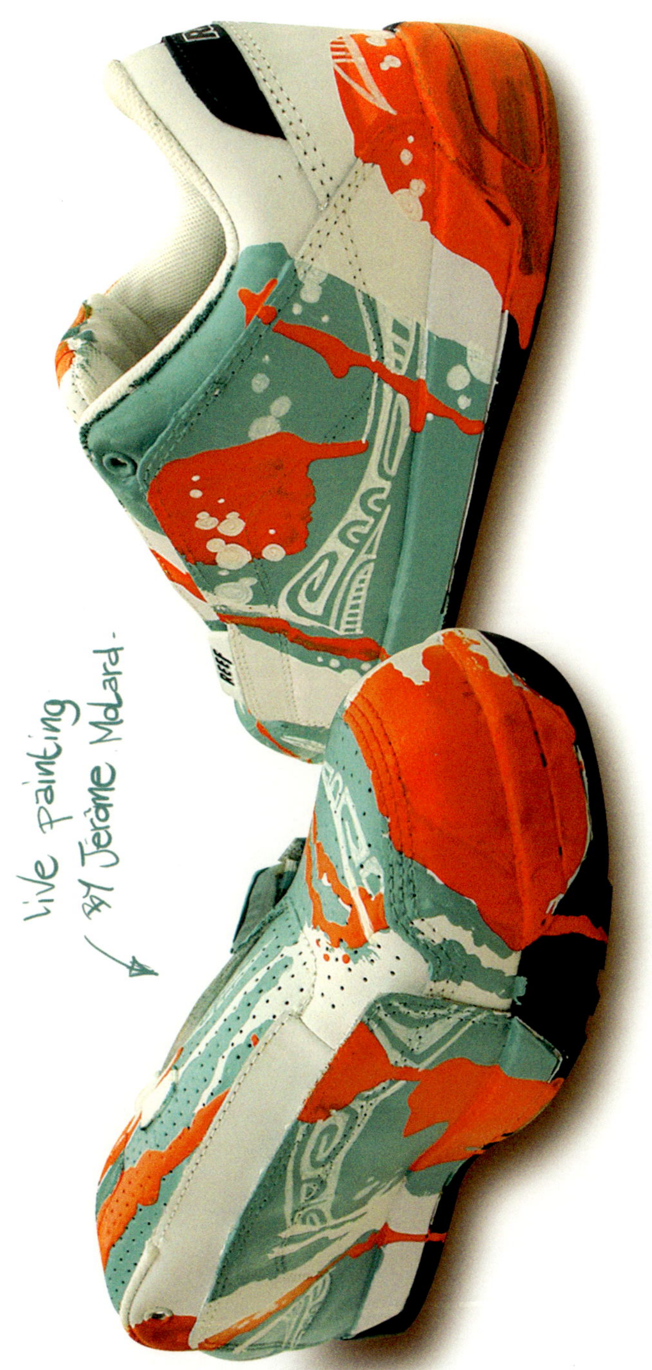

live painting
by Jérôme Mdard.

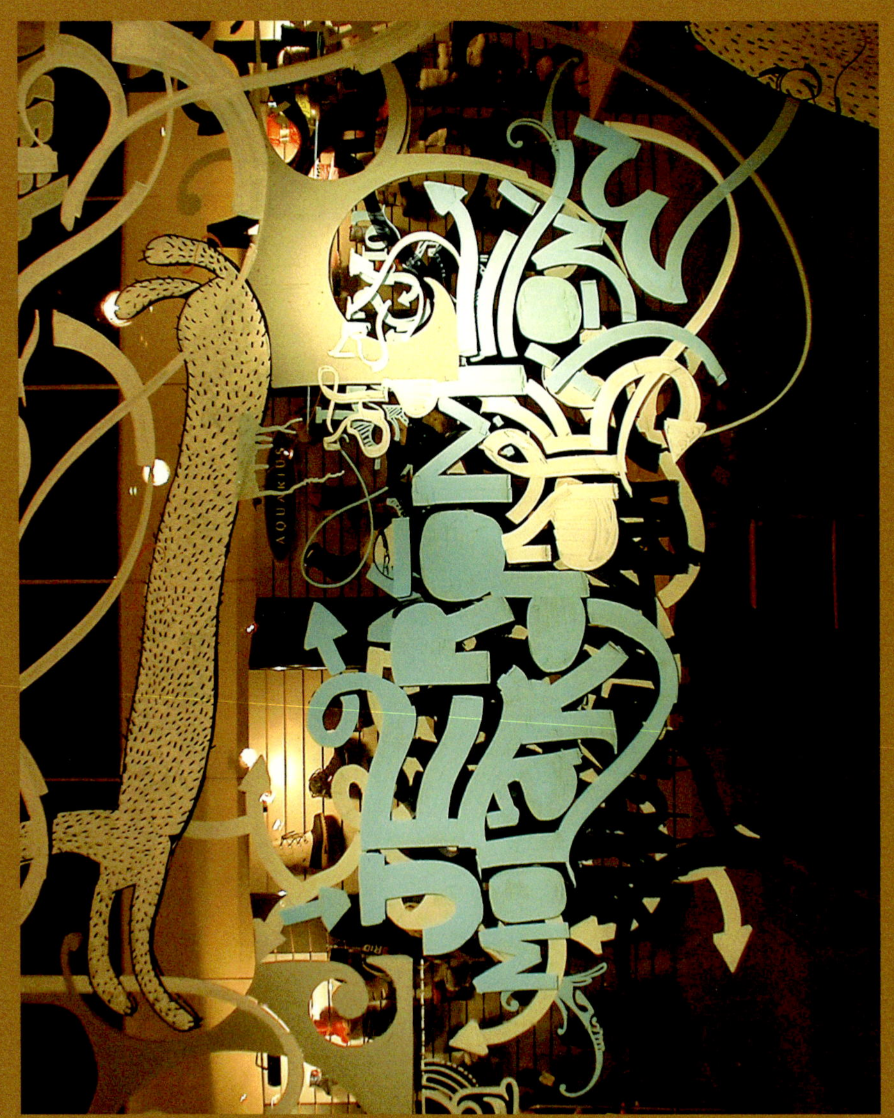

MANCHESTER
february 2005

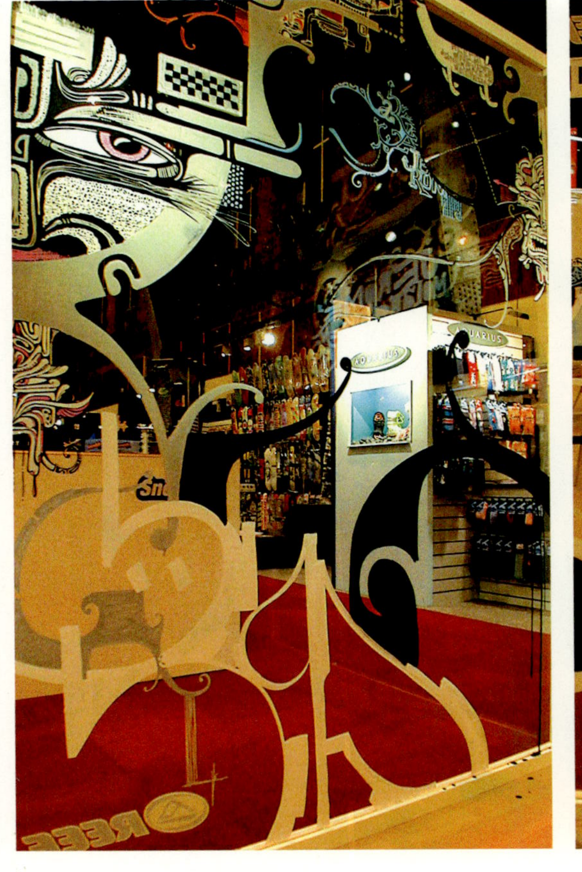

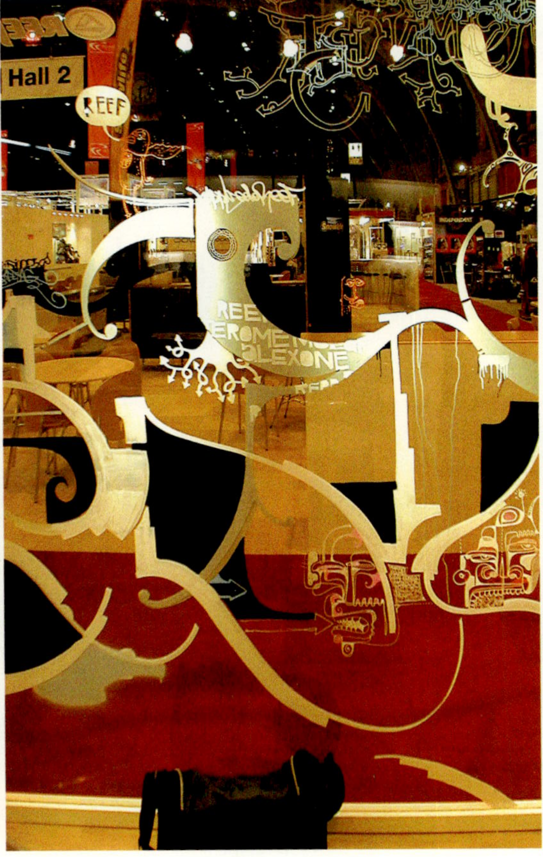

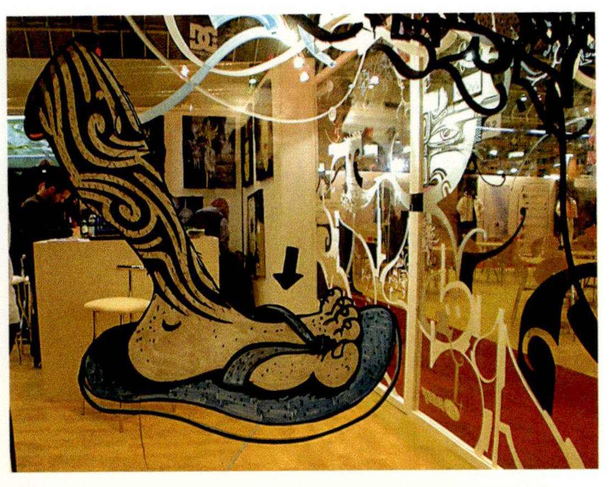

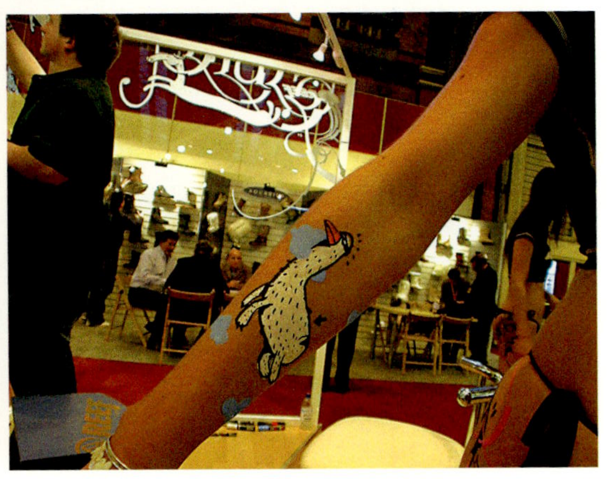

MANCHESTER

121

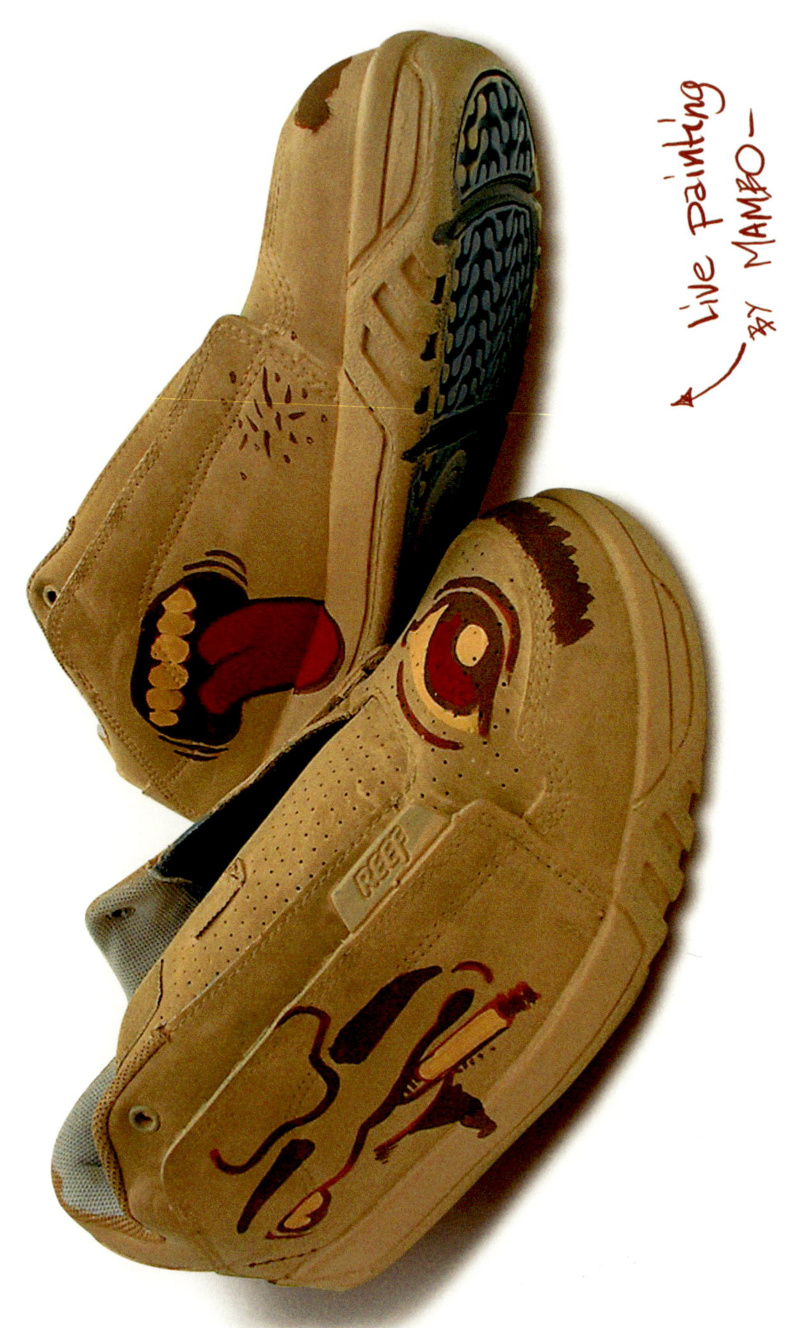
Live painting
by MAMBO—

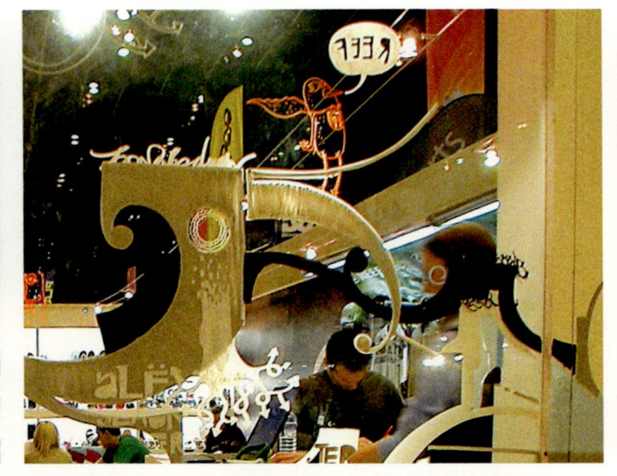

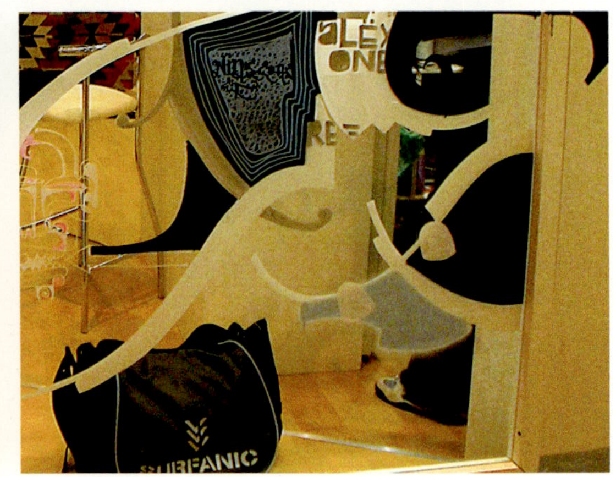

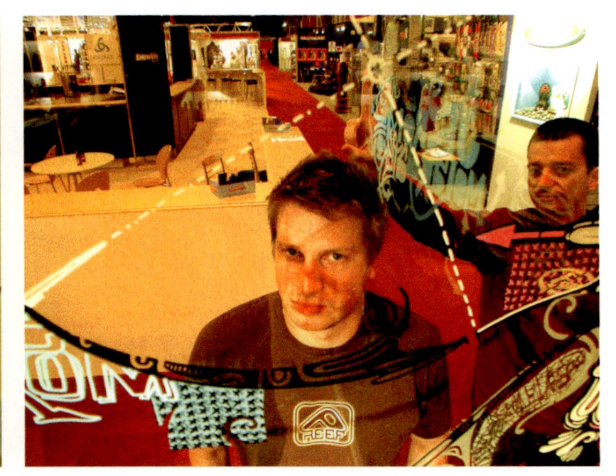

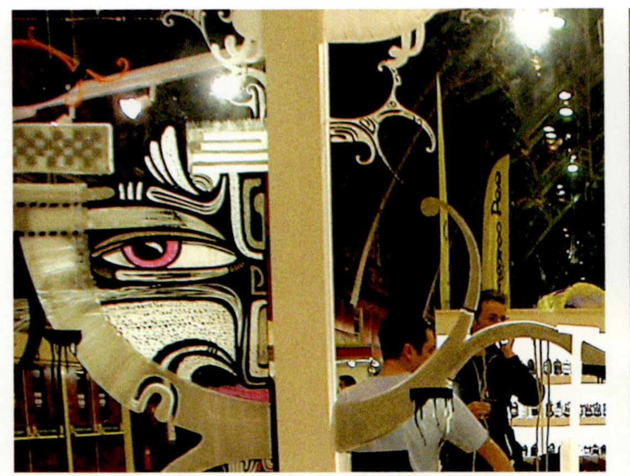

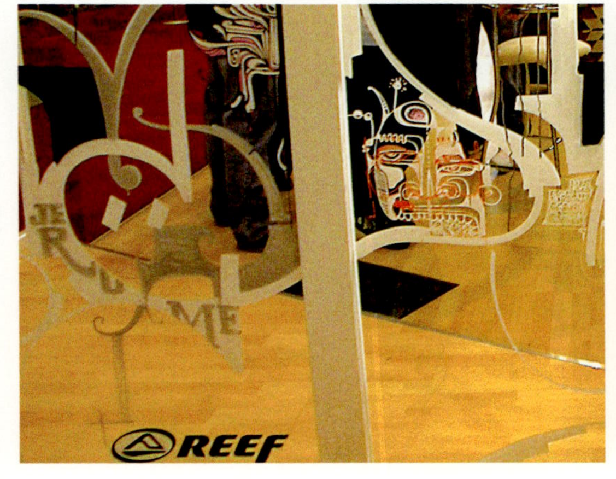

REEF

MANCHESTER

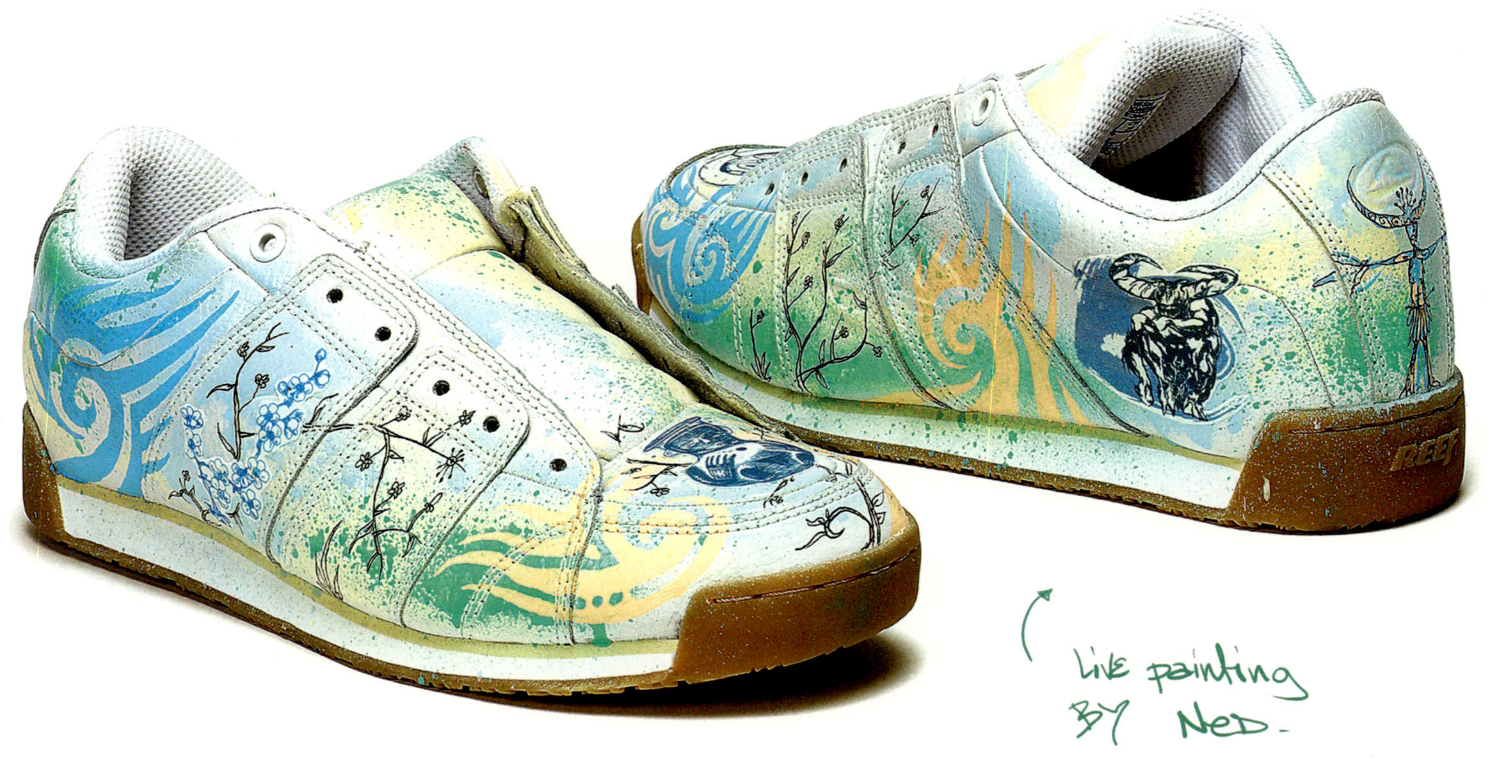

live painting
BY NED.

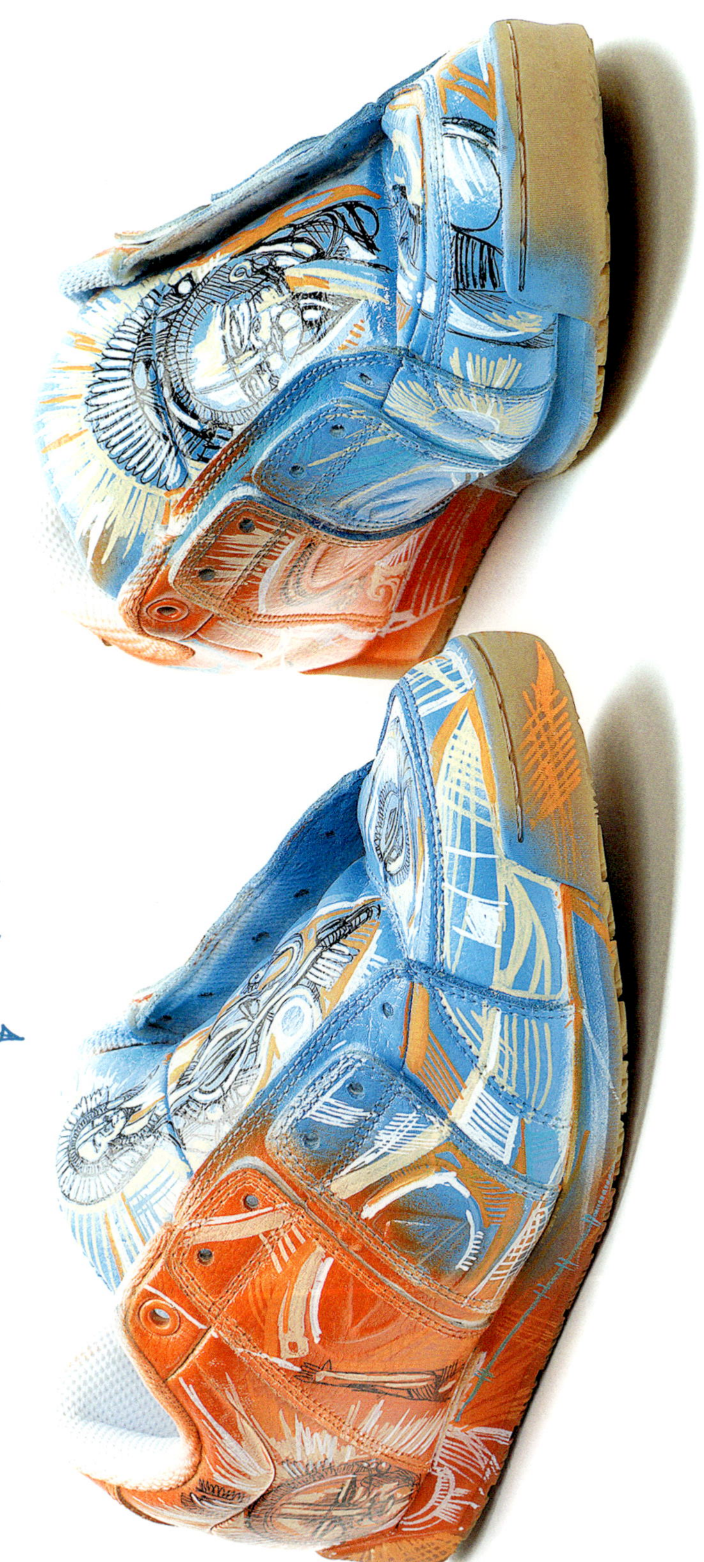

like painting
by steph carricardo -

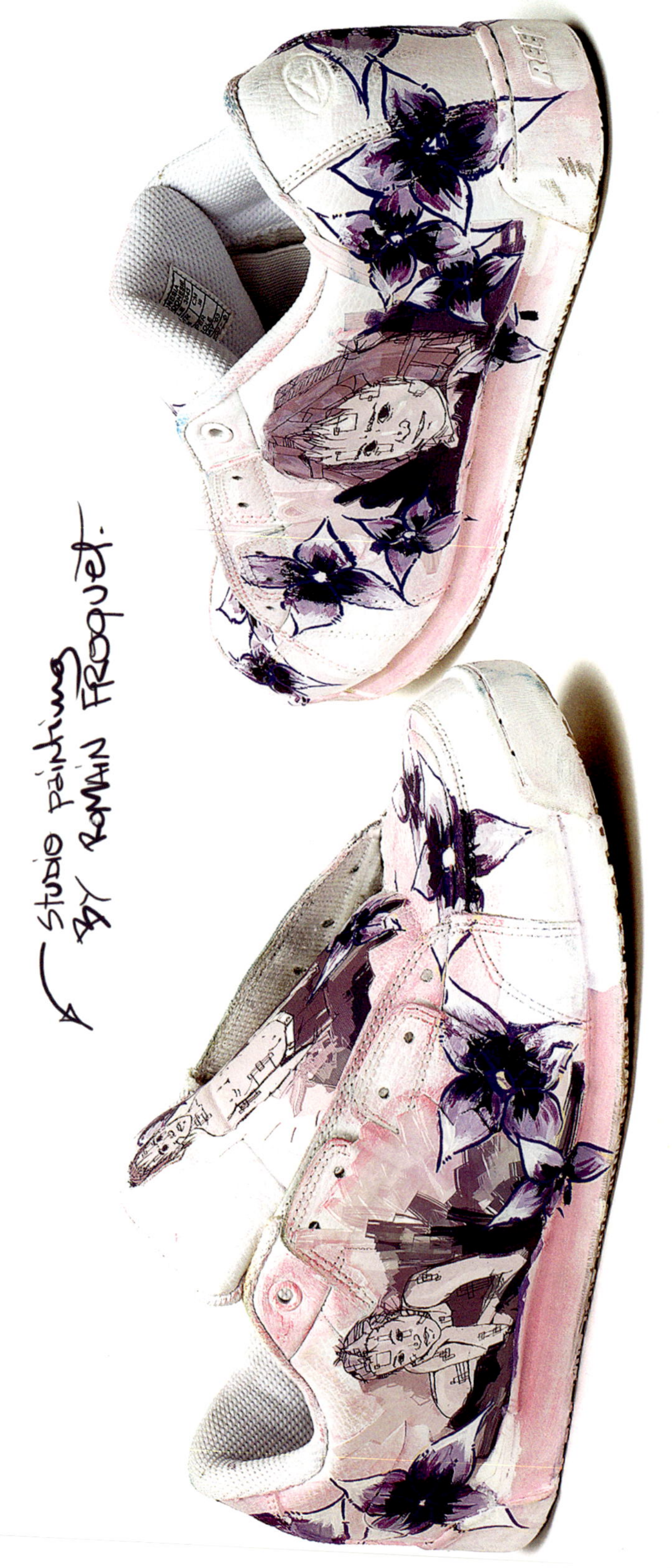
A studio painting
BY ROMAIN FROQUET.

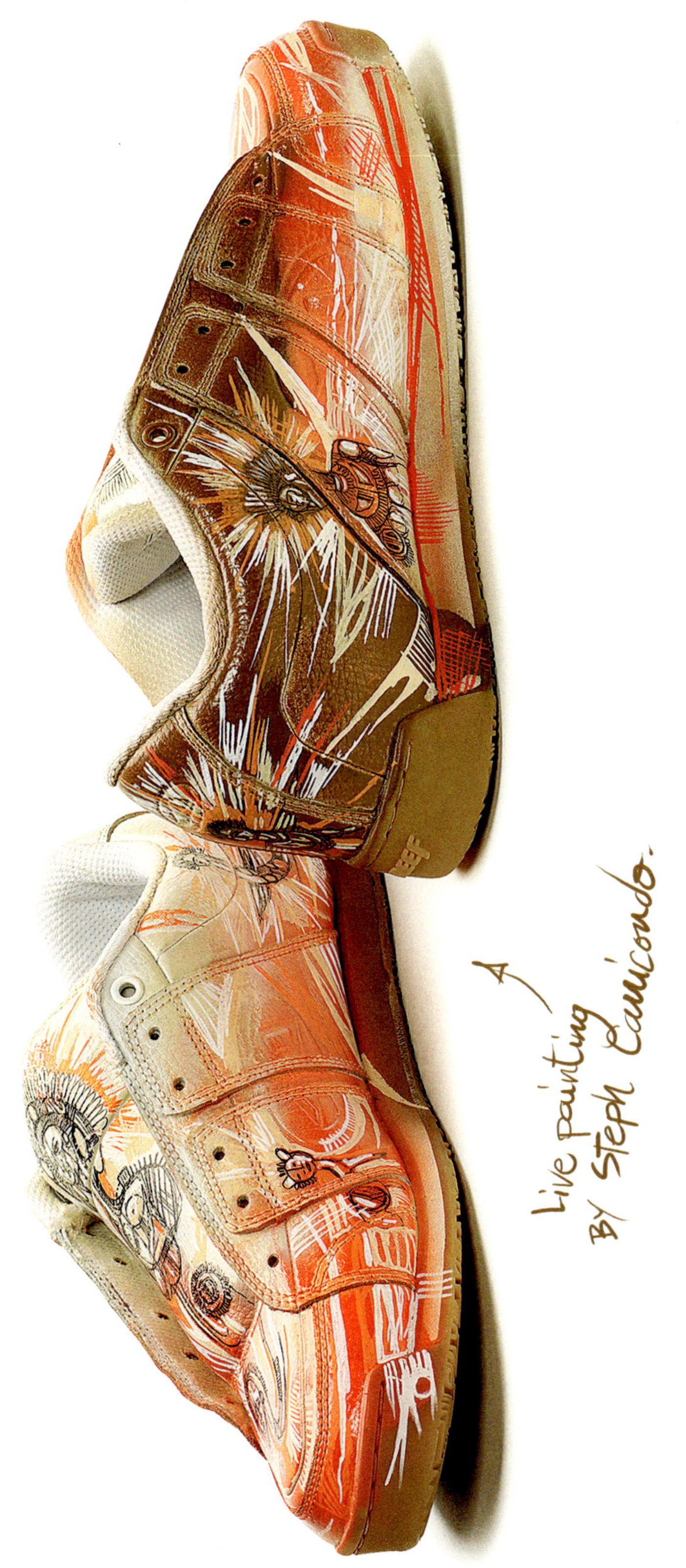

A Live painting
by Steph Cauicondo.

**Le 9ème Concept Peint Pour Planet Reef
/ 9ème Concept Paints for Planet Reef**

Graphic concept & design: Alëxone
Introduction and biographies: Alexis Deforge
Contributions by J.C. Clenet, Mark Price,
Marcelo Bengoechea, Pauline Espagne
photography: Donato Sardella (Hollywood part)
Flindt (Rob Machado), 9ème Concept crew

First published in 2005 by Kitchen 93
Distributed worldwide by Critiques Livres SAS
BP 93 - 24 rue Malmaison
93172 Bagnolet Cedex, France
www.kitchen93.com
kitchen93@wanadoo.fr
Printed in Italy
by LITOGRAFICA FAENZA
ISBN 2-85980-006-9

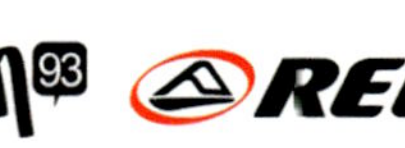
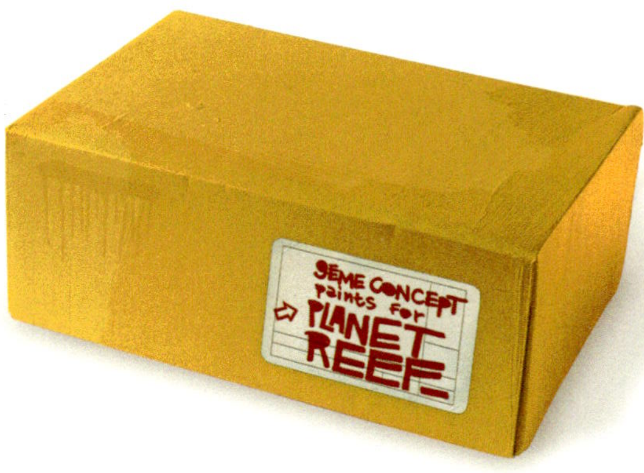